SIX DAYS IN AUGUST

ALSO BY DAVID KING

The Trial of Adolf Hitler:
The Beer Hall Putsch and the Rise of Nazi Germany

Death in the City of Light:
The Serial Killer of Nazi-Occupied Paris

Vienna, 1814:
How the Conquerors of Napoleon Made Love,
War, and Peace at the Congress of Vienna

Finding Atlantis:
A True Story of Genius, Madness,
and an Extraordinary Quest for a Lost World

SIX DAYS IN AUGUST

The Story of Stockholm Syndrome

DAVID KING

W. W. NORTON & COMPANY
Independent Publishers Since 1923

For information about permission to reproduce selections from this book, write to
Permissions, W. W. Norton & Company, Inc., 500 Fifth Avenue, New York, NY 10110

For information about special discounts for bulk purchases, please contact
W. W. Norton Special Sales at specialsales@wwnorton.com or 800-233-4830

Manufacturing by Lake Book Manufacturing
Book design by Daniel Lagin
Production manager: Julia Druskin

Library of Congress Cataloging-in-Publication Data

Names: King, David, 1970- author.
Title: Six days in August : the story of Stockholm syndrome / David King.
Description: First edition. | New York, NY : W.W. Norton & Company, [2020] | Includes
bibliographical references and index.
Identifiers: LCCN 2019058100 | ISBN 9780393635089 (hardcover) |
ISBN 9780393635096 (epub)
Subjects: LCSH: Bank robberies—Sweden—Stockholm—Case studies. | Police—Sweden. |
Hostage negotiations—Sweden. | Hostages—Sweden. | Stockholm syndrome.
Classification: LCC HV7040.S7 K56 2020 | DDC 364.15/52094873—dc23
LC record available at https://lccn.loc.gov/2019058100

W. W. Norton & Company, Inc., 500 Fifth Avenue, New York, N.Y. 10110
www.wwnorton.com

W. W. Norton & Company Ltd., 15 Carlisle Street, London W1D 3BS

1 2 3 4 5 6 7 8 9 0

To Sara, Julia, and Max

Not even Hollywood screenwriters in their wildest imagination could envision the drama that is playing out in this bank in the middle of Stockholm.

—Malcolm McDowell,
actor in Stanley Kubrick's *A Clockwork Orange*

AUTHOR'S NOTE

This is a work of nonfiction based on police files, court documents, newspaper articles, radio and television broadcasts, first-person accounts, and my own interviews. All translations from the original Swedish are my own.

Stockholm syndrome: the psychological tendency of a hostage to bond with, identify with, or sympathize with his or her captor.

This is how it began.

SIX DAYS IN AUGUST

1

The day Stockholm held its breath

—*Aftonbladet*, August 24, 1973

AUGUST 23, 1973

A FEW MINUTES BEFORE TEN O'CLOCK ON A WARM, OVERCAST MORN-
ing, a tall, muscular man in a gray zippered sweatshirt walked into the
main branch of Sveriges Kreditbank, one of the most prominent banks
in central Stockholm. He wore makeup, a ladies' wig, and a pair of blue-
tinted sunglasses. In his hand, he carried a bulky canvas bag.

The lobby was large and elegant, with white marble columns, a grand
mahogany staircase, and a long teller counter where two clerks were busy
helping customers. About thirty people were dispersed throughout the room.
No one paid any particular attention to the man.

He took his place at the back of the line. He set the bag on the floor,
unzipped his sweatshirt, ripped out a submachine gun, and fired a round
into the ceiling.

"The party starts!" he shouted in English. "Down on the floor!"

Many people froze, but a few darted toward the exits. A handful of
staff at the far end of the room quickly retreated out of sight. Everyone else
dropped to the floor, which was now littered with shattered glass and plaster
from the ceiling.

The gunman started running about the room, shouting commands, pointing his weapon at frightened individuals and threatening to shoot anyone who did not obey. He pulled a transistor radio out of the bag and slammed it down. Rock music now blasted throughout the marbled lobby.

He dashed behind the teller counter and stopped near a woman who had ducked under a desk.

"Get up!" he shouted.

Turning to a male employee on the floor, the gunman ordered him to take a knife and a rope from his bag and tie her up. He then had two other women bound by their wrists and ankles. All the while, the gunman's finger quivered at the trigger. One minute he was laughing, one minute he was screaming. He seemed to be crazy, high on drugs, or both.

AT 10:02 A.M., THE METALLIC CLANG OF THE ALARM RANG OUT ACROSS town at the Kungsholmen police station. A radio dispatch then alerted patrol cars to the armed robbery and urged available officers to hurry to the scene.

Kreditbanken was located in a six-story building on the eastern corner of Norrmalmstorg, a bustling square in the capital's financial district. This was just a short walk from Norrbro, one of the famed bridges that earned Stockholm the nickname "Venice of the North," and connected the busy modern commercial hub to its medieval heart with its veritable labyrinth of narrow, twisting cobblestone lanes.

The area boasted several of the country's leading banks, as well as an array of chic boutiques, expensive hotels, and fashionable, high-end stores. There were offices for British Airways, Air France, Lufthansa, and Finnair. Around the corner was an oriental-rug showroom and a cinema that dated back to the 1920s. The high status of Norrmalmstorg is reflected on Sweden's Monopoly board, where it takes the spot of Boardwalk.

The first policemen to arrive were Torgny Wallström and Ingemar Åhman in patrol car 232. A small gathering of people was already standing in the square looking in the direction of Berzelii Park. A larger group of spectators had gathered across the street. Perhaps the robber had already escaped, Wallström thought. As his colleague remained outside, Wallström drew his pistol and entered the bank.

The crime, he soon realized, was still in progress. He took cover behind a nearby counter that served the loans department.

The policeman saw a large figure with a submachine gun towering over the men and women sprawled out on the floor, lying as still as death. He was holding a young blond woman in front of him as a human shield. Two other women bound by their ankles and wrists remained at his side. Wallström heard several voices shouting, and he thought one of them sounded like he was speaking German. Was it an accomplice? How many robbers were in the building?

Above all, why had they not taken the money and run?

When Wallström inched his way forward, the gunman fired a shot in his direction, shattering glass in the door just ahead of him. Wallström flung himself back, hopped over the counter, and then found shelter in a small safe-deposit room used by the foreign exchange department. He joined about ten or eleven bank employees who were already hiding there.

———

SIRENS OUTSIDE SIGNALED THE ARRIVAL OF ADDITIONAL POLICE CARS to Norrmalmstorg.

"What a fucking long time it took for them to get here," the robber taunted, still speaking English.

Unbeknownst to the gunman, Wallström was not the only policeman who had entered the bank. At least four other officers had discovered an alternative access point via a neighboring staircase at Norrmalmstorg 2A. This led to the second floor, where the executives had their offices. From there it was just one flight of stairs down to the lobby.

One of these policemen was Inspector Ingemar Warpefeldt, a fifty-seven-year-old plainclothes detective inspector who had been driving nearby in his gray Volvo when he heard the radio call. A former bodyguard for the children of the prime minister, Warpefeldt entered the building and made his way to the second floor. Bank employees rushed about the corridors. Telephones kept ringing. Rumors circulated that there were two bank robbers, but no one seemed to know what was happening and so he decided to find out.

Warpefeldt descended the dark mahogany staircase, passing three other policemen also making their way down to the lobby. He stopped on the final step, and looked around the corner, shielded by a marble column. His police pistol, a Walther 7.65mm, was in his hand.

The robber was nowhere in sight, though Warpefeldt could hear a loud, dominating voice bellowing throughout the room. The man with the submachine gun then came into view about twenty feet away, moving about on the far side of the teller counter, with the barrel of his weapon pointed upward, or occasionally horizontally.

He had not seen Warpefeldt, but the woman he used as a shield did, and screamed. The gunman, turning quickly, shouted at the man asking if he was a Swedish policeman.

"Yes, I am," Inspector Warpefeldt said in his broken English and told him to drop his weapon.

Instead, the gunman dropped to one knee behind the teller counter, and fired. The detective inspector felt a sharp pain in his right hand and reflexively yanked it back. He retreated up the staircase, leaving behind a thin red trail.

2

_____

When I realized that he was not after money, I had my first real fear.

—Bo Nilsson, bank employee

S WEDEN WAS, AT THIS TIME, AT THE HEIGHT OF ITS INTERNATIONAL renown as a progressive socialist country praised for its peaceful achievements. There was relatively little crime, even less poverty, and, in almost two hundred years, no war. Sweden's cradle-to-grave welfare state boasted myriad benefits, including free health care, free university education, free child care, and guaranteed pensions for life. Vilgot Sjöman's controversial film, *I Am Curious (Yellow)*, with its frank depictions of nudity and rampant sex, catered to another long-standing feature of the Scandinavian mystique: Sweden was a blond and bronzed Babylon, populated with beautiful hunks and sirens.

The prime minister, Olof Palme, drew comparisons to John F. Kennedy. Like the American president, Palme was a young, rich, and eloquent popular leader with an elite education and a well-honed appeal to the working class. Palme had studied at the country's most prominent boarding school at Sigtuna, and earned a degree in economics and political science from Kenyon College in Ohio. For many people to the left, Palme oozed too much affluence; to others on the right, he seemed to be a class traitor.

Palme had worked the last four years, since coming to office at age forty-two, for the extension of state welfare programs, protection of the environment, and the promotion of women's equality. The young leader was focused on an upcoming election, which as the rainbow of campaign posters around the capital proclaimed, was only three weeks away.

Palme's party, the Social Democrats, had ruled Sweden since the 1930s. They had come to power during the Great Depression—the same global crisis that brought Adolf Hitler and the Nazi Party to power in Germany. Sweden's Social Democrats, by contrast, were still in office, enjoying one of the longest periods of uninterrupted rule in a multiparty system in modern history.

It was the Social Democrats who had built the expansive welfare state. Palme's predecessors had transformed a poor country, with a small, thinly spread population into one of the richest and most advanced economies in the world. In terms of per-capita spending power, Sweden ranked among the top four countries (along with Finland, Switzerland, and the United States). It had many large multinational corporations and enjoyed a reputation for high-quality products, including aircraft, automobiles, ball bearings, furniture, and interior design.

The Social Democrats had become as Swedish as the country's more intangible cultural exports, like the films of Greta Garbo, Ingrid Bergman, and Ingmar Bergman, whose latest drama, *Scenes from a Marriage*, starring Liv Ullmann, had been released that spring in the United States. That summer, one of the warmest and most beautiful in years, the seventeen-year-old tennis sensation, Björn Borg, had reached the quarterfinals in Wimbledon for the first time, and a newly formed Stockholm pop band had decided upon a name: ABBA.

By the early 1970s, however, the national idyll was increasingly under strain. The economic boom of the postwar "European miracle" was over. The Swedish currency had fallen hard on the new, floating international exchange rates that were introduced earlier that March. Sweden was also, even before the shock of the first oil crisis, struggling to meet the expensive obligations of a welfare state. Trade was languishing, unemployment rising. Prices for basic commodities, meanwhile, skyrocketed. Palme's political opponents, riding the wave of unease, gained in popularity at his expense, and, many pundits believed, stood a good chance of unseating the Social Democrats. Palme was, in other words, in the fight of his political life.

Now, just as unthinkably, there was a gunman running amok in this celebrated "land of tomorrow."

ONE AFTER ANOTHER, BLACK-AND-WHITE POLICE CARS WITH WHIRLING
blue lights slammed into the square, parking haphazardly amid kiosks,
benches, and café tables with umbrellas. Other patrol cars parked on nearby
streets and policemen jogged toward the scene of the crime.

The gunman had already shot twice at the police. Inspector Ingemar
Warpefeldt had been hit in the right hand. The bullet had entered between
the middle finger and the index finger and shattered several bones in the
dorsum, or back of his hand. The policeman behind him on the staircase had
helped him to safety. Warpefeldt removed his bloodstained jacket and sipped
water. His hand, already swollen, was being wrapped. Blood dripped through
the towel onto the desk.

Warpefeldt had worked with the Stockholm police for thirty-one years
and had faced many dangerous situations, but this was the first time he had
been injured on the job. The gunman, he believed, had fired at his head,
because his hand had been at shoulder height when it was struck. He felt
lucky to be alive.

Back in the lobby, the gunman remained behind the teller counter with
three women at his side. A dark wig concealed his thinning auburn hair.
Tinted glasses hid his blue eyes, and makeup gave him a suntanned com-
plexion. His gray sweatshirt partially covered a bright-red jersey, and he wore
brown suede pants and black gloves.

The gunman angrily rebuked the women for taking cover without his
permission. He seemed nervous and agitated, even more so now than before.
Beads of sweat appeared on his neck. His eyes darted to the left and to the
right. He reacted to the least noise or movement, pointing with his submachine gun wherever he turned. His finger remained on or near the trigger.

He demanded to know all possible entrances to the lobby, where the
corridors led, and other details about the layout of the building. He asked
many questions, but, curiously, not a single one was about cash or deposits.
It did not look like a normal bank robbery—and that uncertainty about his
intentions made the attack all the more terrifying.

The male bank employee who had been ordered to tie up the women was
now sent to look for any other policemen hiding behind columns, counters,
desks, or anywhere else on the large and opulent ground floor. The robber
had asked his name. It was Bo Nilsson; he worked in accounting.

When Bo returned from his search empty-handed, the gunman accused him of lying and started yelling. The bank employee shook his head. There were no police there.

"Bo," he told him, "you are the first one I'll shoot if anything happens!"

The gunman ordered Bo to fetch another box of bullets from his bag. Then he changed his mind and shouted at Bo to go up the staircase where the policemen had retreated to find someone in authority. He wanted to talk.

THE FEW POLICE OFFICERS ALREADY ON THE BANK DIRECTORS' FLOOR were reluctant to enter the lobby. One officer told Bo to return downstairs himself and tell the gunman to put down his weapon and come out with his hands up. The bank employee had no desire to relay such a message to a hotheaded, apparently unstable man with a submachine gun. Perhaps they could find someone with a better command of the English language, he suggested, and remained in safety upstairs. This is where the matter stood when Morgan Rylander arrived on the scene and took charge.

Morgan was a thirty-two-year-old inspector in civilian clothes who worked in the drug-enforcement division of the Swedish National Bureau of Investigation. He had been driving with his colleague Kjell Lundgren and a female police recruit, Carina Larsson, south of the city center when they received the 10:10 a.m. radio call about the robbery. He turned the car around at a hot-dog stand on Ringvägen and sped away to Norrmalmstorg.

Borrowing a Walther 7.65 pistol from Carina, as he had forgotten his own that day, Morgan inserted the magazine, shoved the gun under his belt, and covered it with his T-shirt and jean jacket. He then ducked low and dashed across the square. He drew up next to a policeman lying on the sidewalk under a large window.

"What's happening?" Morgan asked.

"They are inside, and they have shot!" the policeman told him.

Morgan entered the bank through the neighboring staircase and came out on the second floor, where he saw four bank employees crouched down.

"Where are they?" Morgan whispered.

One of the employees motioned toward the staircase.

Morgan slowly descended the steps.

Behind the teller counter was a man with sunglasses and a curly bobbed haircut, wielding a submachine gun. He was adjusting the ropes around the ankles of three women while speaking to them in English.

"Do you only speak English?" yelled Morgan from behind one of the pillars.

"What do you think?"

"I think so."

"Step forward so that I can see you. Are you a cop?"

"Yes, I am," Morgan said, and reached toward his pocket to show his identification.

It was not necessary, the gunman indicated, waving away the formality with his submachine gun. "Are you armed?"

"No, I am not," Morgan said with some hesitation.

After lifting his jean jacket and turning around in a slow, 360-degree motion, his gun still concealed, Morgan was allowed to remain inside the bank.

To Morgan, who had considerable experience with drug users, the robber looked high, probably on amphetamines.

"What's your name?"

"Morgan."

"OK, Morg," the gunman said, with the sweat now running over his makeup. He was ready to state his demands: 3 million Swedish crowns. This was the equivalent of the pre-tax income that an average worker would earn in three lifetimes, a reporter for *Aftonbladet* later estimated.

When Morgan yelled this ransom up the staircase to the policemen who waited on the second floor, he appeared to smile, the robber thought, at the ambitious sum. But it was the second item on the list that would provoke even more disbelief. The gunman was demanding that the country's most infamous criminal, Clark Olofsson, be released from prison and brought to the bank.

3

Who I am does not matter. I am the one you call the robber or the desperado.

—The gunman in the bank

CLARK OLOFSSON WAS A HANDSOME TWENTY-SIX-YEAR-OLD WITH tousled dark brown hair and a short, thick beard. He looked vaguely like Jim Morrison of the Doors, and enjoyed a similar reputation for intelligence and charisma. Clark had recently made a prominent Swedish newspaper's list of the country's most influential opinion-makers.

This was perhaps a peculiar honor for a hardened criminal who had been in prison most of his adult life. Or at least supposed to have been in prison. Clark was notorious for escaping, which he had already done on multiple occasions—six by his own count. "If you do not risk anything, then you won't gain anything," he later said.

Clark's rise to fame had been swift and dramatic. Seven years before, he and a friend had been caught by the police in the middle of a burglary of a sports store in Nyköping. There was a brief clash that left one officer, Ragnar Sandahl, shot. Sandahl would die from the wounds sixteen days later. Clark's friend later confessed to firing the gun, but the police blamed Clark, who then led them on a four-week manhunt that held the country enthralled.

In his antics, Clark did not disappoint. He mocked authorities during the pursuit by recording interviews and mailing the tapes to the police. On another occasion, he showed up at a cinema in a stylish suit, made a show of purchasing a ticket, and then disappeared to a nearby hot-dog stand to watch the chaotic scene when the police emptied the building in a vain attempt to find him. Swedish tabloids covered his escapades in vivid detail.

"Have you seen that they no longer call me Olofsson," he allegedly told a friend, clearly delighted at the growing media attention. "They say Clark now."

Born February 1, 1947, Clark had grown up fast. His father, Sten, an excavator operator, had left the family, and his mother, Ing-Britt, had raised him and his two younger sisters in a small apartment in Trollhättan, an industrial town about 220 miles southwest of Stockholm. By age eight, when his mother had become ill, Clark was placed in the first of a number of foster homes. He had already shown a pronounced rebellious streak. "My enemies," Clark said, "were all those people who locked me in: the police, child protective services, guards, people, society, everyone!"

As a young boy, Clark started looking for ways to make money. As a teenager, he sold vodka and stole cars, particularly Volvos and Opels. He stole one particular Opel Rekord no fewer than three times. He soon moved on to larger and more profitable crimes, such as robbing banks. In May 1973, Clark received his current, six-year prison sentence for doing just that: aggravated robbery, illegal possession of weapons, and motor-vehicle theft.

During his incarcerations, Clark read voraciously. He studied the history of ideas and science as part of his university correspondence course. His favorite subject was the Renaissance. He devoured the essays of Montaigne and the musings of the ancient Stoics. "I like any kind of philosopher who puts good questions on the table," Clark said. "You can drink from their well."

As a prisoner, Clark used his clout to hold personal press conferences. He also started a progressive newspaper for his fellow inmates, *The Concrete Paper*. The publication not only made a profit but caused such an uproar because of its outspoken criticism of the prison system that authorities shut it down. Clark, one journalist said, was always a story.

But why had his release been demanded and, for that matter, who was the gunman?

———

THE POLICE FIRST SUSPECTED THAT HE WAS AN INTERNATIONAL TER-rorist. After all, he had not simply taken the loot and fled, as a conventional bank robber would have done. Moreover, he spoke English, rather than

Swedish, and, as far as anyone could tell, he did not appear to know a word of the Scandinavian language.

It was certainly easier in 1970s Sweden to believe that such an attacker would come from the Middle East, Northern Ireland, or someplace else, such as West Germany. In the latter, for instance, various radical left-wing groups had sprung up after the arrest the previous year of revolutionaries Andreas Baader and Ulrike Meinhof. It was there, too, at the 1972 Munich Olympic Games, that the Palestinian terrorist organization Black September had kidnapped and killed eleven members of the Israeli national team. The gunman at Norrmalmstorg could be from almost anywhere, it seemed, except for Sweden. Such acts were simply not committed by Swedes.

But in fact the gunman *was* Swedish. His name was Jan-Erik, or "Janne" Olsson. He was a thirty-two-year-old expert safe-cracker with a long criminal record of burglary, theft, and one account of assault for attacking an informant with a knife. The most recent of his seven convictions, February 11, 1972, was for grand larceny. He was actually still supposed to be serving that three-year sentence, but a couple of weeks earlier he had taken advantage of Sweden's progressive, rehabilitation-focused prison system, which allowed a temporary release on good behavior, so he fled.

Janne was born April 16, 1941, in Helsingborg, just a short ferry ride across the sound from Helsingør, Denmark, the home of Kronborg Castle, where William Shakespeare set his tragedy *Hamlet*. Janne's father, John-Erik, was a mechanic who worked at a paint manufacturing plant. He was authoritarian and distant, and they had a difficult relationship. His mother, Olga Matilda, on the other hand, showered him with affection. She taught him to dance as a child, showing him the tango and foxtrot in the kitchen of their small apartment. As a boy, Janne liked music, sports, air guns, and girls; his dream was to become a doctor. He had, however, left school by age fifteen.

Taking a job as a mess boy on the cargo ship *Victoria*, Janne had sailed off to an uncertain future. He returned home six months later, and worked, in quick succession, as a bellhop at a hotel, a clerk in a paint warehouse, and a laboratory assistant in a copper plant. In 1957, he enlisted in the navy, and it was there that he learned to handle a submachine gun. He called it his "lawyer."

At age twenty, Janne made his first major theft. He broke into a laundromat with some friends and carried off a heavy safe. With a blowtorch, a cutting blow pipe, and other welding tools that he had learned to use in a training course for blacksmiths and repairmen, he opened it to find 5,000 Swedish crowns. Years later, Janne wondered what would have happened had the safe been empty. In all honesty, probably nothing, he concluded. He enjoyed the adrenaline rush of busting open the strongbox and the thrill of not knowing what he might find inside. Besides, this was a good profession, as he called it, and it paid well.

Earlier that week, Janne had purchased the beige canvas bag at the Stockholm department store PUB and packed it with a map of the capital, a road atlas, a transistor radio, and a rope that he could use to tie up hostages. There was a set of walkie-talkies and fake passports, a change of clothes, a second pair of shoes, two hats, wool socks, and an array of other supplies, including hair dye and an extra wig. The bag was also packed, more ominously, with wires, fuses, blasting caps, and explosive pastes that could, if necessary, be assembled into powerful bombs.

That morning, Janne had woken about eight o'clock after tossing and turning throughout the night. He had eaten a light breakfast consisting of two sandwiches and coffee and then walked to a bench near the Ulvsunda library, where he flagged down a taxi to central Stockholm. Twenty minutes later, he had arrived at Norrmalmstorg. He took a quick walk around the square. Everything was in order. It looked like a typical Thursday.

At a public restroom behind the newspaper and magazine shop, Pressbyrån, Janne had made his final preparations. He applied the Avon bronzing powder and slipped on the wig, sunglasses, and the thin black gloves that he always used in a heist. He inserted the clip with thirty-six shots in his submachine gun, and slung the weapon around his neck, concealing it as much as possible under his jacket. He took a deep breath and approached the bank.

An older woman, leaving the building, held the door open for him. Janne smiled and entered.

4

—

Ugh, how incredibly easy it is to rob a bank. Good thing I didn't realize that earlier!

—Janne Olsson

NORRMALMSTORG WAS ALREADY BEING BLOCKED OFF TO TRAFFIC and pedestrians. Police officers with drawn pistols crawled on sidewalks and crept behind park benches, café tables, and vehicles parked in the square. One young blond police recruit, Barbro Lundberg, crouched behind a police Volkswagen van. The foreign press, less accustomed to female police officers, dubbed her "Gun Girl" and "Miss Sharpshooter."

Inside the bank, the erratic gunman kept three hostages at his side. The woman with the short black hair was Kristin Enmark, a twenty-three-year-old clerk who worked in the loans department office just off the lobby. She rarely came out front and had only done so that morning to bring a letter to her colleague, Bo Nilsson. She had been glad to run this particular errand, she later said, because she thought he was cute.

Kristin had been talking with Bo behind the teller counter for less than half a minute when the submachine gun salvo echoed throughout the marbled room. She had thrown herself to the floor, as ordered, thinking that it was a bank robbery that would soon be over. She looked up and saw Bo still sitting in his chair. *Get down*, she whispered. For a moment, Kristin wondered if she had overreacted. Then the gunman approached and ordered her to stand up.

The robber had then picked Bo to tie her up, her hands crossed in front of her chest and legs extended, with her ankles lashed together. The yellowish rope, typically used for clotheslines, was about as thin as an ink pen. Bo was forced, at gunpoint, to redo the knots when they did not seem tight enough. The blaring music was disorienting, and the telephones kept ringing.

Until that morning, Kristin had enjoyed her job at the bank. The position had been one of the first she had been offered after she left her home in Boliden in northern Sweden more than three years before, and followed her fiancé, John, to Stockholm. Their relationship, however, had ended the previous spring and Kristin had become interested in pursuing a degree in social work. She had hoped to remain at the bank until her classes began for the fall semester, which was only a few weeks away. The previous night, she had been up late with friends drinking vodka and Coca-Cola, and playing Yahtzee.

Now, with the ropes constraining her ankles and wrists, Kristin was terrified that the gunman would make an example out of her or one of her coworkers. She also worried that the police, clearly visible through the large windows, might rush into the lobby and open fire, possibly hitting her or them by mistake, or causing a deadly shootout. All the while, she did not know where to look. She did not want to let her gaze fall on the gunman, whom she feared was completely insane.

Thoughts streamed over her in a sequence that defied logic or reason. She recalled the day when she was four years old and awoke to find her father sitting beside her bed drinking a bottle of brandy. He had been crying and said something about a baby boy dying. The next morning, Kristin learned that her mother had given birth and her little brother had not survived.

Another image that came inexplicably to mind was a religious songbook that her grandfather had given her. Black cover, gold-edged pages—she saw it clearly. She also found herself thinking of her small apartment in the industrial community of Gustavsberg, east of the city center, where she took the 7:45 bus every morning to arrive at work by 9. Above all, she thought of her family: Her father, an employee of a cement company; her mother, a schoolteacher; and her three younger brothers and sisters. All of them seemed so far away.

Kristin had no idea, at the time, why she had been selected—it seemed like it could have been anyone. But Janne had in fact chosen her and the two other employees on purpose because they were women and looked younger than their colleagues nearby, many of whom were in their fifties. Janne did not believe that the police would dare to jeopardize *their* lives. Certainly, the police would not risk shooting at him as long as female bodies remained by his side.

As they waited for a high-ranking policeman, Janne sent Morgan to a black leather sofa in the lobby. He then bent down to readjust the ropes at the ankles of the hostages. Preoccupied with the task at hand, Janne turned to the police officer and said, referring to his own vulnerability: "Now you got your chance, Morg."

Morgan was thinking the same thing. It was certainly risky. He might miss his target, inadvertently hit one of the hostages, or otherwise squander the shaky trust he was starting to build. The gun, for the time being, remained hidden underneath his jean jacket.

ACROSS TOWN AT THE POLICE STATION ON KUNGSHOLMEN, COMMIS-sioner Sven Thorander sat at his desk reading reports about the previous night's crimes in the capital. There had been an attempted rape, a knife attack, two cases of domestic violence, and a non-life-threatening injury when a drug user fell off a balcony.

As chief of Stockholm's Homicide and Violence Squad, Thorander supervised the major criminal investigations in the capital. Reporters often sought interviews with this fifty-six-year-old who was known as a risk taker with nerves of steel. He would later be billed as "the real-life Martin Beck," after the famous fictional detective of the Maj Sjöwall and Per Wahlöö novels.

Thorander had just returned to work from vacation with his family in his summer cottage. It had been a rough transition back to the routine, and he was already looking forward to the weekend. When he heard the alarm, he had called for a car and taken off, speeding through traffic snarls using the emergency lane. He arrived at Norrmalmstorg around 10:30 a.m.

Policemen in the square told him that the robber had opened fire and warned him to keep his distance. Thorander went first to a public-transportation ticket booth near the bank, where he found a telephone and tried in vain to find some valuable information about the crime in progress. At that point, a colleague approached with news that the robber had demanded to speak with him.

"What, does he know me?" Thorander asked himself. He was also surprised because, from what he had heard, the gunman was supposed to be a foreigner.

Thorander entered the bank through the same side entrance that led to the suite of executive offices on the second floor. He spoke briefly with the wounded policeman, Ingemar Warpefeldt, and learned that an unknown number of bank employees and customers were still trapped or tied up. What did the attacker intend to do with these people, and why did he want Clark Olofsson?

Thorander descended the wooden staircase down to the lobby. Given its strategic location, it would serve as the site of many negotiations with the gunman. Police would dub it *snacktrappan*, or "the chat staircase."

Thorander looked out into the large, ornate room. His eye fell on Morgan Rylander, who was still sitting on the leather couch. The gunman was standing off to the side up a few steps on a landing in front of the customer vault, yelling something in English. Morgan confirmed that the new arrival was indeed a prominent policeman. Thorander received permission to enter and stepped away from the pillar into the open.

He removed his jacket, as ordered, and turned around to show that he did not carry any weapons, as he had in fact come unarmed. He then took another step forward.

"Stop right there!" the man yelled, stomping the floor.

Thorander could now see the gunman more closely. He was tall and powerfully built, as both Bo Nilsson and Ingemar Warpefeldt had said, and clearly in excellent physical condition. Above all, Thorander thought he looked irritable, unbalanced, "hyper-nervous" and "especially desperate." Around him were the three young women bound at their ankles and wrists. One of them with short blond hair was being held in front of him.

"Who are you?" Janne shouted.

"Commissioner Sven Thorander."

"Spell it."

Thorander was beginning to think that the gunman's English accent tipped him off not as an Arab, as some policemen had started to speculate, but as an American. His submachine gun, the commissioner also recognized, was a Swedish-made Carl Gustav m/45 used by many American Special Forces in the Vietnam War. No one trained in the Swedish military could use it so confidently, he thought. Was the gunman a veteran commando who had fought in Vietnam?

The transistor radio, switched on to channel P3, was broadcasting the news—and Janne's desire to follow developments in the story was the reason why he brought the radio into the bank. To maintain his pose as a foreign terrorist, the gunman had asked the women hostages to "translate" for him.

At one point that morning, the radio broadcast a live interview with a policeman who described the uncertainty about the situation and reported that Sven Thorander had entered the building to negotiate personally with the robber.

"Thorander, that's you!" the gunman said, and repeated his demand for Clark Olofsson. He gave the police two hours.

Then, abruptly, Janne deemed his own deadline too short and extended it to two-and-a-half hours. He warned Thorander that he would not wait any longer. And if the police did not bring Clark and the 3 million crowns to the bank by the designated time, Janne motioned with his submachine gun toward the three women hostages, leaving no doubt about the consequences.

Thorander promised to see what he could do.

No, the gunman said. "You will not see what you can do! Just bring him here!"

5

One fine day, they will be needed here too.

—Frank "Mickey" Spillane,
speaking about police snipers with a
Stockholm journalist in February 1973

JANNE HAD KNOWN CLARK FOR ONLY A FEW MONTHS. THEY HAD MET in the summer of 1973 at Kalmar Prison, a regional penitentiary on the coast of the Baltic Sea. Janne had been repairing mail bags at one of its workshops when Clark arrived as a new inmate and ended up in an adjacent cell. The two men began to talk.

Janne admired his intelligence, his wit, his renown in the criminal underworld, and his tales of thrilling, lucrative exploits. He also liked how Clark sang and played the guitar, both the six- and twelve-strings. "Clark could be quite charming when he wanted to be," Janne said, and he wanted to be his "gangster buddy." Clark, in turn, enjoyed the attention, and the two inmates started talking about possible heists together. One of them involved Janne taking advantage of his upcoming furlough on August 2, 1973, to help Clark escape from prison.

The plan was to smuggle into the premises a package containing dynamite, blasting caps, extension cables, and a small battery. This would be hidden in the ventilation of the workshop until the right moment, when the explosives would be placed in a certain window. A prearranged phone call from a friend asking to speak to Clark would send the guard to his cell. Clark would overpower him, blow out the window, and hop out onto the roof of the workshop only three feet away. From there he would climb down the drain-pipe, scale a fence, and escape.

Janne would be waiting with a rented car to drive them both to a certain dock, where they would board a rented boat and sail to the nearby Baltic island of Öland. There they would blend in among the summer tourists until Janne's younger brother, Åke, helped them reach the continent.

On August 6, the plot was set in motion. Janne arrived outside the prison, carrying supplies and hoping to pass himself off as a painter. The rented Mercedes was parked around the corner and the Albin Cruiser ready for the journey at sea, which they figured would be less risky than plane, train, car, or other means of transportation.

Unfortunately for Clark, there was a mishap. As he set up the dynamite, the extension cables connecting the battery to the blasting caps were not long enough to reach his cell, where he planned to ignite them. Improvising, he used an adjacent room. When he shut the door to protect himself from the explosion, that motion pulled the blasting cap away from the charge. The detonator then ignited on the floor. The window had not been damaged. Clark made a desperate run, wielding a Mora knife, toward the exercise yard and tried to climb the fence. Given an old shoulder injury, however, he lost his grip and the guards caught him.

Clark was then transferred to the more secure Norrköping Prison, where he now sat in isolation.

As for Janne, he had made his way by train toward Stockholm. He stayed in a small apartment in Ulvsunda, just outside the capital, with a twenty-one-year-old woman who had been one of Clark's girlfriends and was also, at that time, eight months pregnant with Clark's baby.

During the two weeks there, Janne walked with her around the harbor and looked at boats. They went shopping and enjoyed a seasonal crayfish dinner. They often spoke about Clark and the future. One night, they saw *The Godfather*; on another occasion, she recalled, they watched the action film *The Getaway*, which featured a bank robbery, hostage-taking, and Steve McQueen as a former convict on the run from the police. Unlike in many such movies, the McQueen character actually succeeded. The young woman loved it. She called it one of the best movies she had ever seen.

Soon the two of them were visiting various banks. That previous Monday, they had gone to three or four around Norrmalmstorg. One of them was Kreditbanken. By this time, Janne had come up with his new plan to free

Clark. Authorities would have no choice, Janne said, but to hand him over "on a silver platter."

AFTER LEAVING THE LOBBY, THORANDER RETURNED TO THE SECOND floor of the bank and called his supervisor, Superintendent Dag Halldin to report the gunman's demands and seek guidance. He could not be reached. Thorander tried the chief of police, Kurt Lindroth, but he was not available either. Thorander then called the minister of justice, Lennart Geijer, who oversaw Sweden's police and prison system. Yet this, too, was in vain. An assistant said that the official would call back as soon as possible.

Shouts were soon again echoing up the chat staircase. Thorander returned to the lobby to calm down the gunman.

The decision to hand over Clark was not one he could make himself, Thorander explained. It would require approval from the Justice Department. He had contacted authorities, he added, and should have news for him soon.

What about some drinks in the meantime?

Bottles of carbonated water were lugged down the staircase. The robber, however, preferred passion-fruit soda. Each time Thorander entered the lobby, he had to submit to the gunman's vetting procedures: gain permission to come forward, raise his arms, and turn around slowly to show that he was not armed. Janne did not speak in a calm, rational tone but barked his commands in a threatening manner.

When one of the women hostages requested a cigarette, Thorander pulled out his own pack of Camels and slid it across the floor. He also loaned her his own lighter. Janne stuffed it into his pocket.

Throughout the morning, during the long wait for news about Clark, Morgan would try to keep the robber as calm as possible. He whistled, told impromptu stories, and, at one point, sang Elvis Presley's "Lonesome Cowboy." Morgan knew from his eleven years' experience as a policeman that trying "something completely unexpected" can create opportunities for resolving a crisis. Morgan made it all the way through the song. This time, however, there was not the least reaction from the gunman, or anyone in the bank. The standoff continued.

6

We have experienced indeed what is truly a drama without precedent, broadcast live on television.

—Ingemar Odlander, television journalist

"SOME ROBBERS HAVE BARRICADED THEMSELVES IN THE MAIN offices of Kreditbanken at Norrmalmstorg," announced Lennart Broström on the radio news at 11 a.m. Six bank employees were believed to be held inside at gunpoint. A policeman had been wounded, and all available officers were on their way to central Stockholm. Little more was known about the attacker or attackers. It was a "serious crisis," the reporter added before cutting back to the studio.

Radio would broadcast every hour from the center of Norrmalmstorg. Television crews would follow suit in what Swedish tabloids soon dubbed the most thrilling bank robbery in modern history. The drama at Norrmalmstorg—a sudden, unexpected high-stakes development that shook the country—was to be one of Sweden's first media events.

Outside of major sports games, live television broadcasting was still a rare occurrence in Europe. But the Swedish media was in fact already mobilized to expect breaking news because, five days earlier, the country's beloved ninety-year-old king, Gustaf VI Adolf, had been rushed to the hospital for gastric hemorrhage. The popular monarch had undergone a late-night, three-hour operation. His ulcer, however, continued to bleed and many people did not expect him to survive.

As the manager of Sweden's only two television stations, Radio Sweden had sent its TV bus to the royal palace to capture the moment when the national flag would be lowered to half-staff. As they waited, however, the media executives learned of the bank robbery in progress and decided to send the idling TV bus to Norrmalmstorg. The bank drama would be broadcast live across the country and soon, too, around Europe and the world.

One of the many journalists flocking to the scene that morning was Bo Holmström, a handsome television reporter who was prominent and photogenic enough to play himself in the film *I Am Curious (Yellow)*. Holmström had risen to fame in the 1960s when Sweden had only one television channel and he was on it nearly every night, making him arguably more famous or recognizable than most celebrities.

Holmström had been Swedish television's first foreign correspondent to London, where he reported on the famous 1963 train robbery. He later worked in the United States, where he covered the *Apollo 11* landing on the moon. He still focused on international affairs, but he had been back in Stockholm, at that time, to attend an annual conference for foreign correspondents. Hearing the news of the heist, he followed his reporting instincts to Norrmalmstorg. He would not leave again for six days.

Traffic in the city center had already ground to a halt. The nearby thoroughfares Kungsgatan, Sveavägen, and Birger Jarlsgatan looked like a vast parking lot. City buses 46, 47, 50, 55, 61, and 69 were being rerouted away from the congestion. Curious Stockholmers, on the other hand, made detours toward Norrmalmstorg. No one could remember a sensational crime quite like the one taking place at that moment in the capital.

A policeman with a megaphone yelled for the crowds to back up behind the barricades. The number of spectators only grew, and from time to time some of them tried to pass the police lines. Construction workers at a nearby site cheered and catcalled as the police cars raced by.

The police were now pouring into Norrmalmstorg. Policemen wearing helmets, bulletproof vests, and carrying submachine guns, milled about behind cars, vans, and tables in the square. Other officers moved in closer, zigzagging their way forward on the sidewalks. A reporter for *Svenska Dagbladet* compared the center of the capital to an occupied city. His colleague at *Expressen* thought it seemed more like a battlefield.

With television cameras still rolling, an ambulance made its way to the front of the bank. Had the gunman already shot someone else? reporters wondered. Instead, an older woman had collapsed in the lobby. Morgan, enjoying his growing rapport with the gunman, had asked permission for her to leave.

"There are people lying there," Morgan said when he heard her groaning in the employee space behind the teller counter. "Do you need them anymore?"

Janne glanced over in that direction and said, "Let them out!"

Morgan escorted the older woman, who suffered from a heart condition, and the two coworkers near her, out of the lobby. Janne instructed them to take as much time as they needed.

Some policemen in a reconnaissance unit, in the meantime, had taken up position at Pressbyrån's kiosk. They had a view inside the ground floor of the building. The gunman, they could see, moved about with his human shields, showing agitation and making jerky motions, pointing his submachine gun wherever he turned. About 11:30 a.m., however, the robber and his captives disappeared from sight.

———

JANNE HAD TAKEN THE HOSTAGES TOWARD THE CUSTOMER VAULT, which was located up a half-staircase from the lobby. He kept Kristin and her colleague, Elisabeth Oldgren, on the landing outside.

Kristin barely knew Elisabeth, the woman with short blond hair in a white cardigan sweater whom the gunman had held with his left forearm wedged around her neck and the submachine gun pressed into her ribs. Elisabeth had only worked at the bank for about a year. Just one month before, to the day, she had celebrated her twenty-first birthday, making her the youngest of the hostages.

Like Kristin, Elisabeth came from the far north of Sweden, in her case, Vitvattnet near the Arctic Circle. She, too, wanted to return to school, though her hopes were set on nursing. Elisabeth had found her way to Stockholm the previous year after first moving with her family to southwestern Sweden, where her father worked as a principal at a boarding school. That morning, Elisabeth had been talking on the phone at her desk behind the teller counter when she heard the gunshots. She had gone down to the floor when she saw everyone else doing it.

It was when Elisabeth poked her head up for a quick look around the lobby that the gunman caught her eye. He pulled her to her feet and clutched her in front of him, holding her so close that she could read the serial number on the gun: it was 181931. She feared that this man, with his bizarre, unpredictable moves, was "the world's worst desperado who would mow us all down." She tried to distract herself from the sheer terror by imagining the crayfish dinner party she was supposed to be enjoying that weekend at a beach house.

The third woman, Birgitta Lundblad, was ordered to carry Janne's canvas bag into the vault. Birgitta was a thirty-one-year-old bank employee with short blond hair wearing a yellow sweater, green skirt, and a pair of black-and-white low-heeled shoes. She had been verifying a check at her desk near Elisabeth's when all of a sudden she heard what sounded like the ceiling crashing down. She dove under a desk, squeezing into a small space in front of the foot rest. The gunman, alas, found her and forced Bo to tie her up in the middle of the floor near a marble pillar.

Before that morning, Birgitta had only exchanged a few words with Elisabeth and did not know Kristin at all. She had worked at the bank for about six months. She had quit her last job to spend more time with her two young daughters, and worked part-time as an *extern reserv*, or alternate. This position involved covering bank branches or departments as needed, and usually meant working two or three days a week. Kreditbanken had thus far been an excellent fit. That morning, Birgitta had been thinking of going shopping on her lunch break for children's clothes on sale at a nearby store. Now she worried about what would happen to her family should the nervous submachine-gun wielding maniac, visibly on edge, panic and again open fire.

THROUGHOUT THE MORNING, SEVERAL MORE POLICEMEN SLIPPED INTO the building. Morgan, sometimes sitting in the leather sofa or standing next to the teller counter, could see and hear them more than Janne, who now mostly remained on the landing. Morgan talked and whistled, hoping to muffle the noise of their movements.

He also kept trying to assure Janne that Clark and the ransom money were on the way. Time, however, dragged on and nothing seemed to be happening. Janne was growing impatient.

Thorander came down the staircase to suggest that they call the prison so the gunman could speak to Clark himself. It was an improvised move, but he hoped that a phone call would comfort "the desperado," as the media would soon begin calling him, and that their conversation might provide

clues to his identity. It would also buy time as Thorander waited on direc-
tives from the Justice Department and the Stockholm Police. Both the chief
of police, Kurt Lindroth, and his superintendent, Dag Halldin, were en route
to Norrmalmstorg.

Thorander walked over to a telephone and tried to call the prison. The
phone dropped the connection after about thirty seconds.

The authorities have probably tampered with it, Janne told him. Call the
prison with a different phone and ask them to ring the bank.

As Thorander went off to find another line, he hopped over the teller
counter with a dexterity that impressed Kristin. Along the way, Thorander
saw four or five bodies lying completely still between desks, the office furniture, and the empty rolling chairs. He feared that the people, all bank
employees, might be dead, until one of them finally made the slightest move.

The wait on the prison to call back seemed interminable. Then, just out
of sight of the gunman, Thorander saw two policemen in bulletproof vests
sneaking forward with submachine guns and realized that, if the robber saw
them, he was standing in the line of fire. It was the first time that morning
the commissioner felt really frightened.

Thorander asked for a cigarette.

The gunman told Elisabeth to give him one. When Thorander
approached to take it, Janne warned him not to take another step. The burning cigarette was then tossed to the police commissioner. Extinguished in
midair, a second attempt succeeded.

The telephone finally rang. Janne ordered the commissioner to set the
receiver down and slowly back away.

7

I had absolutely nothing to run to, but a great deal to run away from.

—Clark Olofsson

NINETY MILES AWAY AT NORRKÖPING PRISON, CLARK OLOFSSON HAD just sat down with a bowl of pea soup, a traditional Swedish dish enjoyed on Thursdays. He would not have time for the pancakes that typically followed.

A guard approached and demanded that he come with him.

"Can't I at least finish my food first?" Clark asked. "What is this about? What have I done now?"

Clark was led into the Administration Building of the nearly two-hundred-year-old institution that served as the country's oldest penitentiary then still in use. He was taken to the office of the warden. Waiting for him was the acting director, Gunilla Arnerdal, because her boss, like many people in Sweden during August, was on vacation.

Gunilla smoked her pipe. No one said a word until the official informed Clark that someone wanted to speak with him.

"Oh yeah, who?" Clark asked.

"Don't you know?"

Clark wondered what had happened. The prison usually did not interrupt an inmate's meals unless it was serious. He feared that someone in his family had died, he later said. The mood was somber and tense.

Gunilla then picked up the phone, dialed a number, and handed Clark the receiver.

A voice then asked in English: "Do you want to come to my party in Stockholm?"

It was a short, strange phone conversation, Gunilla thought. Clark grunted, mumbled, and spoke mostly in monosyllables without revealing how much, if anything, he knew of the situation. Even Janne on the other end of the line did not think that Clark had recognized him. He had made a point of saying a few words in Arabic that Clark had taught him in prison from his days in Beirut. This would perhaps signal Janne's identity, and, at the same time, contribute to the overall impression to eavesdropping policemen that he was a foreign terrorist.

"What is this?" Clark asked after hanging up the phone. "Is some journalist joking with me or something?"

Gunilla told him about the bank robbery and the demand for his release. Clark said he began to understand.

Given his responses during the call, Gunilla now believed that he'd had no idea of the situation in Stockholm until she explained it to him. Years later, Clark admitted that he had in fact recognized the caller but maintained that he knew nothing of the plot itself.

He had first thought that Janne was calling to gloat about being free while he was not. Then, Clark remembered what he called "the bedtime stories" that he had been telling Janne every night about exciting criminal escapades and possible heists that could be pulled off, including hostage-taking. Janne had listened closely, Clark said, but he had never thought he would actually do it.

———

BY 11:45 A.M., SWEDISH AUTHORITIES HAD CRAFTED A STRATEGY. THE Justice Department had already learned of the matter when Thorander called to relay the robber's demands. An official had heard the news on the radio and went at once to report it to his boss, Lennart Geijer. As minister of justice, the sixty-three-year-old Social Democrat was responsible for the country's prisons and police.

After speaking with his staff, Geijer had decided to grant the police permission to bring Clark to Stockholm as a "precautionary measure." This was important, he thought, in case the gunman started shooting hostages at periodic intervals until his demands were met. Transporting Clark to the capital sooner rather than later could save lives.

But there was an important caveat. The police were not to allow Clark to enter the bank itself unless the robber first released the hostages. The risks were too many and too great. The prime minister, Olof Palme, had agreed completely with this reasoning.

This governmental decision would place enormous pressure on the police. They would have to bear full responsibility for the outcome of the affair without having the freedom to maneuver that negotiations might require. The immediate plan was then to buy time by fulfilling *part* of the gunman's demands. The police would, in other words, concentrate on stalling, with the hope of wearing him down. He might surrender, crack under stress, or make a serious mistake that would enable them to pounce.

And that meant relying on sharpshooters.

So snipers moved into position on balconies and rooftops of nearby buildings, or behind trees and overturned café tables in the adjacent Berzelii Park. A handful of policemen known to be excellent shots prepared to descend the wooden staircase and enter the lobby. The tactical objective was to find Janne, in a careless moment, stepping into the line of fire without the protection of the three women hostages at his side.

ON THE WAY BACK TO HIS CELL, CLARK SAW A FELLOW PRISONER IN THE exercise yard and yelled the incredible news. "You are not going to believe me, but some fucker in Stockholm has taken hostages in a bank and wants me to come there and help him get away."

It was not long before the news on the radio confirmed the fact. Thanks to the media, too, Clark learned that a policeman had been shot inside the bank, and a second officer was missing. Were the authorities really going to let him leave prison to join this desperado?

Clark also wondered if he should let the police know the identity of the gunman. If he did, they would probably suspect him of being involved in planning the attack and then not let him go to Stockholm. If he said nothing, on the other hand, authorities might not dare to hand him over to an unknown and presumably dangerous criminal, who, for all they knew, might intend to harm him. Clark's task was, he said, "to balance on a knife's edge."

Awaiting transport, Clark tried to read and relax.

Janne, too, was waiting. For Clark and the money. The deadline was approaching.

But the police dragged their feet, though not all the delays were intentional. Officials at Norrköping Prison refused to release Clark—and officials at the city police department refused to transport him—without a written order from the government. "We cannot send him there just because you want it," Gunilla told Sven Thorander.

It would take an irate telephone call from the Justice Department to set everything in motion.

Around 1 p.m., veteran policeman Bror Axel Molin, picked Clark up from his cell. Eight other police officers and three cars were waiting outside to bring the prisoner to the capital. Clark sat between Molin and a colleague in the backseat of the second car. He was handcuffed. Clark protested that the minister of justice should instead be grateful to him for coming to the government's aid in this crisis.

Reporters had been calling the prison all morning for information. Photographers and camera crews waited outside the gates for any sign of Clark. Cameras snapped and flashed as his car sped past. Journalists then hopped into vehicles and followed in pursuit.

Clark could not quite believe his good fortune. Did the police really think that he would help them? At any rate, he was not going to protest. He was out of prison. He was on his way to Stockholm. By the end of the day, he might well find a way to turn this extraordinary situation to his advantage.

During the ride, Clark cracked jokes and spoke lovingly of his fiancée, Maria Wallin, a twenty-one-year-old student who lived in Gothenburg. He described his travels around the world with such relish that at least one policeman in the car thought that he expected to resume them in the near future. Clark's high spirits contrasted with the policemen's caution and vigilance. They had to be prepared, they had been warned, in case the demand for Clark was a trap and a prelude to an ambush.

The officers tried to extract as much information as possible about the unidentified robber in the bank. Clark played it cool. He said little, parrying their questions with vague or ambiguous answers. When someone asked if the robber was a foreigner, Clark laughed. He spoke even less as they approached Stockholm. He smoked his cigarette and stared out the window. From time to time, Clark saw people who had heard the news of his release and come out to cheer him by the side of the road as the car passed. Some people held signs, others waved. It must have felt like a triumphal parade into the capital.

Before they reached their destination, one of the policemen mentioned the possibility of helping shorten Clark's six-year prison sentence. Perhaps, too, they could see to it that he earned more furloughs for good behavior. Even the potential of a pardon was mentioned. Was he interested?

Clark said that he would do anything to spend less time in prison.

8

Personally, I believed that he was a mentally sick ... [and] extraordinarily dangerous person!

—Kurt Lindroth, Stockholm chief of police

B Y NOON, A REPORTER FOR *AFTONBLADET* COUNTED SOME THIRTY police cars and nearly one hundred policemen around the square. The crowd beyond the barricades was already estimated at several thousand, and they looked on the action, *Svenska Dagbladet* said, like rowdy fans of Stockholm's Hammarby soccer team.

The chief of police, Kurt Lindroth, had arrived in the makeshift headquarters on the second floor of the bank. Lindroth was then in his third year running the Stockholm force. His career had begun in 1940 as a constable patrolling the streets, and he had worked his way up, earning a law degree and, for a time, serving as a prosecutor. About medium height with blond hair, the fifty-five-year-old Lindroth was known as a hardworking reformer with an artistic and musical bent. His colleagues called him "the kind policeman."

Lindroth's priority was not only to rescue the hostages but also to figure out the identity of the attacker. Given the latter's demand to free Clark, investigators started looking into Clark's known associates and soon had an alternative to the foreign-terrorist or American-commando theories. In fact, the police kept hearing the same name tossed about: Kaj Robert Hansson, a twenty-one-year-old bank robber from southern Sweden who was on the run from the police.

Seven months before, Clark and Kaj had robbed a bank together in Gothenburg. They had then fled the scene in a stolen Volvo, stopping off at a hotel an hour away in the spa town of Ulricehamn. A few days later, Kaj made the mistake of leaving a bag with a loaded pistol out on the bed and a maid discovered it. Later, in another moment of carelessness, Kaj called the hotel and left a message for Clark, giving his real name and telephone number. The police then arrested them both.

Kaj had received four and a half years in prison for the robbery. On July 2, 1973, however, he had escaped. Feigning illness, he had persuaded authorities to send him to the hospital and from there, he climbed out of a window. He made his way back south to the university town of Lund, where bank security cameras captured him robbing yet another bank. He had not bothered to disguise himself. In fact, the robbery appeared to be spontaneous. He had come in to cash a check, but when the teller recognized him and refused, Kaj demanded the entire cash register.

Kaj was regarded as a violent and highly unstable criminal. Perhaps the attack at Norrmalmstorg, police investigators speculated, was an attempt to redeem himself and patch things up with Clark after the blunders that botched their last bank robbery together. Kaj, it was also said, virtually idolized Clark—and Clark, in turn, was believed to be one of the few people who could control him. And so Clark's help, the police concluded, would be vital in dealing with this dangerous and unpredictable attacker.

AS LUNCHTIME APPROACHED, THE POLICE CAME IN TO THE LOBBY WITH a tray of landgångar, traditional open-faced sandwiches with an assortment of delicacies. Janne, suspicious that the food had been drugged, ordered Morgan to start eating.

The policeman feared the same thing, but ate without incident.

Moments later, the gunman tossed one of the soft-drink bottles to Morgan, presumably to gauge his reaction speed. The bottle crashed to the floor. Janne then tauntingly rolled the next one across the floor to Morgan.

After lunch, the door to the Hamngatan entrance flew open and a man in a brown suit walked straight into the lobby. "Guys, I think you should cut it out," he said, waving his arms. "You are not going to pull it off."

Janne was clearly unsettled. He asked Morgan if he knew this person.

"No, I have never seen him before."

The man had heard the news of the robbery and had come to help them resolve the crisis. He had simply stridden through the police lines with such confidence that no one had stopped him.

"Get him out of here!" Janne yelled.

Grabbing him by the collar and the belt, Morgan escorted the gentleman out of the bank. This was the most dangerous moment thus far, Morgan thought, fearing that this unexpected visitor might cause the gunman to panic and start shooting again. The incident also showed that there were some serious flaws with the police lines that supposedly sealed off the square.

With Janne's deadline looming, the police decided to send in the ransom, or at least the first part of it. To carry the money down the staircase, Thorander picked Dr. Nils Bejerot, a fifty-two-year-old psychiatrist who had been called in to advise the police. Bejerot asked Janne's permission before he entered the lobby. Janne glanced toward Morgan as if to ask if the police were sending in a psychiatrist because they thought he was crazy. Morgan nodded. Janne laughed.

Holding Elisabeth in front of him, Janne told Morgan to take the knife and cut open the bag to confirm its contents. It was all in crisp, brand-new bills, numbered consecutively and still with the bands around them. They were worthless, Janne knew, because they could be easily traced. Exchange these for old bills, he exploded, and bring Clark at once.

With assurance that Clark was on the way, Janne soon allowed more people to leave the bank. First out had been Anita Bohman, the teller at window number one, who had sounded the alarm; her colleague, Gudrun Hauffman, who worked at a desk behind her; and Runa Bösman, the other teller working that morning, who told reporters that she had looked right into the face of the attacker and thought, "The robber had kind eyes."

Next to leave were three men, also all bank employees who had been forced to lie on the floor: Herbert Bergman, Ulf Andersson, and Ralf Carteg. It was certainly encouraging to see some hostages walking out of the building unharmed.

One of Elisabeth's relatives, an uncle who worked as an engineer south of the city center, felt confident that she, too, would be OK. The gunman had probably selected her because she spoke excellent English, he thought, and planned to use her to negotiate with the police. He expressed confidence in his niece's ability to deal with the stress. She was both physically and emotionally strong.

At some point in the late morning, Elisabeth had to use the restroom. Janne had first refused, pointing to a small wastebasket, though he relented and allowed her to walk unaccompanied to the staff bathroom, located down the steps and around the corner. Kristin and Birgitta followed one at a time, also without a chaperone.

It may have seemed peculiar that each woman returned to their captor, as reporters noted, when they learned of the fact, but the motivation was rather straightforward: fear of what the gunman might do to their fellow hostages if they tried to escape. A few steps away could be freedom, but the consequences could be devastating for those left behind.

What they saw, on their way back to the vault, was a lobby with police officers hiding here and there, with black helmets, bulletproof vests, and submachine guns. It was a frightening sight. The Stockholm police had borrowed equipment from the military, including an armored car, and surrounded Norrmalmstorg with what Swedish television called an "iron ring." And that ring already seemed to be tightening.

"HERE AT NORRMALMSTORG, A VERY DRAMATIC EVENT OUTSIDE KREDIT-banken," Bo Holmström began shortly after 1 p.m. for the breaking news update for TV2. "The police just now have said that they are going to try, if they can, to shoot the man with the submachine gun in the lobby."

Holmström went on to describe how the robber could be seen from time to time through the large windows, shoving his gun in the face of the hostages. Outside, police and reporters alike took cover behind kiosks and café tables, in fear of gunfire. Holmström was doing that himself, triangulated between two police cars and a police van, as he gave a rundown of the morning's developments.

"We are prepared for a dramatic resolution to the bank robbery at Norrmalmstorg today," Holmström said. "Back to the studio."

Minutes later, a colleague at TV2 followed up with the breaking news that Clark Olofsson was reportedly on his way to Stockholm. "The tense, nervous expectation at the square only continues," the announcer said.

The deadline for Clark and the ransom money had passed more than an hour ago, and Janne was growing restless. He pointed his submachine gun at Morgan and ordered him to "do something."

"I cannot do anything," Morgan protested. "I am standing right here!"

Janne gave him a hard look but accepted this response.

Then, about twenty minutes later, Janne ran down the landing and stopped about twenty feet away from Morgan to take up a shooting position. He aimed his submachine gun right at the police officer.

"Do you think I should miss?"

Morgan picked up one of the bottles on the teller counter, removed the cap, and took a sip. He swished it around in his mouth and swallowed. Coolly and deliberately, he stared at the robber and said with a smile and a shoulder shrug, "Why should you?"

Janne lowered his weapon. He seemed satisfied with this answer.

Not long afterward, as he had returned to the landing outside the customer vault, Janne heard something on the far side of the lobby beyond his view. It was clearly a policeman in the building. Janne sent Morgan to remove him.

Rounding the corner into largely unexplored territory, Morgan passed a couple of smaller offices in the loans department. A young policeman, startled, raised his gun. Morgan quickly grabbed the barrel and pushed it aside. "Don't shoot, dammit," he said, and told his colleague that the gunman wanted him to leave. Morgan escorted him out.

"There are more there," Janne said afterward.

As Morgan went to take another look, he saw his former roommate at the police academy, Håkan Larsson, with his gun, lying in wait under a desk. Morgan, at once, felt more secure. Larsson was a fearless police veteran and an excellent marksman.

Morgan passed Larsson and looked into a corner office, where he found two older bank employees sitting motionless at a desk, staring straight ahead.

"There are people sitting here," Morgan yelled to the gunman across the lobby. "Do you need them?"

Janne said to let them go.

CLARK'S CARAVAN, MEANWHILE, HAD ARRIVED IN STOCKHOLM. THE first stop was the police station at Kungsholmen. Officers and plainclothes detectives bustled about its corridors, popping by to ask Clark if he wanted something to eat or drink. Two policemen soon came to take him to a large, darkened room that turned out to be Sven Thorander's office.

Officers filed in after him and lined the back walls of the room. One of them said that there would soon be a phone call and motioned for Clark to sit down. He was given Thorander's own chair. On the desk beside him, near a giant telephone, a reading lamp shone the room's single stream of light onto a folder. It was labeled "Kaj Robert Hansson."

Did the police, Clark wondered, suspect Kaj was the gunman in the bank?

The police had planted the dossier on the desk with the hope of scrutinizing Clark's reaction as he supposedly "stumbled upon" the name of his old accomplice. Instinctively, Clark had pushed the folder to the side. The police did not miss his reaction. And Clark had not overlooked their scrutiny either. Quick glances and furtive nods by the uniformed men in the back of the room convinced Clark that he was correct in his assumptions.

When the phone rang, Clark answered, as instructed. It was Sven Thorander at Norrmalmstorg.

After confirming that Clark was still willing to help save the lives of the hostages, Thorander told him to expect a second call, this time from the robber in the bank. Clark sensed another trick.

Authorities, undoubtedly, would be listening to, if not also recording, the conversation—he could not have failed to notice the phone-surveillance equipment in the room. Worse, Clark suspected, the police would encourage the gunman to talk on the telephone so that snipers could take advantage of his distraction and render it "game over."

The phone rang. Clark confirmed that he was in Stockholm and ready to come to the bank. He preempted further talk by warning Janne that the call was being recorded. He spoke low and fast, with as few words as possible, and then ended the brief conversation by saying that he would not talk any further on the telephone.

"That was unnecessary," complained a policeman in the back of the room.

As Clark was escorted out of the office, another officer asked if he cared to identify the robber.

He declined.

"You do not have to say anything," the policeman said. "We already know who it is."

9

In this decisive moment . . . a society of laws stands powerless. Lawless-
ness and brutal violence triumph. The criminal with the submachine
gun in his hand dictates the conditions. The authorities are forced to act
against all reasonable intentions.

—*Smålandsposten*, August 24, 1973

A T CHANCELLERY HOUSE, OLOF PALME WAS HOLDING AN ALREADY-
scheduled press conference about the king's health and his own plans
for the upcoming national election. When the prime minister opened
the floor to questions, many reporters focused instead on the extraordinary
events inside the Stockholm bank.

Did the police really intend to meet the gunman's demands and deliver
Clark to Norrmalmstorg? If so, would Palme kindly explain the reasoning, and did he not anticipate that this would lead to a rash of copycat
crimes? Was Clark, for that matter, involved in the plot, and if not, how
could authorities ensure his safety if they did not know the identity of the
desperado?

The priority, Palme said, was to save the lives of the hostages. Police
were already working on identifying the gunman and they would of course
preserve law and order. Palme spoke too long and accepted too few questions, said a *Svenska Dagbladet* reporter.

The hostage crisis at Norrmalmstorg was a veritable minefield. Yielding
to the gunman's demands would make the government look weak, hardly
a desirable prospect on the eve of an election. A hardline approach, on the

other hand, risked escalating the crisis into a bloodbath. Anything the prime minister did—or didn't do—might prove crucial, perhaps even decisive.

The national election risked indeed being hijacked and held hostage by a gunman in the bank.

———

ABOUT A QUARTER AFTER FOUR O'CLOCK THAT SUNNY, WINDY AFTERnoon, three cars arrived at Norrmalmstorg. Out of the second vehicle stepped Clark, wearing a fashionable blue-and-white mottled sweater and blue corduroys. He was handcuffed to two policemen. Cameras flashed all around the square. As one Associated Press correspondent later put it, he looked like a "scruffy Scandinavian mixture of Jesse James and Warren Beatty."

Clark was brought through the crowded street to the entrance at Norrmalmstorg 2A and then to one of the bank director offices on the second floor. Waiting there were a number of high-ranking police officers. Clark recognized Sven Thorander from his photographs in the newspaper. The chief of police, Kurt Lindroth, and psychiatrist, Dr. Nils Bejerot, were also present. Thorander introduced his colleagues to Clark, removed his handcuffs, and offered him a beer. Several of the men began to smoke.

The situation was tense and unchanged, and the police needed Clark's help, Thorander said, gesturing to the square outside, filled with Stockholm police.

The recent ploy by the police to seek confirmation that Kaj was the robber had played right into Clark's hands. Confident that they had identified the gunman, the police leadership exerted no real pressure on Clark to make a difficult choice; that is, he did not have to decide between revealing Janne's identity (and risk being accused of complicity in the plot) and claiming ignorance (and possibly not be allowed inside the bank).

The police appealed to Clark to "do a good deed" and save the hostages. The entire country was watching, Thorander said, and Clark could make a real difference. The more vaguely Clark responded to their overtures, the more attractive the offers became from this "brain trust," as Clark mockingly called them. Thorander mentioned at least one week of furlough and potential police support for a pardon. According to Clark, he went further, offering three weeks of freedom and even hinting, of all things, that he might be able to rob a bank during this time.

Suddenly, according to a confidential police report, a policeman rushed into the room. The gunman, who had heard on the radio that Clark had arrived on the scene, had started to strangle one of the women and demanded that Clark be handed over immediately.

"She is screaming. He is completely desperate down there. What shall we do?"

Thorander and the men stepped away to discuss the dilemma. Moments later, Jonny Jonsson, one of the younger, athletic detective inspectors in the entourage, approached Clark and asked if he would promise to cooperate if they let him into the bank. Jonsson emphasized the risks, including the possibility of death.

Clark agreed to take his chances.

There was no time to inform the minister of justice. A team of police officers escorted Clark down the corridor to the chat staircase.

One of the policemen had earlier asked Clark if he knew the gunman.

Yes, he said, and "he is crazy enough to do anything."

10

If the police had been as cutthroat as I am, this hostage drama would have been over in an hour.

—Clark Olofsson

HAD SOMEONE ACTUALLY BEEN STRANGLED? IT IS HIGHLY UNLIKELY. Janne, of course, denied the allegation. Elisabeth dismissed it as false, as did Kristin and Birgitta. Morgan Rylander, who had been closer to the action thus far than any other policeman, said that it most certainly did not happen.

But a policeman had in fact run into the second-floor room with the warning that a hostage was about to be choked. Clark remembered the incident too. There had been considerable shouting outside the room in the corridor, and he caught fragments of the dialogue, including a reminder that the Justice Department had refused to allow him into the lobby.

The police were confronted with a volatile situation that threatened to escalate at any moment. The gunman had already opened fire, wounding one police officer, and he had hinted earlier that the hostages would pay the price if the police did not comply with his demands. Still, from the perspective of the Swedish government, orders were orders and the police chief had failed to follow them.

As Thorander returned to his makeshift office on the second floor of the bank, the phone was already ringing. It was the Justice Department. Geijer's assistant, Ove Rainer, wanted to speak to the police chief.

He was not there, Thorander said.

At this point, Thorander received a memorable scolding. He would relay the message, he said, and hung up. "We had more important things to deal with just then," Thorander later said.

Releasing Clark into the bank had been a gamble that, in one sense, opened new possibilities for the Stockholm police. Clark *could* be a valuable ally inside the bank. He might use his charm to persuade the gunman to surrender, or even catch him off-guard, seize his weapon, and free the hostages. Even if these situations were long shots at best, they were preferred over many alternatives that the police could imagine.

At the same time, now that Clark had entered the lobby, in deliberate defiance of the government's orders, another thing was clear: If anything went wrong whatsoever, the Stockholm police would take the blame.

ONCE AGAIN, CLARK COULD NOT BELIEVE HIS STROKE OF LUCK. HE HURried down the staircase before the authorities changed their mind. All around him, sprawled out on the steps, were armed policemen in helmets and bulletproof vests.

Clark looked exactly like he did in the newspapers, Kristin thought when she saw him for the first time in the lobby. He was tall, even taller than Janne. His hair was long, his beard was disheveled. He exuded outlaw glamor and rebel mystique. He reminded her of a Swedish Che Guevara.

Clark scanned the lobby and saw Morgan Rylander, leaning against the teller counter.

"Are you a cop?" Clark asked.

"Uh-huh."

"There are too many cops here, you understand," Clark said, and asked him to leave.

Morgan hesitated. Was a policeman really to obey a convicted felon?

Jonny Jonsson, one of the officers who had escorted Clark down the staircase, reassured Morgan that everything was OK. "He is with us."

Morgan did leave the lobby, though he remained at Norrmalmstorg, as Janne requested, in case he was needed.

Clark looked around for the gunman. He would be the first person to know, without a shred of doubt, if the police were correct in identifying the attacker as Kaj Hansson. Then, to his left, Clark saw him, holding a blond woman.

Clark paused.

The robber was tall and athletically built, like Janne, but otherwise bore little resemblance to the person he had expected to find. The gunman's hair, for one thing, was much longer. Janne—in his choice of wigs—had inadvertently come to resemble Kaj.

Come closer, the gunman said, and whispered a nickname from prison: "Shaggy."

"What the hell, is that you?"

Almost immediately, Clark and Janne embraced and huddled off to the side. None of the policemen or the hostages in the vicinity could hear what they said. Janne nodded a few times.

Most likely Clark said what both men later stated on separate occasions: He let Janne know that the police had tried to bribe him if he helped them secure a surrender or capture.

Clark would never reveal Janne's identity to anyone on the police force. He did not let them know, either, that their Kaj theory was dead wrong. Throughout the afternoon, whenever he spoke of the gunman, Clark tended to use an indiscriminate term like "robber" or the pronoun "he." Clark also stressed the attacker's unpredictability and instability. All of this, of course, increased his own importance as an intermediary in the crisis.

11

For too long, we have had the same goal as the bank directors, that is, to obtain for ourselves as much dough as possible. But, you know, I just want to be free.

—Clark Olofsson,
as told to fellow inmate Harri Miekkalinna

NOW THAT CLARK HAD ARRIVED, THE OTHER ITEM ON THE ROBBER'S list of demands was the ransom money. Three large bags of cash from the Riksbank, or national bank, stood in the middle of the lobby, presumably this time in old bills. Clark carried them into the vault. There were 150 bundles, each one with one hundred 100-crown notes that came to a total of 1.5 million crowns, or about $2 million today, which was only half the ransom. Janne began to yell. He sent Clark to confront the police.

Lindroth and Thorander were still dragging out the negotiations with the hopes of wearing down the robber. In the meantime, they increased their arsenal. Automatic carbines with riflescopes and light amplifiers were on their way from a depot in Ursvik, as were two hunting rifles borrowed from the coast guard. These weapons would be far more effective than normal police-issue pistols, particularly at hitting precise targets at short range.

What's more, some of the guns would be loaded with so-called dumdum bullets, or projectiles whose metal casing had been cut to expand and fragment upon impact. Named after the site where first manufactured, by the British in Dumdum, India, these modified bullets had been prohibited in warfare by the Hague Convention since 1899 for the immense suffering they caused. The police used them mainly on moose or other large animals wounded in traffic accidents.

Morgan Rylander, meanwhile, stood on the sidewalk looking through a window into the bank and watched Janne and Clark deep in discussion. On the far side of the lobby, near the foreign exchange and loan departments, Morgan saw a door open and close repeatedly.

With Janne and Clark still near the customer vault, Morgan believed that he could reenter the bank without being detected. Quietly and carefully, he opened the front door and approached the room. The first person he saw was the missing policeman, Torgny Wallström, and with him, several bank employees who had been hiding since the morning.

Motioning for them to follow him, Morgan started leading everyone out, a couple at a time. Sharpshooters watching from Berzelii Park feared for Morgan's life if the gunman found out, but Morgan managed to bring them all to safety.

ALMOST IMMEDIATELY, CLARK SEEMED TO CALM JANNE DOWN. KRISTIN, Birgitta, and Elisabeth all noticed the difference.

Clark's presence meant that Janne no longer had sole responsibility for controlling the hostages and negotiating with the police, all the while avoiding being hit by sniper fire. Clark would roam the bank almost at will. He would make sure to whistle, hum, or talk before he turned corners, so as not to startle the police and cause them to shoot in panic.

Clark went first to look for police officers who had been entering the bank. Some had crept down the chat staircase, as it lay in a blind spot from their position on the landing outside the customer-deposit vault. Others had slipped in through a door in the back. Clark shooed them away, claiming that the police leadership had promised him that they would abandon the ground floor. So many policemen, armed to the teeth, were, Clark said, like "a ticking bomb." Thorander and his staff had certainly not made any such guarantee to vacate the premises, but many police officers left as requested. Within five minutes, Clark estimated, they had cleared out of the lobby.

To make sure they did not reenter, Clark rigged up a homemade alarm at a door to a back staircase well out of sight by using a chair, a couple of empty bottles, and some rope. The door, if moved, would cause the bottles to fall to the floor. The rope came from Janne's canvas bag and the bottles from the drinks that Thorander had carted in for Janne and the hostages.

CLARK PATROLLED THE LOBBY, PAUSING AT CERTAIN DESKS AND RUM-
maging through their drawers. He soon came back, hugging wads of cash to
his chest. A policeman with a view of the landing outside the vault watched
Janne grab a bundle of the bills, sniff them, and laugh with approval. "They
smelled good," Janne later said.

They enjoyed a robber's dream of free rein inside a bank. At one point,
Clark tried to unlock a cash register, as the machines had locked automati-
cally when the employees pressed the alarm. He had no tools, and so improvised with a metal sign that read LOANS. He bent it out of proportion trying to
pry open the register. "It was impossible," he said.

At some other point, Clark returned with a load of cash from some-
where—"Gas Money," he called it. Kristin and Elisabeth helped him count
the loot. They worked at the bank, after all, someone joked, and that was
their expertise.

Handfuls of cash were stuffed into plastic bags that Janne had brought
with him in his canvas bag and then tossed onto the floor in a far corner of
the vault. Another pile of money remained on a small table to the left of the
door. Swiss francs were on top.

With Clark's support, Janne could finally see some results and begin to
relax. In some ways, so could the hostages. Clark was certainly helping comfort them. After the terror of the morning, this calm and unarmed celebrity
had joined them, radiating humor and confidence. Besides, if the authorities
had obeyed the gunman and sent in this high-profile criminal, the police
surely must be less likely to storm the lobby and provoke a shootout.

Still, there was always a risk, and Clark suggested that they move into
the vault itself. He had seen sharpshooters on the rooftops and around Norrmalmstorg. Kristin struggled. The knots, retied around the ankles, made it
difficult to walk. Clark just reached down, swooped her up, and carried her
into the vault, setting her gently down on the floor.

The vault was a long, rectangular, and well-ventilated chamber, even
though it did not have any windows. Cold fluorescent lights shone onto the
marble floor with the maroon runner. The room was 47 feet in length, 11 feet
in width, and 7 feet, 8 inches in height. But given its layout, it seemed much
smaller than that.

It was crammed with office furniture, including a table, four small desks, two filing cabinets, several chairs, and a large steel cabinet containing approximately six hundred safe-deposit boxes. Artwork lined the walls. At the entrance were two thick steel doors, the outer one opening outward toward the lobby and the inner one opening inward to the back of the room.

Birgitta sat inside on a chair. Next to her was the heavy canvas bag that she had managed to lug into the room on Janne's orders, despite the ropes that had been tied around her wrists.

Clark asked Birgitta if she had eaten anything.

It was difficult with her hands bound, she said.

Clark, turning to Janne, asked if it was really necessary to keep the women tied up. Janne agreed to remove the ropes, provided that the women promised to behave.

"Imagine meeting like this," Clark joked as he untied the knots around Kristin's wrists and ankles. He said something similar to Elisabeth. Everything was going to be fine, the handsome outlaw told the frightened hostages. Nothing was going to happen to them. They would soon be allowed to go home. They just had to stay calm and listen to him. He would take care of everything.

Clark raised spirits further by finding a way for the hostages to speak with their families. Birgitta had mentioned where he could find an office phone. On one of his tours around the lobby, Clark picked it up from the desk, brought it back to the vault, and plugged it into a wall jack.

Birgitta went first. Unfortunately, her husband, Per-Åke, a civil engineer, was not yet home from work. Her mother, a retired office worker, did not answer either. Birgitta managed to reach the nanny, telling her that she would be home late that evening because she was, as she put it, "stuck at the bank." She did not use the word "gunman" or "hostage." She left a message for her husband that there were leftovers in the refrigerator for dinner and he should place a piece of butter on the fish before heating it up on the stove.

Then she began to cry.

Janne encouraged her to call again.

Elisabeth called home to her parents at the boarding school where her father served as rector. Kristin telephoned her family in Boliden, a mining town in the north of Sweden. Her mother, Gunnel, had only found out about the robbery two hours before, when she had come home from work and switched on the radio to listen for updates about the king's health. She had been startled to hear that the crime had taken place at her daughter's bank. At about the same time, the phone rang and it was one of Kreditbanken's executives confirming the news.

"You read about things like this in books," Gunnel said, "but I do not believe that we can really understand that this is happening to our daughter."

The Enmarks would stay up all night watching television news and listening to the radio. Gunnel clutched at any sign of hope. Kristin had sounded calm and unafraid on the telephone, she thought, when she told them not to worry. She seemed just as composed as she did when she looked after her younger siblings.

All three hostages were grateful for the chance to speak with their families—a small gesture, which, given the inordinate stress of the day, was magnified in importance. This generosity of spirit, moreover, stood in sharp contrast to the police, who, in their eyes, did not seem to care if the hostages spoke to their families or not. It was Clark and Janne who made it happen.

12

---

*He has captured me by force, he is keeping me against my will, and yet
he imagines that his setbacks fill me with dismay and that his hopes can
cheer me up!*

−Yurii Zhivago,
Boris Pasternak, *Doctor Zhivago*

EVER SINCE THE PHONE CALL IN THE PRISON DIRECTOR'S OFFICE,
Clark had assumed that the gunman had tried to rob the bank and failed,
thus prompting his hostage-taking as an act of desperation to extricate
himself from an impending fiasco. This was a widespread view in the media
too. At some point that afternoon, Clark realized that this assumption was
incorrect. Janne had come to the bank with the intention of taking hostages.

What were Janne's plans after that? He kept the details to himself, but
Clark began to worry about how well thought out the plot actually was. He
also believed that Janne had made a mistake in freeing the first captives. This
was the equivalent of throwing away a strong hand. These hostages would
have been "our ticket out," Clark said. Instead, they sat there with only three
hostages.

Clark watched the women that afternoon. Elisabeth was young, beautiful, and well brought up, with a strong moral compass. Kristin, or "Kikki,"
was spunky with a bold, unassuming directness that both Clark and Janne
found refreshing. Of all the hostages, Clark worried most about Birgitta.
Despite her understandable breakdowns, she showed no signs of panic or
self-pity. He decided that he had to keep his eye on her.

Clark continued to take reconnoitering missions around the ground floor of the bank. He was exploring a small back room stocked with blank checks when, all of a sudden, he jumped back in surprise. A young man was standing there. He was tall and slim with long blond hair and informally dressed in a brown blazer, white shirt, and brown pants. He looked too casual, Clark thought, to be a cop.

This was a twenty-four-year-old bank employee named Sven Säfström. As an *extern reserv*, like Birgitta, Sven went from branch to branch to cover for staffing needs and had just come for his first assignment at Norrmalmstorg. What bad luck, Janne later said. That morning, Sven had gone into the supply room to retrieve checks for a customer when he heard what sounded like someone falling down, or windowpanes being smashed. He first thought it was a terrorist attack, but then someone shouting "Down on the floor!" convinced him it was a robbery. He decided to remain there until it was over.

Sven had worked part-time for many years in the evenings at the opera house, and spent time, too, as a line-order cook on a cruise ship. His parents, both of whom worked for the Swedish government, had been concerned about his lack of direction or ambition, and encouraged him to settle down with a professional position. Sven had reluctantly agreed. What did his parents think now about his career choice, he wondered.

As Sven had stood there, trying to imagine how he would get out, he heard footsteps coming. What was he to do now, he asked himself. He decided to look in the other direction and nonchalantly cross his arms, hoping not to startle whoever was on the way into the room.

"What the hell!" Clark said, taken aback. "You don't have to stand here." His tone was more amicable than menacing.

"You must be very hungry," Clark said.

By this point, Sven had been in the small room for six and a half hours. He had remained as quiet as possible, fearing that the gunman would be able to hear him as well as he could hear the talk in the lobby.

"Look what I found," Clark said, returning to Janne with the young bank employee.

Janne, however, did not seem pleased, suspecting that Sven might be a cop and wondering how he had come into the bank. Janne was also concerned about the prospect of a male hostage, as were the women, who seemed to be uneasy about someone new arriving on the scene.

Clark discreetly encouraged Janne to keep Sven because it would strengthen their negotiating position. At the same time, Clark wanted to make sure that none of the hostages realized that he was the one who had prevented Sven's release. Such a revelation, after all, would undermine Clark's stature and threaten his rapport with the women in the vault.

Reluctantly Janne agreed to keep the fourth and final hostage. He told Sven to join the others and help himself to the sandwiches and beer that the police had brought for them.

"Sven, we don't need any heroes here," Janne said, his weapon still strapped around his shoulder and clutched in his hand. "There are enough of those out there."

WHEN SVEN ENTERED THE VAULT, HE FOUND BIRGITTA SITTING ON A chair in the far corner, her head in her hands and crying. This had caught him off-guard because, from his position in the storage room, he had thought that there were only two hostages.

"Dear God, what is going to happen to us?" Birgitta asked.

Just outside the vault, Janne and Clark stood talking. About this time or probably shortly before, Janne started speaking Swedish. This came as another surprise to the women. All morning, they had been "translating" the news on the radio for him.

Thorander was also surprised when he later heard Janne speak. Not only was the language Swedish—he had long suspected that the gunman understood better than he let on; it was also a distinct southern dialect called *skånska*. Was not Kaj Hansson also from southern Sweden? Perhaps his colleagues were correct after all.

Still, Thorander thought, the gunman seemed older and more experienced than a twenty-one-year-old like Kaj. The commissioner preferred to think of the attacker as an American, though probably one who had lived for years in Sweden.

Janne was soon mulling over a discovery of his own. He had asked Sven about his year of military service, then mandatory for men in Sweden, and learned that Sven had trained specifically with the submachine gun. At one point, probably about an hour or so after Sven's arrival, Janne startled him. He turned the gun around, told Sven to put his finger on the trigger, and placed the end of the barrel into his own stomach. Janne dared him to pull the trigger. Sven shook his head. He was not a killer.

Why did Janne make such a reckless move? Was this test an attempt to prove his own strength and confidence? Years later, Janne would say that he did not know exactly why he had pulled such a stunt. The risk was certainly unnecessary, and, fortunately for him, Sven did not call his bluff.

As the late afternoon wore on, Janne joked about sending Sven out to buy the evening newspapers just hitting the stands. Reporters would probably cover the story, he thought, as indeed they did.

"BANK ROBBER TOOK SIX HOSTAGES today in the middle of Stockholm," screamed boldface, front-page headlines for the prominent national evening tabloid, *Aftonbladet*. Large photographs showed two of the "hundreds of policemen" at Norrmalmstorg, crawling beside police vehicles with their guns drawn.

"A Man with a Submachine Gun took Hostages in a Bank in the City" splashed its influential national rival, *Expressen,* counting the number of captives as nine. "Demand: 3 million and CLARK FREE!"

Relegated to the bottom of the page, in both newspapers, was some other national news. "The King Has Difficulty in Breathing" and "THE KING WORSE."

13

_____

What is the burgling of a bank to the founding of a bank?

—Captain Macheath,
Bertolt Brecht, *The Threepenny Opera*

I T WAS ONLY A MATTER OF TIME, JANNE THOUGHT, BEFORE THE POLICE brought the rest of the ransom money, which he now wanted in foreign currency. This would be harder to trace. As for which currency, Janne did not specify. He did not want to provide any clues to where he planned to go, and besides, he could always exchange them later.

During the wait, Janne added to the list of demands. He wanted "two pistols and a fast car," with Clark as the driver and a guarantee of safe passage. To make sure the police kept their agreement, the gunman wanted two hostages to accompany him. Sven was ruled out because he was a man and Birgitta because she was a mother, narrowing the choice to Kristin and Elisabeth. The women would be released, Janne said, once they were safely away.

Before they left, Janne had another important task for Clark.

Clark went out into the lobby, grabbed a chair, set it down in a corner, climbed up to the security camera, and removed the cassette. He then disabled two additional devices.* Janne would later mock the clumsy equipment

---

* The bank actually had a fourth camera, but it covered the foreign exchange department on the other side of the lobby.

for the loud hum of the motors. It sounded like a threshing machine, he said, and suggested that the bank invest in more sophisticated surveillance technology.

The cassettes of the bank's footage were brought back to the landing outside the vault. The film was removed and then set on fire. Kristin helped. The fire was started with the cigarette lighter that Sven Thorander had given the hostages.

Thorander and several policemen on his staff had already begun to wonder about Clark's true allegiance. He was patrolling the bank, sending away policemen, and negotiating on behalf of the gunman, if not also advising him on how to maneuver. Was he really working for the police? If not, what recourse did they have? Clark was still technically in their custody. And, as Thorander knew, critics would be quick to point out that it was the police who let him inside the bank.

The media waited with anticipation. From their view in Norrmalmstorg, Clark had arrived and the ransom money had been given. The police seemed to have met the gunman's demands. At the same time, snipers remained on rooftops and another sharpshooter had entered the bank, carrying his gun hidden underneath a gray blanket.

A police superintendent, Åke Åkesson, held another impromptu press conference at the Palmhuset restaurant. "Negotiations with the robber continue," he announced to a crowd of journalists. "We will do everything we can to end this drama without bloodshed."

At 6:30 p.m., however, the Stockholm police were ready to make a move. A handful of sharpshooters crept down a second small staircase behind the foreign exchange department, farther away from the vault. Two of them, Karl Gunnar Åström and Lars-Erik Karlsson, advanced toward the lobby with drawn pistols. For a moment, Janne stood away from the hostages as well as from the columns that threatened to produce dangerous ricochet shots.

Clark saw the threat and made a quick movement with his right hand. Janne turned and fired.

Three shots rang out in the marbled lobby and shattered the glass in the window near the Hamngatan entrance. One bullet landed in a nearby wall and another ricocheted off a standing clothes hanger, hitting the staircase. Bits of glass and plaster cascaded onto the floor. The bullets had passed just over Karlsson's shoulder, one of them missing by about half a foot.

"Take it easy, dammit!" Clark yelled at the police. "Are you crazy?"

Janne took this episode as a warning. Moving about the bank without the protection of the hostages was, he said, playing "a game of death."

WORD OF THE SHOOTING SPREAD QUICKLY AMONG THE POLICE AND journalists in Norrmalmstorg. All the safety precautions, which had started to ease after the tense morning, returned. "No one dares to stand upright in the square," Bo Holmström announced on the television evening news. Police and journalists alike sought cover, once again, in fear of a shot coming at any moment from a window in the bank. The robber was, Holmström said, confused and "very irritated."

"Get back!" a policeman shouted into a megaphone at the crowds behind the barricades. "It is dangerous here!"

Few people abandoned their spots, even if it was difficult to see the action in the bank. The mass of spectators was instead growing in size. At one point, a man in their midst collapsed, and a reporter for *Svenska Dagbladet* described him as another victim of the "excitement and exhaustion" that raged among the curiosity-seekers flocking to the unusual drama.

As evening approached, the police directed the electric company to turn off the streetlamps and traffic lights around Norrmalmstorg. They also ordered a giant spotlight to shine on the entrance to the bank. Later that night, it would add an eerie glow to the darkened square.

Back in the vault, with the telephone still working, Clark started reaching out to his contacts in the media. He called Åsa Moberg, a young columnist for the national, left-leaning tabloid *Aftonbladet*. She happened to be watching live coverage of the bank robbery on television when her phone rang.

Clark acted as if he were hanging out with pals. "It is cool and calm here, and we are telling fun stories," he said.

TV2 was telling a different story, Åsa said. Its news program, *Rapport*, portrayed a terrifying image of a madman with a machine gun.

Clark invited Moberg to the bank to check it out for herself.

Eager for a scoop, Åsa agreed to come, though she cautioned that, from her residence outside the city center, it would take at least an hour and a half before she arrived.

"Ah, well, forget it," Clark said. They should be long gone by then.

She asked about the robber. Was he anyone she knew?

Clark doubted it.

Could she perhaps speak with him?

A moment later, Åsa received an exclusive interview with the gunman in the middle of the hostage crisis.

"Hello, with whom am I speaking?" Åsa began.

"Do you think that I can say that?" Janne said in a southern Swedish drawl. "All the telephones in this entire bank are bugged."

The journalist asked about his motives.

The gunman said he was acting on behalf of his fellow inmates who were victimized by a harsh prison system. "I am doing this as a protest against all the shit and the inhumane treatment that they are exposed to."

If that is the case, Åsa said, then it was an ineffective protest.

"You should see how it looks from over here!"

He did not have all the money yet, Åsa reminded him. Besides, his protest would have been more credible if he had not demanded a fortune in ransom.

Janne reminded her that he had already succeeded with something.

"What's that?"

"I have freed Clark Olofsson."

Was he really free, she countered, when they were surrounded by hordes of policemen?

Clark, taking the line again, suggested that she write about why actions like this happen. He then explained it for her: The oppressive authoritarian regime of the prison system made inmates like him desperate; this "terrorism of authorities," as he put it, made such action possible, even necessary.

Janne and Clark were tapping into a view then common among many progressive reformers who blamed prisons for harsh, punishing regimes that exacerbated the violent tendencies of its inmates. Psychiatrist Lisbet Palmgren, for instance, would make Janne and Clark textbook examples of how violence led to violence in a never-ending cycle. Prisons had to find a better way to deal with the incarcerated, she argued, and many people in Sweden agreed with her—and now Janne and Clark, too, as they were making a similar argument.

In her article the next day, Åsa Moberg went on to paint a sympathetic picture of the underdogs in the bank resisting the combined power of the police and the media, all in league to destroy them. Norrmalmstorg had become a morality play. Society had marshaled its overwhelming forces against the defiance of the lone outcast. Clark, enjoying his Robin Hood mystique, was even more irresistible when he struck against the banks, a despised symbol of greed to several of the socialist and left-wing papers.

14

We did not consider ourselves under any obligation to fulfill a promise that had been extorted from us.

—Kurt Lindroth

A S JANNE NOW RELIED ON CLARK TO RELAY HIS DEMANDS, THE police brought in its own negotiator. Bengt-Olof Lövenlo, or "B-O," was a middle-aged policeman who had spent the early morning chasing pickpockets and baggage thieves at the central train station. He enjoyed a reputation for establishing a good rapport with criminals, and his colleagues considered him an expert on prison slang. Or rather, slang as it used to be spoken in the old movies, Janne later said. He and Clark would find B-O's talk alternatively confusing and amusing.

B-O first approached the chat staircase with caution, yelling out his communications from the floor above. With time, he ventured farther down the steps. B-O now came to the staircase to say that the "fast car" the gunman demanded was ready. It was a Volkswagen.

"You've got to be kidding, B-O," Clark said. "Don't you fucking set me up with such wheels."

B-O laughed. He said he had actually gotten them a Ford Mustang with a V8 engine and 140 horsepower.

News that the car was outside raised spirits in the vault. Elisabeth thought that she would be able to attend the weekend party after all. The four bank employees, Kristin joked, had to remember to stamp their timesheets on their way out so they would receive overtime pay.

They would be able to leave in a moment, B-O said, and by *they*, he meant Clark and the robber. The police would give them the keys to the car and a guarantee of safe passage in return for the hostages. Under no circumstances would the women be allowed to accompany them.

Authorities were bluffing, Janne felt. They would have to surrender to his demands because there was no chance, he thought, that the government would risk him killing the women if he did not get his way. The government would never gamble with their lives. Not in Sweden. Certainly not this year, when the prime minister faced a close election.

It seemed that Janne had a point. Less than one year before, on September 15, 1972, members of the far-right Croatian gang Ustaše hijacked Scandinavian Airlines domestic flight SK130 and demanded the release of seven men convicted of assassinating the Yugoslavian ambassador. The minister of justice, Lennart Geijer, had come to negotiate in person after the plane landed at Bulltofta Airport in Malmö, eventually handing over all seven prisoners and the ransom. The hijackers had then increased their demands and the authorities had accepted them as well. After that, the Croatian gang had flown off to Spain, where they were promptly arrested.

But this time, it was different. The Swedish government planned to fight.

After all, in only three weeks, the country would go to the polls. Olof Palme risked being the first Social Democratic prime minister to lose a national election in forty-one years. If he had ever had any desire to compromise at Norrmalmstorg, it was disappearing fast.

So the police went forward with a plan to overpower the gunman. The car they would offer did not have a full tank. The gauge had been tampered with to conceal the fact that it had less than a single gallon of gasoline. The police had also attached a small radar tracking device to the vehicle that would allow authorities to follow its movement. Two helicopters were ready to take flight. Many other policemen waited to pursue in cars and on motorcycles.

Roadblocks, moreover, controlled strategic intersections along the routes out of the capital. Police forces in surrounding towns of Södertälje, Nacka, Jakobsberg, and Täby were on standby. Other officers watched the departure terminals of Stockholm's airports Arlanda and Bromma.

Where was Janne to go?

AT 7:40 P.M., FLASHES FROM THE CAMERAS OF THE PHOTOGRAPHERS LIT
up the windows of the bank. A midnight-blue 1971 Ford Mustang pulled up
outside the Hamngatan entrance. The policeman at the wheel, Kenth Svensson, must have been concerned about more than just his own safety. It was
his personal vehicle that the police offered as the getaway car.

The cameras were rolling.

"The car, a sports car, an American Mustang, is in place," Bo Holmström spoke in his microphone, once again without a script. "It is possible that the dramatic and perhaps violent resolution that everyone had
feared can come to pass at any moment." The cameras zoomed in on the
front door of the bank. Swedes across the country were glued to their
television sets.

That evening, Channel 1 had scheduled an Abbott and Costello comedy,
followed by a dramatization of the Guy de Maupassant short story *The Fly*
and a French series about famous escapes from prison. Sweden's other channel, TV2, had packed its lineup with documentaries about India, Mozam-
bique, and the popular show *Hem till byn*, which dealt with family life in a
small Swedish village. That, at least, was the plan. Both television stations
would repeatedly interrupt their programming to broadcast the latest news
from Norrmalmstorg.

In the bank, meanwhile, it was quiet. The main sound in the vault
was Janne's transistor radio. Clark kept working the telephone. He called
another journalist friend, Rune Johansson of *Dagens Nyheter*, one of the
largest and most respected daily national newspapers published in the
capital.

"You understand," Clark said, "I am only a pawn in this game of chess."

"Do you think of yourself as something different?"

"Yes," Clark said, and wanted to know if he could ask a favor.

Dodging the question, Rune asked about the policeman who had been
shot that morning. In the background, the gunman shouted that the officer
had drawn his weapon first.

Clark went on to praise Kristin, Elisabeth, and Birgitta—and he gave
their first names now, though he did not yet mention Sven. They had behaved
brilliantly. Everyone was getting on well. In fact, Clark said, the women
wanted to come along with them on their departure from the bank. The

phone went dead. Clark suspected that the call had been tampered with, as indeed it had.

Moments later, Clark redialed his journalist friend and asked him his favor: He wanted the private telephone number of Prime Minister Olof Palme.

"What do you have in mind, Clark?"

15

—

Sweden was, despite everything, still kind Sweden, where you do not sacrifice hostages.

— Clark Olofsson

A S THE SUN SET ON NORRMALMSTORG, DARKENED FURTHER WITH-out the usual glow of streetlights and traffic signals, the blue Mustang remained parked outside the bank. Police spotlights and television cameras were trained on the door. The gunman might come out at any moment.

Many people clearly expected them to emerge from the bank and leave, presumably enjoying passage out of the country. The hostages might then be exchanged for an airline crew, guessed *Smålandsposten*. Some airlines, however, had already started canceling Stockholm flights that night for fear that their aircraft might be commandeered by the robber. Swiss Airlines, for one, had rerouted its flights to Helsinki.

It was a test of nerves, wrote the southern Swedish newspaper *Skånska Dagbladet*. "How much is the police promise of 'free passage' worth when [the robber] comes within range?" A sniper at a second-floor window of a nearby building had a clear, unobstructed view of the vehicle.

At 9:45 p.m., the police received a phone call from a man who ran his own aviation company. The pilot, Dan Andersson, had been contacted by an anonymous person wanting to hire an airplane that evening. When the pilot asked about specifics, the caller refused to elaborate and said, abruptly, "See to it only that the plane is ready at ten o'clock."

The police had begun to suspect that Clark and "Kaj" planned to use part of the ransom money to hire a private plane and fly abroad, perhaps to a refuge among Clark's contacts in Lebanon. On one of his escapes from prison, Clark had hopped on a plane and gone there. He was known to love the country and its people.

Was this possibly the plane, and if so, who was helping on the outside? The call had definitely not originated from inside the bank. Perhaps it was simply a ruse to mislead the authorities into looking in the wrong direction, or an unrelated transaction altogether. The police did not know what to make of it.

Pranks and threats were pouring in to both the police and the press. Earlier that afternoon, someone had phoned in a warning: "We are going to take the bank at Stureplan too!" This was of course a real concern because with so many police and so many resources focused on Norrmalmstorg, there were plenty of opportunities for criminals to strike elsewhere.

A journalist for *Dagens Nyheter*, Matt Lundegård, meanwhile, had arrived in the square, wanting to speak with Clark. The infamous bank robber had called the paper to ask for an intermediary, and so the reporter had come to help. The police escorted him up to the second floor of the bank.

Lundegård passed an array of officers in uniform and civilian clothes and a half-dozen others carrying submachine guns and sweating under their thirty-pound bulletproof vests. He was brought to the corner office, which was also packed with policemen. It was a hot, smoke-filled room littered with thermoses, plastic mugs with stale coffee, and plates with half-eaten sandwiches. He recognized Thorander and Lindroth at once and stated his plans.

There was complete silence.

Finally, a policeman standing by the window turned and asked, "And what the hell do we do when he goes down and gets shot?"

The journalist protested that that was not likely because Clark wanted to speak with him. Authorities, moreover, should not neglect any measure that might save lives. He could perform an invaluable service for the police, the women, and everyone involved in the standoff.

Thorander rejected the offer. "We have had enough of hostages," he said.

Lundegård was led out of the bank, fearing that this crisis would end in tragedy.

There were only two possible ways to save the victims, a policeman told him. One was that the gunman succumbed to the pressure and surrendered.

The other was that the police sharpshooters seized upon an opportunity to hit their target. At this point, they could not simply wound him. "We have to kill him," he said.

TWELVE HOURS AFTER THE DRAMA HAD BEGUN, POSITIONS WERE DEAD-locked. Time passed slowly. It was far from clear, *Göteborgs-Posten* wrote, how this crisis would end. Or when. The television cameras were still rolling in case something happened. The crew talked between broadcasts about getting a cup of coffee, or, one person said, a glass of whiskey. Someone wanted a blanket. A producer probably spoke for many people in the square when she said that she hoped something happened soon, so that they did not have to stay there all night.

There was still no stirring from the vault. Thorander eventually asked Clark, "Kaj," and the hostages if they wanted something to eat.

Into the bank lobby came policemen carrying trays of hot dogs and French fries purchased at a nearby restaurant. Some members of the press later reported that they had enjoyed steak dinners, which drew laughter from Janne and Sven.

And then came six bottles of beer. Both Janne and Clark were suspicious, because no one had ordered them. Clark proposed that Sven taste-test the drinks, in case they were drugged. Janne, however, thought of a better solution.

He shook the bottles, placed his ear beside the caps, and heard a faint fizz. The bottles had definitely been opened. Perhaps the police had laced the beer with a sleep-inducing substance, Janne feared, with good reason. Both Lindroth and Thorander later admitted that they had tampered with the drinks, and police files record that Bejerot had in fact obtained an unidentified drug that night from a pharmacy.

About 10:55 p.m., Thorander came down the staircase again, like a waiter checking on his table.

The women wanted to speak with him, Clark said.

Kristin then poked her head out of the vault and said that she and Elisabeth had made up their minds. They wanted to leave with "the boys."

That was not going to happen, Thorander answered, in a firm, matter-of-fact manner.

"Do you not understand that this guy [the robber] is beginning to get really nervous now?" Clark yelled back. "*He* can do anything whatsoever. *He* is completely desperate."

Did the robber not realize, Thorander countered, that he had no choice but to surrender? The entire area was swarming with police. Sharpshooters were positioned around the lobby, square, park, and nearby streets. Janne, however, had drawn a different conclusion. If he left the bank without the hostages, the police would not hesitate to shoot him. Thorander's talk only confirmed that he had to keep his hostages. There was no other way out.

But then someone in the vault had another idea.

———

THE PHONE RANG AT THE PRIME MINISTER'S OFFICE.

When an assistant answered and asked who was on the line, a male voice replied: "Say that it is Clark in the bank."

Clark was optimistic about the possibility of Olof Palme intervening in the crisis on their behalf. He liked the prime minister. He admired his progressive outlook and what he called his "arrogant and intellectual fearlessness." Palme could not help but listen to their point of view, Clark thought, and then order the police to stand aside. This would be the best solution for the hostages, and perhaps also for Palme's own political career.

The prime minister was, in fact, still in his office. He had been there all day, moving between reports about the hostage crisis and the state of the king's health. This was not his preferred method of operation. Palme liked to concentrate on one problem with his full attention before shifting gears. "One hell at a time," he often told his staff.

Palme came on the line. No one had tried to confirm that the caller really was Clark Olofsson and not a prankster.

Clark relayed Janne's demand to leave the bank with the two women, Kristin and Elisabeth, making many of the arguments he had used with his reporter friends. The prime minister listened and then interrupted to stress the importance of law and order in a society. Authorities could not allow such violence onto the street. Clark should persuade the robber to lay down his weapon and free the hostages because the police would, under no circumstances, allow them to leave with the women. That was the government's irrevocable decision.

Janne took the line. He and Clark were leaving the bank with the hostages, and that was the end of the matter. If the government tried to stop them, there would no longer be any of the hostages alive. The scenario had no other outcome, the gunman said, unless of course Palme himself wanted to come to the bank and take their place as a hostage.

Otherwise, Janne threatened, "I am going to shoot this bird!"

A scream was heard from inside the vault.

Palme, known for his quick wit and sharp rebuttals, did not know what to say.

Janne then calmly and firmly repeated the ultimatum. The prime minister had one minute to decide.

The gunman started counting down: 60, 59, 58 . . .

With fifteen seconds left, Janne slammed down the phone.

16

It was impossible to know what went on in his brain.

—Kristin Enmark, on Janne Olsson

JANNE AND CLARK WERE SUPPOSED TO HAVE ALREADY LEFT STOCK-holm with the ransom money. By late Thursday night, however, they were still at the bank with their hostages, and surrounded by the police, the mass media, and a country mesmerized by the affair.

Live television broadcasts continued, with no end in sight. In fact, the more the television stations broadcast, the harder it was for them to stop. The camera zoomed in on the door of the bank, or the getaway car parked outside. The sense of tension and impending resolution was palpable. Yet there was no movement, and the still black-and-white images highlighted the anticipation for action that seemed imminent.

Policemen, journalists, and photographers paced back and forth across the square, trying to stay warm and maintain their spirits with sandwiches, cigarettes, and coffee. Onlookers, still several rows deep beyond the barricades, also watched and waited, as did millions at home. No one had any idea how the crisis would end. Many feared a bloodbath. Television, evidently, was going to capture it all.

The biggest and most ominous development, radio journalist Lennart Broström reported late that night, was that Clark Olofsson had apparently switched sides. He was working with his old friend, the gunman, described variously as the robber, the submachine-gun man, the desperado, and now, too, the young "Swedish-American robber."

Many reporters camped out at the nearby Palmhuset restaurant, which was to become the unofficial media headquarters for the duration of the ordeal. Here, just a few steps away from the bank, reporters would eat, drink, trade stories, and crash on the floor as they sorted through a barrage of rumor and gossip in the race for the latest scoop. The glass pavilion, in which this spectacle took place, inspired a new nickname: "The Monkey Cage."

Other journalists checked into the Hotell Stockholm. Rooms on the top floor, with enviable views over Norrmalmstorg, were quickly booked. Photographers set up camp on the balcony at Nessim's oriental rugs, or the roof above Marinell's fur shop. Binoculars and long camera lenses were aimed at the bank, side by side with the barrels of the sharpshooters.

At a second-story office used by the police leadership, the lights remained on throughout the early-morning hours. Silhouettes of high-ranking officials moved behind the yellow curtains. Some of the men were smoking. Many of them had their heads down, deep in thought and no doubt exhausted. Above them, bright lights on the facade flashed "The Bank for You . . . Kreditbanken."

SHORT OF SHOOTING A HOSTAGE, WHICH JANNE WANTED TO AVOID, IT looked like he, Clark, and the four captives were going to have to spend the night in the vault. Janne turned out the lights. The room went pitch-black. The temperature dropped inside the chamber, as it had outside in the square. Clark secured a coat for Birgitta from a policeman who'd sent someone to pick one up at random from a staff closet.

Everything was quiet in the vault now except for the transistor radio, switched on to Channel P3 for news. Birgitta struggled to sleep on the floor in a far corner near Sven. In the middle of the chamber, Kristin rested her head on a bag of money filled with approximately $620,000. She lay down near Clark, who made room by scooting a small table and chair against the wall.

The door to the vault could not be locked from the inside, but if the police attempted an ambush, they would find Elisabeth in their path. She sat in an armchair near the inner of the two doors. At its foot, Janne had rigged up some explosives from his canvas bag. He then took up his position, submachine gun in hand. He was popping little white pills.

At one point, during the night, Elisabeth awoke, shivering from the chill. Janne placed his gray sweatshirt around her.

Snipers in the lobby, meanwhile, waited for an opportunity to shoot.

IT WAS A NIGHT OF TERROR FOR THE HOSTAGES, AS *AFTONBLADET*, *Expressen*, and several other papers wrote. The longer this standoff lasted, the greater the chances that Janne—already exhausted and on edge—might make a mistake that would result in catastrophe. The police, moreover, were growing impatient. The gunman showed no signs of separating himself from his human shields.

At one point after midnight, the police decided to try something. They would open the door at the staircase at the far end of the lobby and trigger Clark's alarm. The sound of the bottles crashing to the floor would, presumably, cause the gunman to run out of the vault on impulse and perhaps forget to bring a hostage as cover. Snipers might then have an opportunity to fire.

They were ordered to aim for the head. Even a direct hit at the heart may not always be immediately fatal. This had been clear the previous year at the Munich Olympics, when one of the Black September terrorists was shot in the heart and yet continued to fire his submachine gun for another forty-eight seconds. That would be a long time in a confined space like a bank lobby. The police had to make sure that the robber did not have that chance.

A veteran detective inspector, Håkan Larsson, pushed open the door. Sure enough, the bottles fell. There was no response. Larsson then kicked one of the bottles across the floor. There was still no sign of Janne.

Instead, Clark stormed out of the vault, yelling and cursing. He fixed the alarm and then returned. Along the way, he saw several policemen in bullet-proof vests and noticed the muzzle of another submachine gun, peering out behind an armchair. A sharpshooter, too, lay on the floor wielding a moose-hunting rifle with a riflescope.

Janne then stepped out onto the landing unprotected. Clark shouted and Janne ducked back inside. Quite possibly, Clark had again saved his life.

Janne was furious at this maneuver to "murder him," as he put it. Clark was disgusted. "This is dead sick," he said.

17

If you can shoot him, do it. But the first shot must be perfect.

—Kurt Lindroth

ON FRIDAY, AUGUST 24, 1973, THE BANK DRAMA DOMINATED THE headlines around the country. *Svenska Dagbladet* led with a piece contrasting the police sharpshooters, reluctant to fire, with the ruthless gunman, who obviously showed no such hesitation. The paper would keep up this line of investigation into missed opportunities to end the deadlock.

Dagens Nyheter, on the other hand, emphasized Olof Palme's offer of free passage to the still-unnamed gunman in exchange for his release of the hostages. Palme and his cabinet had worked late into the night to arrange a deal—the minister of justice, for one, did not leave until sometime between eight and nine in the morning, when he went home for a shower and a change of clothes. A photographer for *Expressen* snapped a picture of him exiting his office after the "nerve-wracking night."

Rune Johansson, one of the journalists who had spoken with Clark in the vault, wrote an editorial lamenting the increasing spread of violence in society and called for his fellow citizens to take more responsibility to stem the torrent. The rise of "brutal violent crime," he predicted, was going to influence the course of the election, which seemed to be forgotten in the wake of this sensational story that already captivated the country.

It was Radio Sweden and the evening tabloids that revealed to the public the name of the suspect, Kaj Hansson. Both *Aftonbladet* and *Expressen* put his picture on the cover. He looked dapper, with long curly hair and fashionable tinted sunglasses. The photograph was actually taken by a security camera during a recent bank robbery in southern Sweden.

Several papers ran lengthy portraits of Kaj, offering tantalizing details about his background, his string of bank heists, and his flights from the police. Most highlighted the twenty-one-year-old's youth in a foster home, and his adulthood, which a reporter for *Aftonbladet* summed up as an almost unbroken cycle of "crimes, prisons, and crimes again." His list of arrests, a policeman added, spanned the entire eighth chapter of the criminal code, except for rape and murder.

Kaj was depicted as a touchy, moody hothead with something to prove. Former classmates described his technical mind, while his teachers remembered how the suspect harbored a deep hatred of society. "I am Dangerous If Threatened" ran *Aftonbladet*'s headline.

Readers also learned how Kaj had gained his knowledge of the English language. In 1971, after robbing a bank, Kaj escaped to the West Indies, made his way to Mexico, and from there slipped across the border into California. He had then flown from Los Angeles to Honolulu, where he enrolled in the university and got married.

Stories of Kaj kept coming. Reporter Ian Elliot of *Hennes* magazine told of encountering Kaj earlier that month in the university town of Lund in southern Sweden. They had met at a party that had drawn a mix of professors, students, and hippies. Kaj had made an impression. He sang, played the guitar, and boasted of escaping from prison. Earlier that day, he bragged, he had robbed a bank.

This had more than a ring of truth. As police knew, Kaj was suspected of the August 2, 1973, robbery at Lundabygdens Sparbank in Lund. At one point at the student party, Kaj showed off how much he had scored from the haul, spreading the loot across the table. This was, according to Elliot, equal to the cumulative pre-tax earnings of an average worker for five years. Kaj called it a birthday present to himself.

With the reporter hanging on his every word, Kaj had gone on to talk for three hours. A bank robber, he said, required both excellent planning skills and a gift for improvisation. Unexpected obstacles might arise at every turn. Bank staff and customers might panic and there could be any number of other problems, with the weapons, the getaway car, the flight from the police, the hiding spots, and so on. It was a difficult if lucrative occupation, Kaj mused. He then laughed about how he had escaped from prison and sent postcards from his travels to the prison guards.

Kaj had risen, the journalist said, to become one of the "coldest and most talented bank robbers" in the Swedish criminal underworld. He was also an aspiring singer and musician who would later cut his own album on the acclaimed Swedish label Metronome. He only felt compelled to continue his current "job" of robbing banks because once you begin, he said, you cannot stop.

AFTER THE FAILED ATTEMPT TO DRUG OR SHOOT THE GUNMAN, THE Stockholm police were ready to try something else. They were going to send in Kaj's seventeen-year-old brother, Dan, and a childhood friend, Nico Cleyndert, into the bank to reason with "Kaj."

This plan was probably suggested by Dr. Nils Bejerot, the prominent psychiatrist who was often called in to consult when a criminal was believed to be mentally ill or on drugs. A specialist on addiction, Bejerot had developed a reputation as an old-fashioned disciplinarian who had emerged as one of the country's leading advocates of a "no tolerance" approach to drug use. Before that, he had made his name as a vocal critic of violence in comic books.

Both Dan and Nico, then a policeman in Lund, had been flown up to Stockholm on a military plane in the predawn hours. Dan had promised his mother he would not take any unnecessary risks. Still he was frightened. The psychiatrist advised the teenager and the policeman that they had absolutely nothing to worry about. Kaj would not hurt them.

"Kaj, this is Dan," the teenager yelled from the second floor at about 6:10 a.m. "I want to speak with you. Can I come down?" He and Nico descended the chat staircase with Bejerot in tow. As they turned toward the lobby, the reluctant mediators were met by blasts of submachine-gun fire.

Bejerot encouraged them to try again, claiming that the gunman was really not firing at them. Dan was not so sure. One bullet had landed not far from his feet.

"Kaj, Kaj, this is your brother," Dan yelled on his second attempt to enter the lobby. He talked nervously about their mother and childhood experiences, as they slowly went down the steps. Shots once more sent him fleeing to safety.

When Dan refused to try a third time, Bejerot started down the stairs alone. The gunman aimed a round over his head, creating a cascade of dust and debris. One bullet lodged itself in a work of art on the wall. Another took out a chunk of a pillar.

"Get out of here!" yelled Clark, coming around the corner. "Can't you see that he is serious!"

Bejerot retreated to the bank's second-floor conference room. Dan and Nico were in shock. Several officers there could not help but wonder about the threat they faced in the bank. A man who shot at his own brother and old friend seemed irrational and dangerous, to say the least.

The telephone rang in the makeshift police headquarters and a voice in a heavy southern Swedish dialect asked to speak to his "brother."

"Stop that shit about Mamma!" Janne said. "Kaj is not here! Go home!"

Hanging up the phone, Dan yelled at the policemen: "You fucking idiots. You have the wrong guy!"

18

It is not always reason that guides the action.

—Sven Thorander

S THE SUN ROSE ON WHAT APPEARED TO BE ANOTHER BRILLIANT summer morning, many journalists had slipped away for breakfast, another cup of coffee, or perhaps a nap. The recent spate of police press conferences had revealed nothing—that is, nothing that they did not already know, or think they knew, in the fog of rumor that enveloped the crisis. Now the news of gunfire inside the bank brought reporters scurrying back from restaurants and cafés around Norrmalmstorg.

The police had nearly sacrificed two innocent lives, Clark noted.

"Talented cops," Janne later scoffed. "You wonder where they get all this from."

The embarrassing incident was hushed up by the Stockholm police. It received little immediate attention in the national media other than in a highly edited version in which variously identified police negotiators were depicted as being fired upon by an unstable robber with a submachine gun. He was under the influence of stimulants, *Göteborgs-Posten* said; the cross-town tabloid *GT* went further, calling the bandit a drug addict who had brought into the bank a bag full of bullets and narcotics.*

---

* Janne's white pills were actually ephedrine, an amphetamine that replicates the body's

The Stockholm police remained on high alert in case this man attempted a surprise maneuver out of the vault. Police detachments stood watch at intersections in the area and patrolled nearby airports.

At 8:06 a.m., police listened in to Clark's telephone call with an unknown woman, probably his fiancée, Maria Wallin. She told him about the police force occupying the Stockholm airport, as the news had reported. The police would not let them leave, she warned. "Don't believe them."

"No, no," Clark said, and launched into his own complaint about how the police prowled the lobby trying to shoot the robber. Then, when he intervened to avoid bloodshed, they blamed him for sabotaging their work. "It's so ridiculous," he said.

It had been a long night in the vault. Almost no one had slept. The gunman told Clark to complain to authorities about the conditions, particularly the lack of comfort, and demand mattresses, pillows, and blankets. A short while later, policemen dropped the bedding at the foot of the staircase and retreated.

The police chief, Kurt Lindroth, wanted, in return, to be assured that everything was OK with the hostages. Not a word had been heard from them all night. He asked to see them personally.

About 9:00 a.m., Clark brought out Kristin, Elisabeth, Birgitta, and Sven, one at a time. The police chief, as instructed, remained on the landing at the chat staircase. All the while, he kept his back to the wall and positioned his body at an angle, in case the gunman intended to pull a surprise attack of his own.

What particularly struck Lindroth was not the state of the hostages, who seemed fine; it was their demeanor. They acted less frightened than resentful, or even angry—and all that sentiment was directed overwhelmingly at the police.

When Kristin came out of the vault, Clark draped his arm around her shoulders. He did the same for Elisabeth. They seemed like old friends. The women said that they honestly wanted to leave with the robbers and could not understand why the police refused to listen to their wishes. Kristin, it seemed, had scowled at the authorities who wanted to rescue her.

Lindroth regarded this as one of the most curious mornings of his career.

---

natural adrenaline processes, speeding up the heart, opening the lungs, and preparing for a fight-or-flight response. They can also increase anxiety and nervousness.

Kristin later explained that she had been afraid that the police, by moving sharpshooters into the lobby and onto nearby rooftops, might hit them by mistake. They might also cause a shootout, and this fear had turned to anger when the police treated her, she said, like "a little dumb ignorant girl who was not worth saying anything to whatsoever, much less listening to."

The police snub baffled her, just as the hostages' cold-shoulder treatment puzzled the police. It was a veritable cultural clash—or generational conflict. Many of the police leaders, such as Lindroth and Thorander, were in their mid-to-late fifties; Kristin, Elisabeth, and Sven, by contrast, were in their early twenties, and Birgitta, the oldest, was only thirty-two. All four hostages were closer in age to Janne and Clark than they were to the authorities on the chat staircase.

What the police and the hostages did not know was that Clark had also manipulated the situation. Years later, he admitted that he had told the police *not* to talk to the hostages because they were, he alleged, conspiring to take over negotiations from him and he was losing his influence over the robber. Clark clearly exploited the police fear that multiple spokesmen would complicate the talks.

So when Kristin started speaking—and Clark had of course encouraged her to hold nothing back—the police negotiator had interrupted her to say that he would only talk with Clark. Kristin was stunned. The police really did not seem to care. Tears ran down her cheek. She returned to the vault, furious and ready to tell everyone about the disrespect she experienced. This ploy, also, not insignificantly helped solidify Clark's hold over the hostages as their most trustworthy ally and best hope for rescue.

Word of the extraordinary display of contempt—that is, the hostages for the police (rather than, as Kristin felt, the police for the hostages)—spread among the officers who were on the scene, and, in the hothouse atmosphere around Norrmalmstorg, and also to the reporters. They, too, would soon be trying to speak with the men and women in the vault.

At any time, the police could have prevented such contact by disabling the telephone line. This measure had been proposed, debated, and then vetoed. Maintaining ties with the outside world was deemed essential for the mental well-being of the hostages. Another reason for keeping the phone open was that the police wanted to listen in on the conversations, which they could now do legally. The court order for tapping the phones had arrived the previous night.

AS THE MORNING WORE ON, ALL WAS CALM IN THE BANK. CLARK, THE robber, and the hostages were believed to be resting or sleeping in the vault. They played Tic-Tac-Toe and later poker with a deck that had been requested from the police. Still, positions remained deadlocked. The bank drama was like a film, a reporter for *Dagens Nyheter* said, though one without the tight edits and dramatic soundtrack at the right moments.

One of his colleagues asked Commissioner Dag Halldin how long he anticipated the forces to remain at Norrmalmstorg.

"We are here as long as necessary," he said.

Time dragged on without much to report.

About noon, Clark requested lunch for everyone. Janne had told the hostages to order whatever they wanted. The police promptly rounded the corner to fetch steak from the Bäckahästen restaurant. As this venue now lay within the restricted zone, the dining room was nearly empty. Its business came, at this point, from policemen, journalists, camera crews, and now also the six men and women in the bank vault.

As steak was not available, the police ordered Wienerschnitzel.

"That surely must be good enough," Bengt-Olof Lövenlo said. "Send that shit down."

Coffee followed—one cup black for the gunman and one cup with two sugar cubes for Clark. Berndt Beckman, the young man who carried in the refreshments, overheard the two men talking about their plans for departure. Clark seemed out of the loop, he thought. The gunman had refused to say where he intended to take everyone.

Negotiations continued in the "tug of war" between the robber and the government, as *Sydsvenska Dagbladet* put it. Olof Palme, Lennart Geijer, and the cabinet were not about to budge, the psychiatrist Dr. Bejerot had told Clark on one of his visits inside the bank, especially not on the eve of the election. Janne and Clark, however, felt strongly that the government would in the end yield. This was Sweden, after all, Clark later said.

At some point that day, certainly by the early afternoon, Clark came out of the vault to confront the police. Nothing was happening. Did the police not realize how dangerous the situation was?

The robber not only had a submachine gun and a large supply of ammunition, but also an arsenal of explosives.

"He can blow the entire bank to smithereens!" Clark warned.

The police negotiator actually thought this was a bluff, because he had not seen or heard anything about the robber having this materiel. He did not even know that he had come into the bank with a bag of supplies. B-O was also exhausted. He had been working on the scene for nearly twenty-six hours without sleep.

The government would never allow the gunman to leave the bank with the hostages, B-O stated firmly.

"Then I cannot guarantee what will happen," Clark said.

B-O offered to relay the message to the police chief. "Personally," he added with typical bravado, "I think you are bullshitting."

Clark stormed away to the vault and retrieved a large clump of brown explosive dough. "Is this enough?"

19

When you go down on your knee with a microphone and run around like a broadcasting James Bond, I think that you do the matter a great disservice.

—Fritiof Haglund, producer for Radio Sweden

NOT YET PRIVY TO THE INTRIGUES IN THE BANK, MANY JOURNALISTS grew frustrated with the slow, uneventful afternoon. It was the calmest period of the crisis thus far, concluded a reporter for *Svenska Dagbladet*. Traffic lights blinked on streets without cars. Posters on the kiosks were two days old. Café tables sported empty plastic coffee cups and old film-roll canisters. Chairs were pulled up and placed here and there as groups of journalists formed and re-formed to sip beer and wait for something to happen.

Businesses behind the police barricades suffered in the standoff. Sales at the tobacco shop had dropped 85 to 90 percent of its usual daily take, its manager said. His only customers were policemen, journalists, photographers, and television camera crews. Nessim's oriental-rug showroom had the same complaint. At Cloetta's confectionery, employees busied themselves sprucing up store decorations and wrapping gift boxes of luxury chocolates, candies, and nuts.

During the impasse, a reporter for *Aftonbladet* ventured up to the roof of a building overlooking the square and spoke to a sniper, who identified himself only as "Sharpshooter Number 2." The policeman lay on his stomach, propped up on his elbows with his feet wide apart, resting on a borrowed fox skin from the nearby fur store. The barrel of his automatic carbine M15 stuck out among the long lenses of the photographers around him.

The sharpshooter had been at his post since Thursday morning, or nearly thirty hours. He was tired, though still confident. "I only shoot when I am completely certain," he said. "I am not going to miss."

The radio and television broadcasts went on unabated. Was the extensive coverage really necessary, asked Macke Nilsson in *Aftonbladet*. The programs could, of course, disseminate breaking news, but they could also spread errors, unfounded rumors, and a misleading one-sided account of the affair. This risk was magnified in the intense competition for scoops and the looming pressures of deadline. News was becoming entertainment—and the telling of the story, perversely, was starting to influence the story itself.

Live broadcasting of the ongoing bank drama, no doubt, increased the pressure on the police, making them more susceptible to mistakes, such as sending Kaj's brother and friend into the bank. At the same time, the media coverage was awakening what Nilsson called the inner "hyenas" in the audience. Many law-abiding citizens called openly for the attacker to be shot. The excessive media attention reminded his colleague at *Dagens Nyheter*, Kurt-Olov Eliasson, of a notorious stretch of a road with a dangerous curve, where locals were said to come out every Saturday with sandwiches and coffee thermoses to wait for the inevitable collisions. Norrmalmstorg was like that, he thought: It appealed to the darker instincts of the masses.

About 100 meters from the square, beyond the police lines, the crowds were still thick and lively, and growing larger again during the lunch break. There had never been more people on the streets, thought a reporter for *Kvällsposten*. Everyone seemed to follow the latest developments, and few were shy about speculating on the motives of the robber, the allegiance of Clark, and the ultimate end of the crisis. The atmosphere here was warm and convivial. This was no longer "a city in shock," *Dagens Nyheter* wrote, as it had been on Thursday. It was more like a summer carnival.

AT 3:17 P.M., THE TELEPHONE RANG IN THE BANK VAULT. THE JOURNAL-ist Gunnar Fagerström, of the Radio Sweden news program *Dagens Eko*, wanted to speak with either Clark or the robber. Fagerström excelled at winning the confidence of his interviewees and, in the process, gained revealing answers that sometimes eluded other reporters.

"Am I calling at a bad time?" Fagerström asked.

"No, on the contrary, it is quite good," Clark said with his usual humor. The journalist asked about the state of negotiations.

"Yeah, well, it is like this," Clark began. "The government has, five minutes ago, given its so-called absolute last offer that we could leave if we would only take with us one hostage, a girl, but the fact was that the girls protested wildly. Either they would both follow or . . ."

The next thing the journalist knew, Kristin came on the line. Speaking slowly and firmly, she confirmed much of what Clark had said. She did not want to leave without Elisabeth, and Elisabeth did not want to leave without her.

Had the government, the reporter asked, made its final decision?

"Yes, they say that, and they are so cowardly that they do not want to speak with me either." Kristin was not "the least afraid of Clark and the other guy," she said. They all sat and talked. She trusted them completely. "I could go around the whole world with them."

If all was so well, the reporter asked, why couldn't she or Elisabeth go with them by herself?

"Ah, but we want to leave together. One always wants to be two, right? It is always better." Besides, Kristin asked, "Are we not worth more than three million crowns [approximately $4 million today]?"

"What do you think is going to happen now?"

"I don't know."

The reporter asked if they had talked about where they would go. Kristin hesitated and then asked for clarification. He repeated the question.

"No we haven't, but I trust these boys. I really do."

Kristin went on to call the Swedish prime minister "a big jerk," though this part was edited out of the broadcast. Her critique of the media, on the other hand, aired in full. She accused them of sensationalizing the crime with accounts of the hostages, "sitting in a corner, crying, with two desperadoes."

"But you are not doing that?"

No, she said, adding that they had played Tic-Tac-Toe. "It can hardly be all that desperate then, right?"

After agreeing that her taped words could be broadcast, Kristin handed the receiver back to Clark, who had a few things to add. The police expected the robber to accept their "word of honor," but they had not proven themselves trustworthy. The authorities had said one thing, then another, repeatedly reversing themselves and flat-out breaking their word. The police had promised not to come in and shoot, Clark said. Yet snipers were in the bank, on the sidewalks, around the square, and everywhere in the area, it seemed.

So if the police insisted on ignoring both the dictates of reason and the wishes of the hostages, then Clark wanted to be taken back to prison immediately. He did not want to die. This decision was not one he took lightly, because, he added, the women desperately wanted him to stay.

For some time now, journalists had been wondering about Clark. Was he, as *Expressen* asked, "a hero or villain"? Some believed that he was helping the police, others that he hurt them, or betrayed them, literally laughing "all the way to the bank." Many people were beginning to see Clark as an ally of the gunman. Perhaps he had resorted to his usual antiauthoritarian instincts, succumbed to temptations of the moment, or just executed the role in the plot that he had helped concoct. Or maybe he was pursuing his own agenda altogether.

Gunnar Fagerström had the famous criminal on the line and asked him directly: Whose side are you on?

Clark's answer was true to form: "I am on the poor girls' side."

AS THE SIXTEEN-MINUTE TALK STARTED TO WIND DOWN, FAGERSTRÖM asked Clark another question on the minds of many listeners and policemen involved in the stand-off: Was not the best and simplest solution for the gunman to surrender?

"This dude has taken on a kamikaze mind-set," Clark said. "He doesn't give a shit about anything." Clark described him as sitting in the vault happily rigging up his explosives.

The reporter asked if Clark could do anything.

"The police believe that I can persuade him, but it is like talking to a wall."

Clark then exploited the still-widespread mistaken identity of the robber as Kaj and reminded the listeners that he had shot at his own brother and best friend. A man like that was never going to surrender. Just give him "his damn money!" Clark said. Three million crowns was a pittance compared to the lives of the young hostages.

20

[In] 999 cases of 1,000, the sharpshooter hits his target, but it is the one-thousandth case that made me nervous.

—Elisabeth Oldgren

THE EVENING PAPERS NOW HAD THEIR HEADLINES. "DRAMATIC Interview with Clark," splashed *Kvällsposten*. "RELEASE THE ROBBER OTH-ERWISE HE WILL BLOW US ALL UP." Kaj, the paper continued, was a delirious professional criminal, prepared to cause untold destruction rather than abandon his almost hopeless endeavor. A conclusion to the bank drama was imminent, the reporter believed. But would the hostages be released, or would the country witness a monumental act of violence?

The Gothenburg tabloid *GT* did not hazard a prediction on how the standoff would be resolved other than speculate that the risk for tragedy increased with each passing hour. National and regional newspapers around the country published long excerpts from Clark's sensational radio interview.

Many people criticized Radio Sweden for broadcasting this piece. It was only one side of the story, *Upsala Nya Tidning* noted, without any filtering or digestion of the raw material. There was no context, or background, either. The director, Otto Nordenskiöld, admitted that he had first opposed running the interview. Asked why he had changed his mind, Nordenskiöld had no comment. The ratings of the program, meanwhile, rose off the charts.

Other journalists decided to call into the bank vault as well. At 4:36 p.m., the evening television news program *Aktuellt* rang for an interview. This time, it was not Clark who answered. It was Elisabeth.

"I feel in good shape," Elisabeth told the reporter. "We have been well looked-after here by the robber and Clark. They have been real gentlemen toward us." The hostages had only one fear, she added, and it was the police. They might try to storm the vault, or attempt some other maneuver that risked their lives.

But didn't she think that the police were employing an "exhaustion tactic"?

Yes, they were, Elisabeth said, but she feared that this method would prove to be futile. After repeating Janne's demands, she confirmed that she was happy to leave with Clark and the robber. She knew they would later release her and Kristin "completely unharmed."

"So you are sitting there, you four . . ."

No, Elisabeth said. "We are not four, but six." She now included herself and her fellow hostages in the same group as Clark and Janne.

SITTING THERE WAS IN FACT A MORE REVEALING DESCRIPTION THAN the television reporter or the audience realized. That afternoon, Janne told the hostages that, given the presence of more policemen in the bank, he had no choice but to keep them inside the vault. They would no longer be allowed outside, even for the bathroom. From now on, the toilet would be one of the plastic wastebaskets in the back of the room.

Birgitta was sadder than ever, longing to see her family. Janne, then sitting in the armchair beside her, comforted her. He had two children as well, he said, and even if he had not seen them in some time, given his prison sentence, he understood how sad she must be. Everything would be OK, he stressed, if only the police would allow them to leave. Someone wanted to smoke. Janne pulled out a pack of cigarettes brought in earlier by the police and offered it around.

Smoking was not allowed in the vault, Birgitta said, citing bank policy. She had also recently quit.

Not knowing that, Janne pushed the pack to the group: "The vault is mine. You may smoke."

Birgitta eventually took a cigarette. Sven, who had also recently quit, took one as well.

There was no ashtray, Elisabeth protested.

"The whole floor is an ashtray," Janne said.

The good times that the hostages had described to the media, however, seemed long gone.

Elisabeth had begun to feel claustrophobic and tried to fight it by thinking of the crayfish party she was missing that weekend. Over and over she imagined the dress she would have worn, the items on the menu, the seating arrangements, the decorations, the songs, and the festivities. Anything except the new reality that had overtaken them.

That afternoon, Janne let her out of the vault one last time. He grabbed a rope from his canvas bag, cut a piece with his knife, and looped it around her neck. Elisabeth now walked out with this approximately 30-foot-long leash.

Elisabeth was grateful to the gunman for granting this permission. "I couldn't go far," she later said, "but I felt free."

Upon seeing the police in the lobby, Elisabeth yelled in desperation, "Why can't you go?"

21

Palme was under incredible pressure. He wanted to have as quick an ending as possible to the hostage drama.

—Carl Persson, chief of Swedish National Police

THE TRANSISTOR RADIO ON THE TABLE ALLOWED THE NEWS UPDATES to enter the closed world of the hostages and the robber, whom the police still inexplicably insisted was Kaj. After the interviews of Clark and Kristin aired, the men and women in the vault received a surprise with the *Dagens Eko* segment that followed.

"Kaj, this is Mamma speaking!" came a voice in a southern Swedish dialect, interspersed with sobbing and sniffling. A reporter had established contact with Kaj Hansson's mother, who wanted to give a message to her son.

"You have to give up this terrible thing you are doing," Kaj's mother said in a heartrending plea. "Think of the innocent people in the bank. Let them go free! Give up, Kaj, for your own sake and for the sake of everyone else!"

Since Kaj had been mistaken as the robber, his mother's telephone had rung almost nonstop. Reporters camped out on the staircase outside their apartment. Neighbors began to shun her. She was even receiving death threats. Now, hour after hour, she heard how her son had supposedly taken four innocent people hostage. She feared for his life, her anxiety manifest in the urgency of her appeal.

"I beg you one last time, Kaj, Do as your mamma says!"

Janne stared at the radio dumbfounded. With a huff, he turned it off.

Kristin later said that this apparent disgust made her think that the gunman might in fact be Kaj. Clark also looked perplexed, as if he did not know whether to laugh or cry. When Kristin later asked him who the gunman was, Clark refused to say anything other than she should be glad it was not someone worse, like the violent and feared Swedish bank robber Lars-Inge Svartenbrandt.

It was probably later that afternoon that Janne rubbed off his makeup and removed his wig. As long as they remained in the vault, there was no longer a need to keep up the disguise. Besides, he could don it again when they left, which he hoped would be soon.

The hostages saw Janne now for the first time unmasked. Sven, for one, was surprised when the gunman took off his wig. His hair had looked funny, he later said, but it had seemed real. Janne, without his disguise, he added, looked kind and unthreatening.

WITH THE HOSTAGE CRISIS STILL LOCKED IN A STALEMATE, JANNE AND Clark had not given up on the prime minister's help. Even if he had not listened to either of them, perhaps he would take to heart the appeals of one of the hostages. Kristin was the obvious choice. Young and articulate, she was also a member of his own Social Democratic Party.

At 5:02 p.m., the telephone rang at Chancellery House. It would be a long and extraordinary telephone conversation, certainly one of the more memorable in the history of Swedish crime.

"Yes, my name is Kristin Enmark. I am sitting here as a hostage in Kreditbanken and I would like to speak with Olof Palme."

"One moment, please."

"Thank you very much."

Palme was actually taking a nap. It had been a long night, dealing with the unexpected crisis at Norrmalmstorg.

Kristin started to explain why she was calling when the official interrupted. "He is coming now. We are getting him."

When the prime minister took the phone, Kristin introduced herself. "I am actually very disappointed in you," she said.

"Oh, really, why?" asked Palme, still groggy from his interrupted sleep.

"I have been a Social Democrat my entire life, you know. But I think that you are sitting here now and playing chess with our lives."

"Why's that?"

"Yeah, you know, I trust Clark and the robber fully and completely. I am not the least afraid of them. I am not the least desperate. They have not done anything to me, except been very helpful." What she was afraid of, she added, was the police attacking the vault.

The police will never do that, the prime minister said.

"But can't you allow me and Elisabeth and Clark and the robber . . ." Kristin began, before she repeated Janne's demands for foreign currency, two pistols, and safe passage. She wanted that as well.

"Put yourself in our position," the prime minister said. "They [sic] have gone in and robbed a bank and shot at a policeman."

"No, now I am going to tell you something. The police drew their weapon first."

"That doesn't matter. They have, in any event, shot a policeman, hadn't they?" He was a fine and decent fellow, Palme said. "It is not so much fun for him to sit now with a gunshot wound in his hand."

"But what do you think is better, that he has a gunshot wound in his hand or that six people die?"

"They [the captors] will die, if they pull a weapon and start shooting!" Palme then went on to ask Kristin why the robber can't simply lay down his weapon.

"Lay down the weapon? He wants to get out of here . . . He says, you know, that he has nothing to lose, right?" At any rate, if the robber released everyone, it would be "boom, boom, boom," Kristin said, imitating the sound of machine-gun fire. She recounted several instances in the bank where the police resorted to sharpshooters ready to kill. "I beg you on my knees," Kristin said, to let Elisabeth and her go.

Kristin became increasingly familiar and informal in tone with the prime minister. "But darling Olof," she said. A moment later she pleaded with "dearest Olof, sweetheart."

The risks were too great to let them leave with the robber, Palme insisted. Besides, why did she want to go?

"Because I trust them." She again defended Clark and the robber, reminding the prime minister that the latter had not hurt any of the hostages, despite having had plenty of time to do so.

The talk went on without anyone persuading the other. Kristin appealed to the prime minister as the most powerful person in Sweden: "You are the one who can save my life."

The best way to do that, Palme said, was "not to let them out on the roads."

"Please, dear sweet cutie, let me go! Let Elisabeth and I leave with these two . . . I beg you . . . I take it at my own risk."

"It makes no difference," the prime minister interrupted. "We have to take responsibility for everyone."

"But please, Olof dear, don't you understand that I am sitting here asking you for my life?"

"No violence, you know, will befall you from any authorities. You understand that, don't you?"

Kristin first agreed and then countered by telling of several instances in the bank when the police had been less than trustworthy.

As the dispute went on, Palme said he could hear someone beside her telling her what to say. Kristin denied it, but Palme said that he heard it.

Kristin then reminded the prime minister of the demonstration that evening, and how it would not be pretty. There was no other way to resolve the dilemma peacefully than to let them leave—that is, except for one thing. Palme could come to the bank and take their place.

"That is interesting," Palme said, and then repeated these words a second time as if trying to think of something to say. "We shall see, but . . ." He did not finish the sentence.

Around and around it went. Palme said the robber should lay down his gun and let them leave; Kristin replied that he was not going to do it because Clark and the robber did not, for a minute, believe the police when they offered safe passage. They needed the hostages for protection.

It was the police that were protecting them, Palme said.

"But they can't do that, as long as we are here inside [the vault]," Kristin objected. If anyone was protecting them, she added, it was Clark and the robber.

"But do you really perceive the police as an enemy power?"

"Yes, I do."

A female official came on the line to say that the prime minister had an urgent call.

"This is also urgent!" Kristin protested.

With Palme still on the line, Kristin made a reference to an assertion they had heard from Bejerot that the real reason the government would not let the hostages leave with the robber and Clark is because then "the election would go down the toilet."

"Yeah, but this has nothing to do with that," the prime minister said.

"Well, [if it did], then one would actually be very angry."

The conversation returned to the shooting of a policeman Thursday morning. Palme reminded her that the officer was only doing his job; Kristin said that she, too, was doing her job when she was taken hostage and the prime minister should now do his job, as well, and let them go.

"Umm," Palme said, and emphasized the need for society to uphold law and order.

"You can tell me about society another time," Kristin interrupted. She was "beginning to get really angry," she added, and told Palme to call down to the police at once to tell them to honor their wishes to let Elisabeth and her leave with Clark and the robber, with the rest of the ransom money, and the two pistols that he demanded. Otherwise, she wanted to see the prime minister come to the vault and take their place.

"Goodbye, and thanks for your help!" Kristin hung up. It was 5:44 p.m.

The stranglehold the man placed on a woman . . . became a symbolic stranglehold on society's authorities.

—*Dagens Nyheter,* August 24, 1973

CLIPS OF KRISTIN'S FORTY-TWO-MINUTE HARANGUE ACCUSING THE government of "playing chess" with her life would be played and replayed on the radio and television. Janne, sitting in the armchair, was thrilled. "I liked Kristin for a lot [of reasons]," he later said, "but most of all when she cleaned Olof Palme's clock." Clark agreed. Kristin's eloquence made the prime minister sound like the "village idiot."

Not everyone shared this assessment, and one person called the vault that evening to say so. It was Kristin's mother, Gunnel. The police allowed the conversation to proceed, despite its risks for upsetting the hostage or the gunman.

"To whom am I speaking?" Gunnel asked when Janne picked up the phone.

"They call me the robber."

"May I speak with my daughter, Kristin Enmark?"

"She is sleeping. Shall I wake her?"

When Kristin came to the phone, Gunnel let her know that she was upset at her daughter's almost flippant tone with the prime minister. It was a good thing for both of them that Gunnel had not heard the censored part of Kristin's earlier interview where she'd called Olof Palme "a big jerk."

Kristin's father, Tore, took the phone and asked if Kristin, a lover of poker, had been winning many games in the vault. There must be a lot of money there for the pot, he joked. Off the phone, he was far less composed. He feared that his daughter had been hypnotized or brainwashed. In fact, the Enmarks had already left their home in northern Sweden for a 500-mile trek to the capital.

Gunnel Enmark was upset with Radio Sweden. Kristin's words were never meant to be broadcast all over the country, she said, and accused radio executives of taking advantage of the abject terror of an innocent child in a crass bid to increase ratings.

Evidently there was one other part of the interview that would have caused even more of an uproar. According to Kristin, the prime minister had responded to her fear with the words: "Would it not feel good to die at your post?"

Olof Palme later denied asking such a question, and it does not appear in the taped recording of the call. But both Janne and Clark said that Kristin was correct, and several minutes of the telephone call are in fact no longer extant. No explanation was ever given for this mysterious editing. Significantly, too, no one on the police surveillance team in the bank has publicly denied the allegation, and probably with good reason. The dialogue that Kristin remembered fits almost seamlessly into the lacuna of the transcript.* It is difficult to avoid concluding that Palme probably regretted saying such a thing to a twenty-three-year-old woman who feared for her life.

LIKE KRISTIN'S PARENTS, ELISABETH'S FATHER, ERIK OLDGREN, thought of going to Stockholm to be near his daughter. Elisabeth had discouraged it. It will be OK, she told him, when they spoke briefly on the phone. He had first decided to stay home, though he and his wife, Estrid, would soon change their mind.

Elisabeth's older brother, Stephan, a thirty-year-old who lived in Stockholm, had already come to Norrmalmstorg. He had also offered himself as a substitute hostage for his sister. She had sat there long enough, he said. After the robber refused to accept the exchange, Stephan had remained nearby, pacing the square and sipping coffee at Palmhuset among the policemen,

* For more, see Notes.

journalists, and camera crews. "I can only hope that no one inside the bank loses his head," he told a reporter.

Now the Oldgren family waited on each update, vacillating "between terror and hope," as Elisabeth's father put it. The same could be said for Sven's parents, Stig and Wera Säfström. They knew the crisis could worsen at any moment, but they, too, expressed confidence in their son, who had only two weeks before survived a harrowing storm while sailing with a friend near the island of Åland. Wera's biggest fear remained that the police would lock themselves into a rigid position without any room for maneuver and cause the robber to panic.

Across town, Birgitta's husband, Per-Åke, concentrated on trying to keep life as normal as possible for their young children. He had gone to work as usual, because he knew that he would not get any peace at home. His office was also closer to Norrmalmstorg, in case something happened.

That evening, Per-Åke came home with milk, blood pudding, and a package of diapers. It was a terrible ordeal for the family. "The worst is the uncertainty," he said. He had not told his children about their mother. Karin, age three, and Susanne, eighteen months, were too young to understand. All they knew was that their mother had not been home in "the world's longest time."

Birgitta's husband was also growing angry. Neither the police nor any of the directors at the bank had bothered to notify him that his wife had been taken hostage. He had tried to call Kreditbanken for information all day Thursday, and had only found out the news by reading *Aftonbladet*. Could they not have at least let him know?

It was going to be another long, dreary night of worrying and lack of sleep for all the families whose loved ones were still held hostage at the bank.

AFTER KRISTIN HAD HUNG UP THE PHONE WITH THE PRIME MINISTER, there was a vague sense of optimism among the men and women in the vault that the crisis might soon be resolved. Once they pulled off the evening's "demonstration," Palme would likely relent and order the police to stand down.

Clark, again, wondered how well Janne had thought out the scenario. Janne had still not told him many details, and Clark drew his own conclusions.

The four of them, as Clark saw it, would have to depart in the Mustang. No doubt, they would need to stop at a gas station as soon as possible because the police would not be stupid enough to give them a full tank, no matter what they promised. He knew a good place south of the city center. But if this did not work—and it would not be easy to fill up with the police in pursuit— he had a backup plan.

He would drive fast through the capital, losing his police pursuers, and find a suitable car to force off the road. After switching vehicles, they would head for a discreet pathway off a forest road that he knew about 75 miles west in Hälleforsnäs. No police car could follow him there, he was sure. At a safe and secluded spot, Janne would disembark with the bags of money. Clark would drive back to Stockholm with Kristin and Elisabeth and release them unharmed, enjoying the gratitude of the country. He would be cheered as a hero and receive the rewards that the police had offered him.

Of course, that was what he said later. Another possibility was that he would join Janne and share the loot—and freedom. The police, meanwhile, would be looking for poor Kaj.

But unfortunately for Janne and Clark, the police showed no signs of yielding. Despite the imminent threats to the lives of the hostages, they remained at a standoff. Neither the government nor the robber came forward with any tempting counterproposals. The call to Olof Palme had not yet produced any concrete results either. The police still occupied the lobby.

Frustrated at the stalemate, Janne enforced his new rule that no one would leave the vault. Then, as the time of his proposed demonstration neared, he made another announcement. To prove to the police that he was serious, he was apparently going to have to do something that he had hoped to avoid. He was going to have to shoot someone.

23

He still stood there with his submachine gun in a firm grip and looked like a comic-book superhero who had the situation under control, when in fact it was as close as it could be to catastrophe.

—Clark Olofsson

JANNE'S WARNING HAD UNDERSTANDABLY SHOCKED AND FRIGHT-ened the hostages. Who would be the victim? It was probably going to be Birgitta, *Kvällsposten* observed, referring to the rumor that she would be blown up with dynamite. Janne, however, had something else in mind.

"I cannot harm the girls," he said, and turned to Sven.

Janne promised Sven that he would only graze him with a single bullet, making sure to hit the thigh. Nothing more than a scar, he said. To prevent this act from being in vain, he would send Sven to the chat staircase and then shoot him in front of the police.

Surely Sven could understand his dilemma, Janne said. Negotiations were not going well, and the police would not agree to his demands unless he showed them he meant business. Actually Sven did understand. He made no protest, and surprised, even impressed, Janne and Clark with his composure.

"I do not know if I was afraid, but I did not feel very brave," Sven later said.

In fact, Sven said that he felt grateful because Janne was trying to make the most of a dreadful situation. "I thought it was very human," Sven said. "In this desperate situation, he could have hurt me even more."

Janne lay down to rest in preparation for the night's demonstration. As

Clark had informed the press, it was supposed to take place between 7 and 8 p.m.

The atmosphere—which had improved so much with Clark's arrival—was darkening fast. The temperature both outside and inside the vault dropped. Police patrolled the square as usual. Journalists hurried back to Norrmalmstorg from cafés, restaurants, and hotels for the display of strength, or whatever it was the gunman planned to do. Some curiosity seekers had climbed atop the roof of a nearby building to watch. A few shouted at the gunman. The crowd did not budge from the barricades.

The time for Janne's demonstration neared. Janne told Sven that he could drink as much beer as he liked.

Sven sat in the vault and drank. "OK, he is going to shoot me," he thought. "I can survive that."

"It's only in the leg," Kristin told him.

Years later, Kristin emphasized how much she regretted that comment. Fear and stress had clearly warped their ability to reason, she said.

AT 7:34 P.M., A BOOM ROCKED THE LOBBY.

"Roll the cameras!" yelled reporter Bo Holmström, microphone in hand as he ducked for cover behind an automobile.

A policeman, on the chat staircase, was startled and had fired his submachine gun by accident into the wall. His colleague, Jonny Jonsson, came running down the stairs to find the bank's ground floor filled with smoke and the smell of burnt fuses.

The police and press in the square were taken aback. The lack of damage to the windows or the furniture visible through the windows made *Göteborgs-Posten* wonder if the explosion had occurred inside the vault. Perhaps one or more of the hostages had just been blown up on television. *Svenska Dagbladet* described the scene in the capital as straight out of a nightmare.

Fortunately Sven had not been blown up, shot, or otherwise harmed. Asked why he changed his mind, Janne later said, "My heart bled for him. I did not want to do it; I could not do it." Clark was relieved, too, because he said that shooting Sven had been his idea and he felt "so ashamed" when Sven accepted his fate so calmly. At any rate, by the early evening, Janne had found a better plan.

He sent Clark out to rig up explosives on the long counter window in the lobby. The demonstration was timed to coincide with the start of the evening news. It would, Janne hoped, put pressure on the authorities to yield. At the same time, Janne and Clark's action accomplished something else that no one at the time guessed. The bomb had been placed near the locked Cash Register No. 1 and blasted a hole about the size of a fist in the almost ten-inch-thick fiberboard desk. The cash register drawer had opened enough that a hand could squeeze inside.

An undetermined amount of cash was brought back to the vault.

Janne and Clark then celebrated their success by calling the police and ordering coffee and ice cream for everyone.

24

The drama is beginning to take on purely mythological proportions. Election campaign? What damn election campaign? Here, it is about . . . three princesses and a frightful dragon, a beast with a head named [Janne] Olsson and a tail named [Clark] Olofsson, or the other way around.

—Esko Korpilinna,
Finnish playwright in Stockholm,
September 16, 1973

ABOUT A QUARTER OF AN HOUR AFTER THE EXPLOSION, OLOF PALME made a public statement. He reaffirmed his "full confidence" in the police and encouraged his countrymen to show patience and understanding for their difficult task of protecting society while also safeguarding human lives. There would, in short, be no deviation from their position. The robber would not be allowed to leave the bank with the hostages.

Such a move resonated with many people who did not think it was dignified for a prime minister to negotiate with an escaped convict. If the situation had taken place in the United States or the Soviet Union, one of Palme's critics said, the crisis would have been resolved in thirty minutes with the bank robber defeated or dead. Palme should show some backbone.

Actually, *Expressen*'s P. O. Enquist thought Palme was already taking on too much risk when he called for "absolutely no concessions." There was no way, Enquist wrote, that Palme would have struck such an uncompromising pose if it were not an election year. The columnist feared that the people who would pay the price would be the hostages.

"How many lives is your career worth?" one person telegrammed the prime minister.

That night, Channel 1 showed the Marx Brothers' comedy *A Night at the Opera*. The hilarity of the film had then spilled over into the hysteria on the news program that followed, *Expressen* noted. Television cameras zoomed in on the bank's entrance, or the Mustang parked outside, while excited reporters commented on the ongoing crisis. Hallmarks of the profession, such as fact-checking and sound interpretation, seemed to be forgotten. It was "pure farce," the columnist concluded, and a parody of a news broadcast.

TV2, by contrast, received praise for sticking with its nature program and social documentary on the lives of Pakistani girls trying to navigate between rural and urban life. Still, from time to time, the broadcasts were interrupted with breaking news from Norrmalmstorg. "Such a [crime] does not happen here," could have been said a few years ago, but alas that was no longer the case.

The king's health, meanwhile, was deteriorating further and the royal family was asked to gather at his bedside. At any moment, the popular ruler might pass away. The old Sweden—safe, neutral, and secure—seemed to be dying with him. Was a new, uncertain, and far more menacing Sweden being born on live television?

THE INTERVIEWS OF KRISTIN, ELISABETH, AND CLARK OFFERED A unique and disturbing perspective on the ongoing crisis. That evening, however, the media helped the Stockholm police make a real breakthrough in the case, when Janne, too, granted an interview that aired on the national television news program *Aktuellt*.

"Who I am does not matter," Janne said. Robbing was his profession. "Yeah, I come in and will, yeah, do the robbery, you know, that is my job."

Janne said that he had wanted to speak with a policeman and state his demands. Instead, the officers had come at him and the hostages with guns. "What should I have done?" he asked. He had shot. Now Janne emphasized that he wanted to avoid violence and make a deal.

There was one fundamental problem with Janne making this appeal on the airwaves. As he had not bothered to disguise his voice, everyone from Kalmar prison guards to Helsingborg policemen would recognize him. The ability to exploit the police's mistaken theory that he was Kaj Hansson would soon be over. The telephone interview was clearly a blunder.

One viewer who heard the broadcast was Kaj's mother, who called the police to say that the gunman in the bank was certainly not her son. Another person who contacted authorities was Janne's younger brother, Åke. The twenty-seven-year-old auto-body painter had been watching the news in the family's hometown of Helsingborg when he heard Janne's unmistakable southern drawl—and then, too, his hearty laugh when the reporter asked Janne where he intended to go. Åke now had no doubt who the gunman was.

Be careful, Åke urged the police. He had seen his brother two weeks before and had been struck by his state of mind. He seemed "desperate and tired of life." Åke wanted to speak to Janne in person, claiming that he was the only one who could talk sense into him and save the innocent lives of the hostages.

The police, however, rejected his offer, deeming it too risky. They feared that this might be a trick to help Janne pass along money from the bank, or other valuables stolen from the safety-deposit boxes. They also suspected that Åke might be trying to relay messages or provide some unidentified additional support to his besieged brother.

Åke decided to go to Stockholm anyway. He feared a massacre, he said.

———

AFTER THE EVENING'S EXPLOSION AND THE UNEQUIVOCAL STANCE OF the prime minister not to yield, the police remained on high alert in case the robber attempted to make a desperate breakout.

A reporter for *Göteborgs-Posten* received a sharp rebuke from a policeman for crossing Norrmalmstorg and potentially alarming the robber. Each movement in the square could cause the gunman to panic, the policeman explained. "We don't know what he is capable of," and so everyone had to show the utmost restraint.

But Janne was not preparing to force his way out to the getaway car. He later said that he had wanted to leave, but Clark had refused. "I could not do it alone," Janne said, referring to the task of carrying the submachine gun and the three bags of money while also using the hostages as shields so that he would not be mowed down, Bonnie and Clyde–style. Clark had opposed it for that very reason. Sharpshooters were in the park with a clear line of fire at the car. Janne, however, did not think that they would dare to shoot at them, with the hostages beside them, in the center of Stockholm.

There was one other problem: They did not have the keys to the car. If they'd had them, Clark said, or he had known how to hotwire that particular model, then he would have proposed himself that they rush out. Both Clark and Janne had also spoken of using a large blanket, or sheet, to cover Janne and the hostages as much as possible. Clark would then lead them out. This was something, Janne said, that they only thought of afterward.

Barring a last-minute and unforeseen breakthrough, Janne and Clark instead prepared for a second night in the bank. To make sure that the police did not catch them off-guard, they shut the inner door of the vault, leaving it slightly cracked, and moved a heavy, almost six-foot-tall cabinet to block the entrance. Sven was ordered to help them.

If the police tried to attack, Elisabeth remained out in front in the arm-chair, its foot still wired with explosives.

Janne switched off the lights.

As Birgitta lay alone under the table, she felt someone come up next to her. It was Janne.

There are conflicting accounts of what happened next.

According to Janne, the two of them started talking about life in prison, sex behind bars, and the length of time since he had had sex himself. "Pity we did not meet ten years ago," Birgitta was said to have told him, and snuggled up to him. She kissed him hesitantly, he said, and soon unzipped his pants and started to give him oral sex. She wanted to go further, but he claimed that he stopped her.

Birgitta, on the other hand, told a different version. After Janne appeared under the table, he had asked permission to stay there and volunteered that he had not seen a woman in twenty-one months since the beginning of his sentence and asked if he could "hug" her. She elaborated:

> I thought that if I could establish a small sense of intimacy with him, I could get him to give this up somehow or perhaps he could relieve some tensions in a way that put him in a different frame of mind and not want to carry out this [act] any longer. We had our clothes on the whole time, but he was allowed to hug me . . . then he got to stroke my breasts and hips, but again, the whole time, it

was on top of our clothes. He became rather excited and wanted to continue.

She stopped him, as delicately as possible, and Janne honored her wishes. But as he remained aroused, she suggested that he take matters into his own hand. Traces of semen were later discovered on a wadded-up piece of paper tossed under the table in the vault.

25

Under psychological pressure, you try to do everything to survive. I tried to tell myself that it was not so dangerous, despite the fact that it was perhaps extremely dangerous.

—Elisabeth Oldgren

T HE STREETLAMPS AND TRAFFIC LIGHTS AROUND NORRMALMSTORG had once again been shut off on police orders, creating a surreal, almost ghostly ambience. A handful of Stockholmers, probably tipsy from the evening's revels, climbed atop a nearby building and shouted encouragement to the boys in the bank.

One man somehow made his way past the barricades and strolled right up to the entrance. Was he a friend of the robber or perhaps someone seeking vigilante justice? Police in bulletproof vests pounced. The intruder turned out to be another intoxicated man who wanted a closer view of the action.

Otherwise it was a pretty slow Friday night and Saturday morning. Sven Thorander had left early to get some rest at his home in Vällingby, north of Stockholm. Police chief Kurt Lindroth also disappeared for a nap.

Then, about 1:50 a.m., two shots rang out from inside the bank.

Police on the second floor feared that Janne had started firing his submachine gun, possibly executing a hostage. The shooting, however, was too loud to have come from the vault. It sounded like the lobby or the staircase. Perhaps Janne had rushed out of his stronghold, some people on the second floor wondered, attempting to force his way to the getaway car.

As journalists outside watched, the police officers again crawled on sidewalks, crept around vehicles, and crouched behind the white cast-iron benches in front of the bank. Snipers remained in position with their AK-4s aimed at the front doors to the bank, or the blue Mustang, still parked outside.

What had happened was that several policemen had grown frustrated with the lack of progress in the police operation and decided to make something happen. One of them had approached Morgan Rylander, who had been serving as a sentinel on the staircase, and told him to "wake" the robber.

After all, what good was an exhaustion strategy that allowed the gunman to rest?

Morgan told his colleagues on the staircase to make sure no one entered the lobby, then he took up his position, and waited on his signal. When it came, he descended five or six steps toward the lobby and fired twice, aiming at a wooden bench to avoid a ricochet. The hope was to lure the gunman out of his veritable fortress and into the range of the sharpshooters.

There was still no response from the vault.

Instead, Detective Inspector Jonny Jonsson rushed out from a second-floor room to see what had happened.

"Was that you who shot?" Jonsson asked, clearly upset. He had been organizing his own team of four snipers, and lashed out at Morgan, "Put away your weapon and get out of here!"

Morgan was sent to the conference room to explain his actions. A colleague had advised him to claim that the shots had been an accident, but Morgan took full responsibility. He had been asked to wake the gunman, he told the commissary on duty that morning, Bert Levinsson. As for the damage, he had been told that the bank would have to be renovated anyway.

"Are you tired?" the commissary asked.

Morgan said he was. He had worked long hours since Thursday morning with little sleep.

"Are you very tired?" asked Levinsson, leaning forward and putting his arm on Morgan's shoulder.

He then sent Morgan home to rest.

AS SATURDAY MORNING DAWNED, NORRMALMSTORG ONCE AGAIN DOMI-nated the headlines. Television cameras shooting the "thrilling drama," as

Svenska Dagbladet dubbed it, broadcast nightmarish images nonstop into homes around the country and the continent. From Madrid to Munich, audiences were gripped.

Prime Minister Olof Palme urged his countrymen to trust the police, *Dagens Nyheter* led, while the opinion pages and letters to the editor reflected a swirl of dissent. The police had several times acted in a clumsy manner, concluded a reader from the northern city of Sundsvall, and they had spent too much time on negotiations and press conferences. "Shoot the robber" was the advice of one fourteen-year-old in Janne's hometown of Helsingborg. A telephone repairman in Falun suggested that they poison him instead.

Other readers urged authorities to end the standoff by allowing Clark and the robber to leave the bank with the hostages. This viewpoint was particularly strong with women and younger readers, noted *Aftonbladet*. Older generations and men, on the other hand, pressed for a strict, unyielding approach. Exceptions to these generalities, of course, abounded as the debate was just getting started.

What were the prime minister and the minister of justice doing, bargaining with a criminal? many people asked. The left-leaning *Dala-Demokraten* interpreted this as another example of the government's lack of vigor and vision. No wonder, *Västerbottens-Kurier* added, that Palme's regime adopted such a passive stance at Norrmalmstorg, given how it had failed to tackle the national crises of rising unemployment, inflation, and high taxes on pensions in a stagnating economy. The leadership looked paralyzed. Some readers mocked the administration. If a single gunman could incapacitate the entire Swedish government, one reader shuddered to imagine what an enemy force of ten people might accomplish.

The problem was not Palme or the police, noted others. It was the media.

While the authorities were doing the right thing, namely, focusing on saving the lives of the hostages, reporters were busy glorifying the criminals. One critic, Fritiof Haglund, called the emerging national obsession an absurdity. Television and radio in particular, he thought, exploited the entertainment value of the crisis and crowded out real news from their programs. It was a "pornography of violence," as *Aftonbladet* would soon dub the coverage.

Calls for moderation and restraint went on in tandem with the wild and reckless reporting. Norrmalmstorg was becoming a "grotesque drama," concluded Kalmar's *Barometern*. "Real Gentlemen" ran the startling headline in *Östgöta Correspondenten*, putting Elisabeth's praise of Janne and Clark on the front page. *Västerbottens-Kuriren*, the largest newspaper in northern Sweden, also stressed her fear of the police. *Sydsvenska Dagbladet* went further: "The Hostages Take the Robbers' Side?"

Commissioner Sven Thorander was appalled. When he arrived back on the scene Saturday morning, he lashed out at the media for its lack of discretion. When were the journalists, *Expressen* remembered him asking, going to stop feeding the robber all the details of the police operation? All this coverage was complicating their rescue mission and prolonging the suffering of the hostages. Clark and the gunman were listening to every broadcast. "We are not dealing with idiots here," Thorander said.

But the media drew the bulk of its coverage from the police, Bror Jansson of Radio Sweden countered. If the authorities did not want the robber to anticipate their plans, then maybe they should not be so eager to parade them so openly at the press conferences. It was the media's job to report the news, not censor it, and besides, his team had run several stories by the police before publishing them.

Fingers continued to point in many directions and everyone, it seemed, had an opinion. One of the many issues about the police action was, of course, whether the authorities had acted wisely in handing Clark over to the gunman. They had no choice but to trust him, some people said. Others argued that Clark had only compounded the problem the police faced in overpowering the robber and freeing the hostages. Now they paid the price. Clark, the media darling, was enjoying his newfound platform, speaking directly to the entire country. The infamous bank robber had become "a saint and a superstar."

Crank calls and bomb threats, meanwhile, continued to come in to the Stockholm police. At 6:45 a.m., an anonymous caller claimed to have kidnapped Clark's mother. "Tell Clark that he knows where she is," a voice on the phone said, and hung up. The police ordered the call traced and the matter investigated. Clark's mother, it turned out, was safe.

ABOUT FIFTEEN MINUTES LATER, A WELL-TRAINED MAN WITH A THICK mustache and long sideburns ran across the square and entered the building through the same staircase that led to the bank directors' offices. This was Håkan Larsson, a detective inspector who had returned to duty after leaving his post about seven hours earlier.

Larsson made his way down the chat staircase.

The lobby looked almost deserted, with overturned chairs, fallen plaster, and broken glass scattered about helter-skelter. On the teller counter near window No. 1 was a blown-up cash register littered with coins, papers, dust, and debris. Everything was ominously quiet. Larsson scanned the room. There was no sign of Clark or the gunman.

Perhaps the robber was still sleeping, Larsson thought. On the other hand, the outer door to the vault remained wide open with the inner door cracked at an angle. It was therefore possible that the robber was watching him. At any moment, a barrage of bullets could come his way, and he had not worn a bulletproof vest because it would have made too much noise as he moved about the lobby.

Larsson sensed his opportunity. He thought he could dash across the room to unlock the front doors. This would allow the police to move in to secure the ground floor, and then, if he left the door open, sharpshooters would gain a more favorable opportunity to hit the gunman without the thick plate-glass windows deflecting their shots.

Confident that he could make it across the lobby undetected, Larsson removed his shoes and took off in his black socks.

The maneuver worked.

Still the vault was quiet—too quiet. Even the microphone, which the police had mounted on a column near the chat staircase during the night, was not picking up any noise.

The police began to worry. Perhaps the gunman had carried poison in his canvas bag and forced everyone to take it. Maybe he had brought some tools and somehow escaped through the other side of the vault. Larsson and his colleague Jonny Jonsson left to search the cellars of the building, on the off chance that the gunman had, incredibly, found a way out.

With no trace of the attacker, the police needed to know if they were still in the vault. And if the gunman was in fact only asleep, who was holding the submachine gun and preventing the hostages from escaping?

About 9:30 a.m., one of Larsson's colleagues, Jack Malm, came down the chat staircase with a cigarette in one hand and an approximately 8-foot-long iron rod in the other. The latter was a tool that was used to open and close awnings. Malm moved slowly across the lobby. When he reached the teller counter, he snuffed out his cigarette and inched his way closer to the customer vault on the landing. Then, Malm stood on a chair, and, with the help of the long pole, pushed open the inner door to the vault by about half a foot.

Janne, who had drifted off into a deep sleep, awoke at the noise of falling bottles from an alarm they had earlier rigged up, and started shouting. Someone on the inside of the vault slowly closed the inner door again, leaving only a gap of an inch.

26

It is, of course, a game of poker. I realize the risks [we are taking] ... but those risks cannot prevent us from acting.

—Kurt Lindroth

BY THIS TIME, THE STOCKHOLM POLICE HAD TO CONFRONT THE DIS-heartening possibility that their supposed ally, Clark Olofsson, might have "defected."

Despite their praise of Clark in public (and really, also, a defense of their own risky gamble of releasing him into the bank), there was no indication that he had made the slightest attempt to disarm the gunman. He had opened cash registers, destroyed security footage, and criticized the police in his interviews. He had even warned the gunman as sharpshooters had him in their crosshairs. Such action sabotaged their work, many policemen complained. In the parlance of military intelligence and law enforcement, Clark seemed to have been turned.

As disappointing as that conclusion was, Lindroth and Thorander took some comfort in the fact that the robber had been tentatively identified by the police as Janne Olsson. Preliminary research indicated that he was a convict with a high standing among his fellow prisoners. He felt utter disdain for criminals who preyed upon women and children. Janne did not seem to be a vicious, cold-blooded lunatic who would harm the hostages.

This assessment of the gunman was shared by the psychiatrist, Dr. Bejerot. Now, too, Bejerot made another point that encouraged the police. The more time the gunman spent with the hostages, the greater the chances were for a nonviolent resolution to the crisis. Janne would come to know his captives not as objects but as human beings with distinct hopes, fears, dreams, and struggles.

Indeed the police hoped that the gunman, Clark, and the hostages would develop what Dr. Bejerot called "a bond of friendship." This phenomenon already seemed to be emerging. Clark had come out of the vault the previous morning with his arms around Kristin and Elisabeth. Kristin had frowned at the police and criticized them on the phone with the prime minister; Elisabeth had yelled at the authorities to leave the bank.

By about 9:40 a.m., the police had decided to gamble that Bejerot's analysis was correct and launched a risky operation that would certainly raise the stakes in the standoff. Journalists outside in the square saw the sudden rush of excitement as policemen sprang into action. Everyone, a *Svenska Dagbladet* reporter noted, thought that they were going to storm the bank, but that was not the case.

The police were hoping instead to lock Janne and Clark inside the vault.

SUCH A MOVE–IF IT IN FACT SUCCEEDED–WOULD ELIMINATE THE GREAT fear that Janne would attack the police in the lobby by surprise. At the same time, the risks of the venture were high. The hostages would, after all, end up trapped along with the robber. The police had better hope that the psychiatric portrait was correct.

They had better hope that the gunman was, as Bejerot had concluded, a rational, professional criminal who calculated his actions based on maximizing his self-interest, not a hotheaded desperado or a madman who played by a completely different set of rules. What's more, they had to hope that the gunman—when he realized that he was going down—did not decide to drag down Clark and the hostages with him, not to mention the chief of police and the prime minister himself. There would certainly be enough blame to go around if this gamble failed.

At 9:51 a.m., Jack Malm repeated his earlier maneuver. Håkan Larsson and Jonny Jonsson volunteered for the mission, too, no surprise, because both of these men seemed to have been the first to support the idea. Very quietly, the three men approached the landing. Malm used the iron pole to push away a chair, a wastebasket, and some cardboard boxes from previous food deliveries, and closed the outer door. Larsson and Jonsson raced up the short staircase to latch it shut. Later they would jam a piece of wood under the lever handle, essentially locking the vault.

Janne had been taken by surprise. He switched on the lights. Realizing what had happened, he began heaving long metal safety-deposit boxes at the door. Each one landed with a loud thud. Screams and curses wafted up through the ventilation holes.

One policeman, Stig Sandström, turned to Jack Malm and asked, "What have we done?"

The hostages, who had felt a tenuous sense of optimism after the Friday-night demonstration, were now more terrified than ever. The police, it seemed, would charge into the vault at any moment. Elisabeth was on the verge of panic.

Janne returned her to the front line of defense in her chair, rigged up with his detonator, fuses, and explosive material. Janne then sat back, behind Elisabeth, submachine gun in hand, and felt as desperate, as he put it, as "a rat caught in a trap."

27

I never found out the answer . . . What was their plan in locking us in with the robber?

—Sven Säfström

T**HIS HIGH-STAKES GAMBIT HAD CHANGED THE POLICE OPERATION.** In the early hours of the hostage crisis, the bank's ground floor had resembled a kind of trench warfare with a veritable "no-man's-land" separating the police, who controlled the lobby, from Janne, who occupied the vault. Now it approximated a siege. But in this case, Janne did not have access to food, water, or any other basic necessities. He did not even have openings from which to shoot. Janne was, in short, locked up tighter in this new prison than he had ever been in his life.

Janne let the police know that, if they planned to storm the vault, they would find an obstacle course of safety-deposit boxes blocking their way and an entrance mined with explosives. The police, in turn, decided to strengthen the defenses on the outside of the vault, in the unlikely case that Janne might find a way out. They hauled in more sandbags and piled them up against the door.

At this point, the police also seized control of the telephones. All calls into the bank would now be routed through their headquarters on the second floor. The authorities also disconnected the vault's outgoing line. Clark would no longer be able to charm journalists with his headline-grabbing antics, nor would the hostages complicate police procedures with unpredictable behavior, like calling the prime minister. From now on, it would be the police who would control the flow of information. The "distribution of power" had changed, as Lindroth put it, and that would alter both the style and substance of the negotiations. Janne was going nowhere now, the police leadership concluded, except to prison—that is, if he got out alive.

WITH THE OUTER DOOR OF THE VAULT SHUT, THE POLICE NO LONGER HAD to fear Janne's submachine gun and moved about the lobby with a new sense of safety.

To confirm the identity of the robber, they collected trays of leftovers on the landing outside the vault and looked for fingerprints: Six plates, fourteen plastic cups, thirteen soft-drink bottles, along with an array of empty beer bottles, apple-juice containers, and cigarette packages. There was also a coffee thermos, a towel from the bank's restroom, and a piece of paper with games of Tic-Tac-Toe. The police would not find the evidence they sought. Janne had been careful not to remove his black gloves.

The police also took advantage of their newfound control over the lobby to increase their surveillance. Around 1 p.m., they obtained a small microphone from SÄPO, the Swedish security service, and installed it in one of the ventilation holes to the right of the entrance to the vault.

It was a primitive system. They simply attached the device to a pole and shoved it into the ventilation shaft. Three officials sat in a cloakroom, just off the lobby, with two everyday analog cassette-tape recorders, listening and taking notes. A direct line remained open to the police leadership upstairs in the conference room. The "Watergate apparatus," as *Expressen* dubbed it, would be a valuable source of information for the wiretappers.

Not long after essentially locking the vault, detective inspector Bengt-Olof Lövenlo called down to ask if Janne and Clark were ready to surrender.

"It's me, B-O," the policeman said. "I want to speak with Clark."

"No, you are speaking with me now," Janne said.

"You run your mouth too much. I don't want to speak with you."

"Go to hell!" Janne shouted.

Clark came on the line.

"Hey, how is everything?" B-O Lövenlo asked, as if taunting them.

"Pretty good."

The inspector reminded Clark that they had closed the door to the vault.

"Yes, sir," Clark said, but they had closed the inner door.

"And how the hell are you going to come out?"

"Do you really think that we are in a hurry? We can celebrate the election in this chamber."

The national election would take place in three weeks, on September 16, 1973, when voters went to the polls. An unresolved hostage crisis dragging out day after day, Janne and Clark knew, would hardly be in Prime Minister Palme's interests.

"Are you being nice to the girls?" B-O asked, changing the subject.

"You know that you can trust me," Clark said. "But you have to arrange something to eat and drink." Clark asked for some beer and whiskey. Seagram's, he preferred. They wanted something nice to treat the women.

"I'm making a note of what you want to have. How do you spell 'Seagram'?"

———

AT 2:20 P.M., AFTER A FEW HOURS WAITING IN VAIN FOR FOOD AND DRINK, Janne and Clark finally received a call from the police. B-O blamed the delay on the fact that the stores had closed and it was, as he put it, hell to find anything on a Saturday.

Janne, taking the phone, asked permission for each of the hostages to call home.

B-O shrugged off the request by saying that he had personally phoned the family members to let them know that the hostages were fine.

"I think it is strange that they can't speak themselves," Janne said. He then asked for a small portable toilet and copies of the day's newspapers.

How was he supposed to send them in, B-O asked sarcastically. "Through the ventilation holes?"

Just open the door, Janne said. "Nothing is going to happen."

The police refused, pleased that Janne was contained.

Janne countered with a warning that the police should not attempt to drug them again when they did send in the food and drink.

"No, no, no," B-O said.

It was clumsily done, Janne said.

"Yes, it was bloody clumsily done," B-O agreed.

Janne also warned the police not to try to attack them either, presumably by using the requested items as a pretext or decoy. "This gun is heavy.

You know how much it weighs fully loaded," Janne threatened. "Bring the newspapers here!"

B-O promised to call back in fifteen minutes.

The fifteen minutes came and went.

That afternoon, Janne pulled out a set of walkie-talkies from his bag, extended the antenna through the ventilation, and started talking.

"Hello . . . hello . . . This is from the vault . . . Anyone hear me?"

28

The country was at a standstill. No one could think of anything but the bank drama.

—Sven Thorander

OUTSIDE IN THE SQUARE, REPORTERS, CAMERA CREWS, AND UNI-formed officers roamed anxiously waiting orders or updates. At least eighty policemen milled about the area. Fortunately, there was not much crime elsewhere in the capital, someone noted. Perhaps the criminals had stayed home, like many other Swedes, to watch the news.

The police presence grew throughout afternoon. Thirty-four additional policemen arrived from Solna; many others had just come there on their own, in their civilian clothes, on their day off, after watching the news on television and wanting to be a part of the operation. The desire "to be there" was irresistible.

Criminal inspector Ingemar Krusell would later criticize the policemen who came to the bank more, he thought, for the action, the camaraderie, or perhaps the free beer and well-stocked buffet tables on the second floor. He called it an "open house." Worse, he was struck by the lack of order and organization. Lines of authority were imprecise. Police officers just seemed to wander around and work wherever they wanted. Evidence disappeared as souvenirs. Guns were not secure. Law enforcement at Norrmalmstorg seemed like the Wild West.

All of these policemen standing about, moreover, were free to speak with journalists, even if not all of them were privy to the state of affairs inside the bank. Many of them actually seemed to know *less* than the general public, marveled Falun's *Dala-Demokraten*. No wonder rumors flourished. Journalists then traded stories with one another, and the tales often grew in the retelling. The atmosphere shifted at a moment's notice, *Dagens Nyheter* said, from the surreal to the chilling to the absurd.

As if broadcasting the crime live were not enough, the two television channels would also interrupt regularly scheduled programming—even if only to report that the situation was still unchanged. Nightly coverage of Norrmalmstorg would go on to top the charts for the most-watched programs of the year, beating film, sports, and everything else.

Many continued to question the engagement of the mass media. "Is it really in society's interest to fix everyone's attention on a few serious crimes and criminals?" asked *Östgöta Correspondenten*. The result would be an unmooring of the individual's respect for the law and consideration for society. It would also, no doubt, inspire unstable minds to emulate the action. At the same time, the paper noted, the Norrmalmstorg drama was exactly what the people wanted to see, hear, and read about, and papers had a duty to report the news, even if not everyone could tolerate the violence.

Other journalists sought psychologists to help understand the bizarre public attraction to this hostage crisis. The intense media coverage—along with the growing crowds on the street—showed, *Svenska Dagbladet* suggested, that a safe and secure welfare state, like Sweden, harbored a thirst, or even a need, for danger, if only a vicarious experience from the comfort of one's living room. The crowds beyond the police barricades recalled the cheering audiences at a Spanish bullfight, or a violent ice-hockey match. There was no sign, either, that this excitement was dissipating.

The spectators still stood and stared as if they could see something other than the activity of the police. Others sought out better views from nearby bridges, or at elevated places, such as the roof terrace of the nearby NK department store. No one counted the number of people, but a reporter for *Göteborgs-Posten* estimated it in the tens of thousands.

Just behind the barricades, a gray-haired man played the clarinet. Another man set up shop, near a department store, to sell his illustrated poetry chapbooks. At the front of the red lines, where a mounted police officer stood watch, children petted his horse, whose name was Shah, after the ruler in Iran. A long line waited for ice cream or hot dogs.

One policeman was photographed sitting on a chair, feeding pieces of a hot-dog bun to pigeons.

"Nothing new at Norrmalmstorg" became the refrain on the regular television broadcasts.

When a brief rain fell in the afternoon, Danish Radio announced that the only thing changing at Norrmalmstorg was the weather.

INSIDE THE BANK, HOWEVER, IT WAS A DIFFERENT STORY.

Stockholm police chief Kurt Lindroth called a strategy session in the second-floor conference room. Discussion quickly turned to the question of how to force Janne and Clark to surrender.

Some members of the staff were growing impatient with the slow war of attrition. Sure, the police had conquered the bank, but it sometimes seemed, as Göteborgs-Posten put it that day, that the robber and Clark were calling the shots. Now, they were threatening to hold out for three weeks. How long were the police supposed to wait before acting with decisiveness?

Lindroth, Thorander, and their key advisers weighed the options. Attempting to drug the food and drink might work, though it had failed last time when Janne discovered the ruse, and it was reasonable to expect him to be on his guard again. Such a maneuver, moreover, would backfire if Janne forced one of the hostages to taste the goods first.

What about using gas?

Anesthesiologists, immunologists, and chemists were called in as consultants. The police would need a powerful, fast-acting, and preferably painless substance that carried the least possible risk. Unfortunately, the most potent substances posed considerable health concerns and could even be fatal in an overdose. The safer gases, by contrast, might not be strong enough to produce the desired effect.

Hydrogen sulfide was one possibility. Its main disadvantage was the fact that it gave off a smell similar to rotten eggs that would alert Janne and Clark to the threat and might drive them into taking revenge on the hostages before it forced a surrender. It was also flammable, and, being heavier than air, it would fall to the low spaces of the vault. Laughing gas was an alternative, but it produced an almost euphoric feeling that might lead Janne and Clark to overestimate their strength and launch a desperate attack.

Tear gas emerged as the leading candidate. A variant known as CS (Chlorobenzalmalononitrile), or K62, as it was called in Sweden, was available. Used to counter street riots in the United States and Northern Ireland, this substance attacked the eyes, nose, throat, and respiratory tract, and caused a choking sensation and a feeling of pressure in the chest. It also made the eyes and skin burn, and could lead to dizziness, nausea, and vomiting. Such a gas, however, was not without its risks in the small, confined space, even with physicians waiting to care for everyone immediately afterward.

One thing was clear: If the police were going to invade the vault, they could not risk orchestrating an ineffective assault that succeeded only in giving Janne and Clark an opportunity to counterstrike or retaliate against the hostages. They needed a plan that could be implemented with as little advance warning as possible.

29

That was our world . . . Whoever threatened that world was our enemy.

—Kristin Enmark

THE DOUBLE FLUORESCENT TUBES IN THE CEILING CAST A COLD, blue light throughout the bank vault. The transistor radio blared the latest news and commentary about the standoff. This not only continued to provide an invaluable source of information about police movements and possible plans; but it also remained a lifeline to the hostages and, as Birgitta put it, a reminder that despite everything, the world had not forgotten them.

The hostages, in the meantime, had to wait on the police to make the next phone call in the drawn-out negotiations. They busied themselves as best they could. They tidied their clothes, fixed their hair, reapplied lipstick, and moved the smaller furniture around to pass the time.

Birgitta missed her husband and daughters. This was the longest she had ever been away from them. What would happen to her family if she died? Would her husband remember her life insurance? Janne told her he understood how she felt and they looked at pictures of her daughters. Birgitta later said that she was sure that the gunman would never have taken her as a hostage if he had known she was a mother.

At one point, when Birgitta mentioned that she had studied psychology, Janne asked her to give him a personality test. A series of questions followed. Birgitta took notes and drew diagrams. Then, everyone listened with amusement when she rated Janne superior in intelligence and vitality, but then failed him on "stability" or impulse control.

Still the harsh reality kept returning. Janne wiped a tear from Elisabeth's cheek. He told her, at one point, that there would be other crayfish parties she could attend. He later gave her a bullet as a souvenir.

Everyone was getting hungry. They had not eaten for half a day, and their latest request for bread and soup had not been granted. There was no sign of any nourishment coming, either. Janne surprised everyone by pulling out three pears from his pocket that he had saved from a previous meal.

He took a seat at the customer table and split the fruit into six parts. Elisabeth ate slowly, taking small bites and hoping to make the meal last. They tasted delightful, she later said. Gestures like this underlined Janne's humanity, which stood in sharp contrast to the portrait of the desperado being painted in the media. Even the prime minister had called him "crazy." Janne, they saw, took the smallest piece of fruit for himself.

A real sense of community was emerging in the vault. With the outer door locked and the entrance to the inner one blocked with obstacles and mined with explosives, Janne was prepared to protect the group against an attack from the outsiders—that is, the police.

Janne, sitting in a chair, fell asleep. Almost everyone else dozed off as well. Kristin remained awake, despite her exhaustion. She looked over at Clark, who slept next to her. "It was hard to believe he was a criminal," she said. "He looked so peaceful."

The ventilation fans cycled on and off throughout the day. The radio, too, was increasingly switched off in between the regular news segments to save batteries. The vault became quiet. The only sound, at one point that night, was breathing. Kristin remembered everyone almost breathing in unison and worked to time hers with the others'. "That was our world," she said.

———

REPORTERS BEGAN TO SEEK OUT EXPERTS TO EXPLAIN THE SURPRISING behavior of the hostages. When Kristin and Elisabeth said that they wanted to leave with the robber, they were not pretending, nor merely acting under the pressure of the gunman, explained Dr. Jan Agrell of Stockholm's Military Psychological Institute. It was more likely that they had experienced a sense of communality in being in "the same boat" with Clark and the robber. They were being united by "a common outside threat." All six of them were, in other words, constructing their own "social community." They really did see the police as the enemy.

Shifting their confidence to the captor, by contrast, gave the hostages security. Agrell compared the experiences of the bank employees to people trapped in a mine, or cohabiting in the closed world of a shelter. "We always have a need to speak with each other, and one cannot tolerate sitting quiet," he said.

The captor, in turn, avoided succumbing to fear and maintained his mental balance by focusing on the immediate task at hand. This was not unlike fighter pilots or astronauts, *Dagens Nyheter* reported, citing unnamed American studies. Perhaps the gunman coped this way by concentrating on limited, short-range objectives to avoid dwelling on the great odds and possible fatal consequences. All this emphasis on tangible gains, such as freeing Clark and obtaining the ransom money, also helped him overcome exhaustion and increase resilience in the face of opposition.

Agrell was not the least surprised at the appeal of Clark Olofsson. He was a highly intelligent person with considerable charm. That was often the case with "great criminals," Agrell added, and cited Al Capone as an example. Perhaps this abundance of charisma was a prerequisite for becoming a gangster on that scale, he suggested.

But as Saturday wore on, the hostages watched with concern as Clark became more serious than usual. At times, he was aloof, even melancholic. He seemed lost in his thoughts. He whispered with Janne, off to the side. He hummed Roberta Flack's latest hit, "Killing Me Softly with His Song."

Clark found some blank forms lying around the vault and started taking notes to preserve the state of affairs:

> The girls absolutely want to contact their relatives and they spoke with B-O about that. He promised them they could expect a call from one relative. Of course he lied to them, as always, and nothing happened.

It was, in short, "only small, short irritating mind games." The police strategy consisted of promising everyone one thing, like newspapers or telephone calls to their family, and then, either not delivering, or trying to wear them down by waiting.

The hostages, Clark also wrote, had begun to understand that the police planned "to sacrifice" Janne and him, and sought only to find a credible "excuse to give after the massacre." The police would, in other words, manipulate the situation so that it appeared that Janne and Clark had started a fight and authorities had only defended themselves.

Clark's situation had clearly changed. His chances of gaining furloughs, pardons, or other rewards were fading fast. How could he possibly avoid returning to prison, let alone receiving additional punishment when the police accused him of prolonging the affair? All this, of course, assumed that he survived, which no one in the vault could take for granted anymore.

———

ONCE AGAIN JANNE, CLARK, AND THE HOSTAGES WAITED WITH FRUSTRA- tion for the police to call back as promised. B-O was still dragging out the length of time between calls.

"Idiot!" Janne later said.

When the police finally did call at 5:40 p.m., they refused to allow newspapers, food, or drink through the door. Instead, B-O said, they were going to drill a hole in the ceiling.

"No, you are not," Janne said, realizing that a hole could be used for distributing more than food and drink. "There will be no hole drilled in the ceiling here."

How will you have food then? asked B-O.

"Not through a hole in the ceiling. That is the same thing as if you were going to storm the vault."

Clark was overheard saying the same thing. A moment later, he took the phone.

"Listen," Clark began, "I am beginning to understand now that I am going to pay for this too."

"What do you mean?"

"You are going to shoot me too."

Clark's anger was growing. He told the police to come on into the vault. "Drill a hole in the ceiling. Do whatever the fuck you want." But the moment the police killed Janne, Clark threatened, he would take his submachine gun, along with all the dynamite, and defend himself to the end.

And if any policemen planned to storm the vault, Clark warned: "I'm going to clip every fucker I see!"

———

THE SATURDAY-EVENING TABLOIDS HIT THE STANDS. *AFTONBLADET* LED
with its scoop of the previous morning's near debacle when the police had
tried to use Kaj Hansson's younger brother as a negotiator. "The Wrong Man
was Brought into the Bank" ran the large front-page headlines—and that
error nearly cost this man's life. The Stockholm police had clearly made a
mistake about the identity of the robber. They had "allowed themselves to be
misled," Christer Renström wrote, "by a false mustache."

Such was the state of affairs as the circus of Norrmalmstorg finished its
third day. "Every hour," *Expressen* wrote, "the drama increased." That statement still seemed true to Stockholmers outside the police barricades that
night, watching many vehicles pull up to the bank. Men carried everything
from sandbags to spotlights, mirrors to periscopes. They hauled in jacks,
saws, blowtorches, crowbars, welding units, and a range of power tools,
prompting speculation that the police planned to force open the vault door.

The temperature dropped again. The journalists were still there, as
Expressen's P. O. Enquist put it, both shivering in the chill and shuddering at
being frozen out of the action. They knew they were in the middle of something big. But what exactly that was remained as uncertain as ever. Editors
pressed for details, seeking to fill up page after page of copy in what was
being billed as the story of the decade.

30

Hard yet charming, calculating but impulsive, the robber in the bank vault is a living enigma.

—*Expressen*, August 26, 1973

NORRMALMSTORG WAS THE COUNTRY'S FIRST "BANK ROBBERY" broadcast on live television. With so many foreign media outlets arriving on the scene, the crime-in-progress would air in about thirty countries around the world. The public was mesmerized. The bank drama was compared to a play, an action film, and a serialized television show. It would later be billed as one of the first news soap operas and "reality television" programs, where, unlike the latter, the unscripted action really could, at any moment, come to an abrupt, violent end.

For the last year or so, the Stockholm police had worried about this particular crime: A robbery in connection with hostage taking. The rules of engagement were uncertain, and now, too, with modern media technology, people at home could follow the events in a more direct way. Live broadcasts fostered the illusion of participation; interviews simulated intimacy; information poured in with an unprecedented sense of immediacy. A new chapter in Swedish criminal history was being written.

But what responsibility did the media have, beyond trying to cover the news as accurately as possible, particularly if their work made the police rescue operation more difficult? What, too, for that matter, was the media's responsibility toward the hostages? Reporting police plans—or broadcasting speculation about their intentions—might cause the robber to panic or empower him to launch a preemptive strike. At the least, he could adapt his own strategy. The debate on the role of the media in society gained momentum.

———

EARLY SUNDAY MORNING, ONE OF KURT LINDROTH'S MEN INQUIRED about the possibility of using firefighting foam to defeat the robber. The idea was soon abandoned when the chief of the fire department explained that the material could lead to the suffocation of everyone in the vault. Gas, by contrast, seemed a more viable option.

Stig Jackson, an expert on chemical and biological weapons who had been called in to consult with the police, worried about the effect of tear gas in the vault because it would take too long to incapacitate the aggressors. That would give the captors plenty of opportunity to counterstrike. He advised the police against trying it.

But if they persisted, the key to the success would, of course, be determining the accurate dosage.

Erik Lögdberg, head of Stockholm police's Technical Department, worked on figuring out the dimensions of the vault. The architectural blueprints and records at city hall showed that the late-nineteenth-century building had been renovated twice in the last twenty-five years. On one of the projects, begun in 1964, the bank had reinforced the vault with thick armored doors. The room, he calculated, was approximately 150 cubic meters.

Bank employees contacted by detectives filled in other details about the room. Of particular concern was any object that might be used to improvise defenses. The police knew that there were two large steel cabinets, one of which Janne had already used to block the entrance. But even if the authorities could open the door with a powerful jack, or a blowtorch, the possibility remained that the gunman might mine the entrance with explosives.

All this, of course, was why the police chief preferred to drill holes in the vault ceiling, which was, in fact, what he, Thorander, and their team decided to do.

Overseeing the drilling process would be Bror Erik Österman, the director of the company AB Hålmetoder. He had contacted the police to volunteer his services after following the news at home and let them know that he had one of the largest core drills in the country. It was an electric 310mm with a hollow steel cylinder and a sharp, jagged diamond edge.

Police technicians estimated that the vault's armored reinforcements spanned 23.6 inches (60 cm) thick, with an additional, almost 3 inches (7 cm) of flagstone on the subfloor. There were also electric lines running to the fluorescent lights and a rat's nest of cables that led to the bank's telephone network.

Österman's team carried the several crates containing the drilling equipment into the bank, up the staircase, and into the narrow corridor just outside the telephone operator's room. They went to work reassembling the drill. Chalk marked the spot where its diamond blade would hit the parquet floor.

SUNDAY MORNING OPENED RELATIVELY QUIETLY IN THE VAULT—MUCH like a regular Sunday, Janne said. Journalists in the square agreed. After the spurt of activity, bringing the drill into the bank, everything had again become calm. "Worryingly quiet" concluded *Svenska Dagbladet*. By the morning, the same paper spoke of a summertime idyll.

Around 8:20 a.m., four ambulances pulled up and men in white coats carried six stretchers into the building. Policemen sprang into action. At least ten sharpshooters were spotted at Berzelii Park, hiding in bushes or behind overturned café tables. Mounted police sealed off the perimeters from the public. Something, it seemed, was about to happen.

Commissioner Dag Halldin downplayed the significance of the activities. The police were still negotiating with the robber, he said, and they could of course hold out longer than the criminal could. "We are not in a hurry," Halldin told reporters.

The crowds beyond the street barricades were growing restless. Many called openly for the police to attack, observed a reporter for *Sydsvenska Dagbladet*, and the pressure was increasing. Several people argued that the police "exhaustion strategy" would succeed only in prolonging the suffering. The hostages' families were also frustrated with the lack of progress. "Why don't the police do anything?" was a question heard on the streets of Stockholm as well as an increasing number of editorial pages around the country.

That morning, if any doubt remained that Kaj was not the prime suspect in the hostage crisis, it was put to rest when the Stockholm police received a long-distance phone call from Honolulu. It was from Kaj. He was not happy about the lies and slander, nor the fact that his photograph had been plastered all over the world. What would his family think, he asked.

"I'm perfectly capable of blackening my own reputation," Kaj later said.

Before Kaj hung up, he made the mistake of telling the police of his intention to return to Sweden, and authorities promptly made plans to arrest him. By September 6, Kaj was behind bars, serving his previous sentence and awaiting trial for two bank robberies he was accused of committing that summer. In November, Kaj would receive another four years in prison.

Clearly not wanting to repeat the fiasco of accusing the wrong person, the Sunday-morning newspapers were more careful with their accounts of the robber. *Svenska Dagbladet* came close to revealing the identity of the new suspect when it asked if a still-unnamed thirty-two-year-old Helsingborg native who had escaped from prison could be the real robber in the bank. The police *believed* that to be the case, the paper added, basing their *guesses* on the fact that he was a well-known expert in explosives who had also been an inmate with Clark at Kalmar Prison.

By the afternoon, the national tabloids were more confident in painting a portrait of the gunman. *Expressen* used Janne's full name, describing him as a cold-blooded, calculating criminal with a violent, impulsive streak. Strong in body and will, he was also an excellent shot. "He is hard, very hard, but at the same time charming and experienced in the ways of the world." He was in one word, the paper said, using capitals: "DANGEROUS."

Aftonbladet, likewise, printed Janne's name. In a front-page article entitled "The Beginning of the End of the Bank Drama," the paper emphasized the new suspect's stubborn will to resist and his own bold prediction that he would in fact "get away with the money." Police were quoted as confirming that the robber would "fight to the last drop of blood." His wild threats to blow up the bank, it reported, were scaring even Clark.

31

He says that it is easy as hell to die. You don't feel a thing.

—Clark Olofsson

NOT EVERYONE AGREED THAT THE DECISION TO USE GAS WAS THE proper course of action. Several police officers wanted to starve Janne and Clark into submission. Thirst and hunger could be powerful weapons, agreed the tabloid *GT*. The exhaustion tactic was wrong, other policemen countered, preferring to take direct action and overpower the culprits as soon as possible.

Authorities had in fact already had such an opportunity, *Svenska Dagbladet* wrote, and wasted it. Police sharpshooters could have shot Janne as early as Thursday morning. When he spoke on the phone with Clark, one sniper had Janne in his sight, with no risk to a single hostage. He had not fired because it was against orders. Later in the day, when the orders changed, they had lost their chance. Janne was then more careful to keep human shields in front of him.

The blame game was just getting started. A reporter at the paper had also spoken with a policeman, Bertil Ledel, who did not mince words about who was at fault: Olof Palme and the Swedish government. The first error had been allowing Clark Olofsson to leave the prison and come to the bank, becoming in effect what *Vestmanlands Läns Tidning* called the robber's assistant. The meddling of the authorities had continued to harm law enforcement's efforts and "politicize" the operation. As a result, no one in the police hierarchy wanted to take responsibility. Chaos and confusion reigned everywhere. The public would soon be laughing at them, Ledel said in disgust.

That is, if the operation did not end in tragedy.

For Stockholm psychiatrist Jan Agrell, that was a real fear. What worried him most was the lack of basic necessities, like food, water, and contact with the outside world. "The hostages find themselves in a terrible situation," Agrell said. He compared their symptoms to those of brainwashing, which involved deliberate efforts to break down a person's mental health and reorient his or her way of thinking.

The term "brainwashing" had been coined by the OSS operative Edward Hunter for his book of the same name that investigated a coterie of American POWs held in North Korea during the Korean War. He described the effects of mind control on a victim memorably:

> Those who interviewed him were bewildered and horrified not only by what he said . . . but by the unnatural way in which he said it. His speech seemed impressed on a disc that had to be played from start to finish, without modification or halt. He appeared to be under a weird, unnatural compulsion to go on with a whole train of thought, from beginning to end . . . [He was] no longer capable of using free will.

The subtitle of the study was "The Calculated Destruction of Men's Minds." Novels and films had popularized the concept, most notably Richard Condon's thriller *The Manchurian Candidate*, which depicted a former captive who had been programmed to kill on behalf of a totalitarian regime.

Whether the hostages were being brainwashed or not, Dr. Agrell thought, it would only be a matter of days, or probably even less than that before they suffered serious psychological damage. The risks were, of course, worse for the bank employees than for Janne or Clark, who were not only used to surviving threatening situations but also had more power to influence the events. The hostages, by contrast, were at their mercy.

Another expert offered more hope. José Gonzalez, a forensic psychiatrist at Stockholm's Långholmen clinic, believed the Norrmalmstorg drama would end more favorably than the police or press feared. Gonzalez had examined Clark several years ago, he said, and described him as gifted and not the least dangerous to the innocent hostages. The psychiatrist did not know the gunman, but suspected that he was not threatening either. If he were sick, or deranged, everyone would already know that. In fact, he thought that the robber had acted mostly with reason and moderation.

No one had ever killed a hostage in Sweden, Gonzalez further said, and he saw no indication to believe that such a tragedy would occur now. What's more, the longer the crisis lasted, the less likely the hostages would suffer harm. The most dangerous time—the first few hours—had passed. The six men and women in the vault had gotten to know one another.

At the same time, he cautioned, the situation could change without warning.

"What will happen if the police storm the room or if some other dramatic or threatening change [occurs], no one can predict."

32

_____

We heard the screams. We heard the howling . . . I have never encoun-
tered fear so blatantly as it was in there.

—Håkan Larsson

BY SUNDAY EVENING, A CREW OF TECHNICIANS AND POLICEMEN
were almost done setting up the core drill. Stockholm hospitals were on
standby. Ambulances pulled up again near the entrance. At 9:08 p.m.,
the drilling began.

The loud, cranking vibrations rocked the vault, echoing around the
chamber and stabbing the bodies of everyone inside like "sharp knives," as
Janne put it. He turned up the volume on the radio in the faint hope to
distract everyone from the pounding. The many repeated breaking news
updates, he figured, might also shed light on what exactly the police were
intending to do.

Three minutes later, after penetrating four to six inches into the solid
concrete, the drilling stopped. The machine had overheated and needed
more coolant. At 9:20 p.m., the piercing roar started again.

What the microphones picked up then was frightening.

"Help! . . . Stop! Don't, don't . . . Stop, stop!" A woman's heartbreaking
cries ended in sniffles and sobbing.

The police listening in the surveillance room feared that Janne had
attacked one of the hostages.

"He's raping her! He's raping her!" one policeman shouted.

But what they did not consider—or want to consider—was that Kristin was screaming not at Janne or Clark, but for the police to end the deafening cacophony. [In Swedish her cries of "*sluta borra*" (stop drilling) were taken by the police as "*sluta bara*" (just stop)]. One detective inspector, Gunnar Arvid Strandberg, recognized the real cause of her distress, but he was ignored.

At another point, police microphones picked up Kristin again screaming, "Stop! Stop!" Janne yelled over to Clark, who lay next to her: "What the hell are you doing?" Actually, as Kristin later explained, she was having a nightmare. Clark had then held her hand and comforted her. "It made me feel enormously secure," she later said. Rumors of sexual assault, however, spread, making their way from the police to the press, where they would be more prominent, at first, in foreign newspapers.

The drilling began again to drown out the conversation. Several observers saw the excruciating racket as an end in itself. The "inferno of noise," as *Kvällsposten* put it, would wear down the robber physically and psychologically, and force his surrender. Janne, however, sensed a different purpose.

To his great horror, Janne suspected that the police were making holes in the ceiling in order to deploy gas. Damage to his eyes, lungs, skin and brain would be permanent, he feared, and he was prepared to do whatever it took to prevent that.

Janne started to rig up an explosive charge in one of the ventilation holes.

Clark urged Janne to stop. This countermeasure could blow up everyone in the vault.

Janne ignored him and went on setting up the bomb.

———

THE DRILLING IN THE VAULT WOULD INAUGURATE "THE FINAL ACT OF the bank drama," concluded *Dagens Nyheter*. Observers had already predicted that the ordeal would end Thursday, and when that did not come to pass, the resolution was projected to be Friday, then Saturday, and now Sunday. Few people thought it could last much longer.

By 9:40 p.m., the police had drilled almost eight inches into the nearly 27-inch-thick vault ceiling. The grinding thrusts of the diamond blade grew louder as it penetrated closer to the frightened hostages. At 10:28 p.m., the core drill had cut twice as deep into the concrete.

The drilling slowed from time to time as the operators paused to repair the machine, add more coolant, or clean out the debris. The latter resulted from a newly created layer of gravel-like bits of concrete—and this gravel, combined with water from the coolant, formed heavy clumps of material that clogged up the drill.

The technicians estimated that they would complete the hole by midnight.

During one pause in the drilling, probably just after 11:30 p.m., the police heard the hostages screaming into the microphones in the ventilation duct that they had to speak with someone.

B-O called into the vault.

"You fools!" Janne yelled at him.

"Stop drilling, please stop!" yelled a woman in the background. "We stand up here . . ."

"What the hell is it?" B-O interrupted.

Janne informed the police negotiator that he had wired an explosive device in the path of the drill. The moment the machine's blade came through the ceiling, he would ignite his charge.

"You are crazy!" B-O said.

"Stop! Stop!" yelled another woman, terrified.

"You're a bastard for abusing the girls!" B-O said, referring to the police interpretation of Kristin's screams.

"Me?" Janne said. "I have not touched them at all, not at all."

B-O repeated his accusations.

"He has not done anything to us," shouted one of the women hostages in the background, probably Kristin. "You are the one who is going to cause us to die. Don't you understand what you are doing?"

"I am not the one who is abusing them," Janne said to the negotiator. "What a shitty thing to say, you know. I have never abused a chick in my life!"

"What are you doing now, then?"

"You fucking terrorist!" Janne said. "You are the terrorist, not me."

"Take it easy and walk out [of the vault] dammit."

Birgitta took the receiver and asked the police to accept the gunman's demands. The drilling was excruciating. "We are all going to die down here!"

B-O did not answer.

Birgitta pressed for a response.

"Yes, yes, I hear what you keep saying, but what the hell should we do?"

"[Let Janne and Clark] leave with the hostages, as we said." Birgitta promised the police that the gunman would not shoot anyone if they could only leave the bank together. "Please!"

Janne came back on the line to say that Elisabeth, Kristin, and Birgitta were now placed directly underneath the police drill. Concrete would likely fall on them, he said, if the blade cut its way through the ceiling.

"Janne, we must make a hole," B-O said.

"What for?"

"Let us make a hole!"

Janne said that he would never allow them to pump in gas.

"There is no gas. You don't have to be afraid."

Hang on for a minute, Janne said. He had to light *something*.

But Janne had not only placed explosives on top of the fluorescent lights in front of the blade and made the women lie underneath the spot where the debris would fall. He also ordered Sven to stand on a chair with his head in direct line of the blade.

"If I see the smallest little hole, then the charge will go off!"

"Sven is standing only a half meter away!" Clark confirmed.

One of the women screamed in terror.

"Give me the lighter, Clark!"

"Take it easy, dammit," B-O said. "You are crazy!"

Screams reverberated throughout the vault.

"We are drilling that hole in the ceiling. Do you understand?"

Clark reminded the police that Sven was standing in the way.

"Yes, yes, but we are going to make a hole in the ceiling."

"Sven is going to fly away, you know," Clark warned again. "Sven is going to go up in smoke!"

"What the hell should we do?" asked B-O.

"Talk with him," Clark said, referring to the gunman. "I don't give a shit."

"I have nothing to say," Janne yelled.

"Listen," started B-O, but the phone went dead.

33

We didn't know what was true . . . we were grasping at straws.

—Birgitta Lundblad

A S THE DIAMOND BLADE OF THE DRILL BORE INTO THE ARMORED
steel, Janne, at the last minute, moved the hostages to the back of the
vault. They huddled together under a blanket that they held over their
heads. Everyone covered their ears.

No, Janne said. It was better to shield their eyes and keep their mouths
open because that would protect their eardrums.

"Why can't the police be considerate like that?" Elisabeth remembered
thinking.

About 11:45 p.m., a blast blew up a cloud of dust and mortar. A chunk
of concrete crashed down to where, moments before, the three women had
been lying. Something else was soon clear: The explosion had damaged the
drill. Janne celebrated the triumph by taunting the police with more insults
and curses. Some of the hostages began to worry about him. Sven asked him
to settle down.

As the police investigated the damage to the drill, Janne, Clark, and the
hostages found a break from the agony. The room went very quiet. The six
men and women remained on the far side of the vault, away from the coat of
chalk and mortar debris that covered the floor. They spread out blankets and

tried to rest as much as they could. The fan in the ventilation system spun in the background. The radio was again turned off to save batteries.

Some slept. Birgitta started dreaming. As she later recalled, she saw herself in an opera house surrounded by family, friends, and classmates from her youth. Everyone wore seventeenth-century silks and satins. The stage's spotlights cast a blue light on the scene, perhaps like the ceiling's fluorescent lights. She walked out of the opera house, where she had been under a staircase, and found a golden carriage with horses outside. She thought she saw her daughters waiting in the vehicle. Then loud vibrations woke her up to the reality in the vault.

The police had renewed their drilling. The large core drill was too damaged to continue, but they had obtained a second, smaller air-pressure drill. On and on, the police pressed for about four solid hours until they had cut a hole in the vault ceiling about 10 inches in diameter.

Immediately, as one technician removed the machine, two other policemen covered the exposed hole with a Plexiglas shield. This was a necessary precaution in case Janne tried to fire his submachine gun through the opening. The hard shield was essentially bulletproof, a technician said. It would take three shots in the exact same spot to penetrate it.

With a hole finally in the ceiling, B-O called down to the vault and gave the ultimatum: They were going to send down a wire with a hook through the hole, B-O said, and Janne was to hang his submachine gun on it. The police would then lift the weapon out of the vault and return the wire for his bag of explosives. This was how he would have to surrender.

"Stop it!" Janne scoffed, dismissing this demand as ridiculous.

Take this opportunity, B-O told him, because it would be his last chance. He had twenty minutes to decide.

———

AS THE POLICE DEADLINE FAST APPROACHED, THE VAULT SUDDENLY went dark. Clark felt his way to the ringing telephone.

"Turn on the lights!" he shouted into the receiver.

"Have they gone out?" B-O asked.

"Yes, there is no light here . . . It is pitch-black."

B-O said that the drilling must have cut through the electrical wiring. He promised to take care of the situation.

Clark requested that they also send down "some tampons and water."

One of the women had started to menstruate. Kristin heard a few of the policemen laugh at this news.

The drilling started again. The pounding, shaking, and vibrating resumed with a vengeance.

"We need some menstruation pads!" Sven shouted over the din. "Do you know what that is?"

"Tampons!" Clark said.

Cigarettes too, someone else added.

At 2:14 a.m., negotiations were over, noted national police chief Carl Persson. The gunman had refused all offers of surrender, and the police now prepared to end the crisis.

The "gas group" readied its flasks of tear gas—despite more than a dozen promises thus far not to use it. The "break-in group," which would storm the vault to apprehend Janne and Clark, assembled outside the entrance; the "sharpshooter group" stood on alert behind a barricade of sandbags. The "doctor group" waited just beyond them with six stretchers. Spotlights borrowed from the Swedish military lit up Norrmalmstorg in a surreal glow.

But what happened next was so desperate and shocking that virtually none of the policemen, politicians, journalists, or millions of people watching the drama on live television predicted it.

Janne reached into his canvas bag and pulled out four lengths of rope. Each one was tied in the form of a noose—no one had seen when they had been made in the pitch-dark vault. Janne then ordered the four hostages to stand and slip the ropes over their heads. The ends were then fastened high on the wall to one of the top rows of the safety-deposit boxes.

So, now, if the police insisted on using gas, the hostages would be the first to die.

34

The more inhuman a person is depicted, the greater the risk that someone does something rash towards that person.

—Eric Rönnegård, policeman at Norrmalmstorg

THE STOCKHOLM POLICE FOUND OUT ABOUT THIS DISTURBING development around 3:15 a.m., Monday, when B-O called back to the vault to hear if Janne had accepted the ultimatum. Clark answered and immediately accused the police of plotting a gas attack.

"No, there is no gas at all," B-O said.

"They said it on the radio."

B-O denied once more any plans to use gas. "You hear what I am saying?"

Clark started to tell the police about the new threat to the hostages, but B-O ignored him and repeated his demands that Janne surrender. Rejection of the offer, he added, might force the police to drill more holes and "possibly use gas."

After the talk continued without progress, Sven took the receiver. "If you send gas down here now, then we have no chance of making it!"

B-O did not pay any attention to him, either, and asked to speak with Janne.

Sven kept on talking. "We are tied here to the bank-deposit boxes so we are going to be hanged and choked and, besides, you cannot come in here because they have barricaded the door."

B-O still appeared not to listen in the slightest. "How are things with you?" he asked.

"All's well with him," Janne said, taking the receiver.

"Really?"

"Yes, he is well," Janne repeated. "He should have a medal."

"Oh, how classy you are."

Moments later, when Sven came back on the line, B-O asked him again how he felt.

"I feel bloody shitty."

"Listen, I understand. We are on the way to get you out of there as best as we can."

"Yes, well, if you turn on the gas, you do not have to get us out," Sven said. "You can bury us here in the same place."

"Why is that?"

"Because we are being hanged!"

"What do you mean?" B-O asked, as if finally hearing them.

"Send down something and look through the hole that you made in the ceiling, if you want. Then you can see."

B-O asked if Janne was really hanging the hostages.

"Yes, he is!" one of the women screamed. "You cannot use any gas."

Back and forth it went until Janne started to laugh.

"Listen," B-O said. "You've had enough playtime now."

"Have I?" asked Janne.

DID JANNE'S THREATS TO HANG THE HOSTAGES POSE ANY REAL DANGER? Thorander was skeptical. Still, it was important to confirm or refute these claims.

Policemen slowly removed the sandbags covering the hole drilled into the vault. Then, as quietly as possible, two men scooted the Plexiglas to the side. A colleague lowered a periscope-like device used in cardiac surgery. There was not much time for a detailed look and visibility was poor, but it was enough to confirm that Janne was apparently not bluffing. The hostages had nooses around their necks.

The chief of police, Kurt Lindroth, appeared shaken. More than sixty hours of unrelenting stress had taken its toll. He had not eaten well and slept even worse. The same went for many members of his staff, some of whom were still wearing Thursday's or Friday's clothes. Janne's surprise maneuver had knocked them off balance.

"What are we going to do now?" Lindroth was reported to have asked with tears in his eyes.

He needed to make a decision. How could he order his team to pump in gas and invade the vault when the hostages might be hanged? Would the police really have time to free them from their makeshift gallows and remove them from the chamber before the gas caused significant damage or Janne panicked and shot them? Janne might not be a killer, as they had assumed, but the police were no longer sure. They did not know what to believe, much less what to do.

Besides, what if Janne had also mined the entrance to the door, as he had threatened? What else did he have in his canvas bag? What weapons, real or improvised, had he found or managed to stow away in advance, if he had planned ahead and rented one of the vault's safety-deposit boxes? It was difficult to predict. Janne and Clark were clearly resourceful. Lindroth's assistants urged for a reprieve in the strongest terms.

———

SHORTLY AFTER FOUR O'CLOCK, THE PHYSICIANS, NURSES, AND MEDICAL staff poured out of the bank, filed into the waiting ambulances, and drove away. The firemen returned equipment to their trucks and boarded their vehicles. Policemen exited the lobby en masse. Journalists, surprised by the sudden exodus, waited for answers. The police had promised a press conference.

At 4:45 a.m., as Kurt Lindroth appeared in the square, reporters came running from all directions, surrounding him like a football huddle. Journalists in the back stood on chairs they grabbed from the outdoor seating of the restaurant and snapped photographs.

"Our negotiations with the robber are now concluded," Lindroth announced to an array of microphones shoved in his face. "I believed that he would take reason to heart, but it is impossible to speak with him."

Lindroth looked pale and exhausted. His eyes were red, his face was unshaven, and his clothes were disheveled. The police chief hesitated, sighed, and then hesitated again before he dropped the bombshell revelation.

"They tied them up so that they would be hanged?" asked television journalist Arne Thorén, thunderstruck.

"Yes."

"You said 'they,'" noted *Dagens Eko*'s Göran Rosenberg. Did this mean that Clark had definitely teamed up with the robber?

Lindroth believed that that was the case. By this point, many reporters had already drawn the same conclusion.

Lindroth announced that the police had established contact with the hostages, who were, fortunately, still alive, even if he could not speak to the quality of their condition. They had "begged for their lives."

Another reporter asked if the police had heard the hostages' pleas themselves.

Yes, they had, Lindroth said.

"Have the police misjudged the situation?" asked another journalist.

It had certainly been risky to lock Janne and Clark in the vault along with the hostages—and then start drilling into its roof and threaten to launch a gas attack against an already desperate gunman. But Lindroth stuck to his position. They had not been mistaken, he said. The police had known that they were dealing with "a very serious psychopath" and "a completely inhumane person."

"What plans do the police have now?"

All further activity would be postponed. Lindroth and his team would reconvene at 2 p.m. to discuss how to proceed. Until then, they would go home and rest. After four stressful days and nights, he feared that, as he later put it, "our power of judgment and our balance might be disturbed by the lack of sleep."

35

It was easier to predict the conclusion of the Cold War than Norrmalmstorg.

—Per Svensson, journalist

SUCCESS IN THE RESCUE OPERATION SEEMED AS DISTANT AS IT HAD been Thursday morning. All the hard work of the last seventy hours had been in vain, one policeman said with tears in his eyes. In fact, in many ways, the prospects now looked worse. The hostages were not only still held in captivity, but they were also locked up with a gunman in a pitch-dark vault awaiting a gas attack with nooses around their necks. The marbled bank had become "a torture chamber," *Dagens Nyheter* wrote.

It was no longer normal fear, agreed *Kvällsposten*, it was sheer terror. The paper ran a piece about Birgitta's family that included a photograph of her youngest daughter, Susanna, smiling in her dad's lap, happily unaware of the threat to her mother. "Thank God that they do not understand," Birgitta's husband told the reporter.

The psychiatrist Nils Bejerot, whose advice had encouraged the police to lock the vault, was also worried. "It was a thoroughly disgusting scene," he said, describing the hostages as "tired, hungry, exhausted, and dirty." They had also changed their attitude toward Janne and Clark. The Robin Hood mystique that had enshrouded the affair, Bejerot thought, was shifting into the horrifying reality that they were dealing with "dangerous men."

What should the authorities do now?

All weekend long, callers lit up the police and media switchboards with advice. The proposals varied widely in value and practicality. The director of the petrochemical conglomerate AB Nitro-Nobel offered to loan the authorities a small explosive device that could blast a hole in the wall approximately 2.5 feet by 2.5 feet. The police would then have no problem, he said, entering the vault and apprehending the culprits.

One of the most common responses was even more direct: "Shoot the bastards." Many people volunteered to do just that, if the police would send them into the vault. One marksman boasted that there was no way the robber could do more than graze him before he shot the assailant dead. Alternatively, authorities should drill many holes so that the gunman could not avoid coming into range. Fifty should suffice. Infrared light and a rotating staff of sharpshooters would keep constant pressure on him.

A large number of other people offered to become hostages themselves if the robber would accept them in exchange for the others' safety. Elisabeth's brother Stephan had been one of the first. Even though his offer was rejected, Stephan had remained optimistic about Elisabeth's chances for survival. But that hope was fading. Stephan grew sharply critical of the police after they had locked his sister in the vault with her captor.

Two policemen had also tried to substitute themselves for the hostages. To show that they carried no hidden weapons, they promised to enter the vault in their underwear. This was politely declined, as were the pleas of a forty-nine-year-old woman who wanted a chance to overpower Janne. She would not reveal the details of her plan, but she assured everyone that the gunman would not stand a chance.

Another possibility came from a translator familiar with covert operations in the Second World War. The Stockholm police should drop adult-sized mannequins through the newly drilled hole as a diversion to encourage Janne to waste his ammunition. Once he did that, they could enter the vault to defeat him with ease. They could also, someone else proposed, drill a thin line across the middle of the room and wait until Janne separated himself from the captives. At that moment, the police could insert a steel plate through the crack to keep them apart. The hostages would be safe; Janne would be at their mercy.

Sven Thorander thanked the public for their suggestions, which continued to stream into the police, as well as the hotlines for major media outlets. Kurt Lindroth actually encouraged everyone to keep the ideas coming.

"We are not, in any way, supermen, who can think of everything," he said. Someone in the general public might hit upon the perfect solution, and he promised that each proposal would be considered by a member of his staff. Lindroth would have to bring in reinforcements. Eight people were soon answering the phones.

The police could fill the vault with radiation, or gas, or as one engineer from Lidingö suggested, carbonic acid. The latter would knock everyone out in eight seconds. Authorities would have ten minutes to save everyone. They could also drug the attackers, others encouraged, though this had not worked before and Janne was expected to be on his guard.

A variant tactic involved sending in food on a special tray that had been rigged up to emit an electric charge, or a telephone constructed to give off 40,000 volts. There was "a little James Bond" element to some of the suggestions, thought *Kvällsposten*. But a more immediate problem was how the police could ensure that Janne, and not a hostage, would be the recipient of these attacks. Perhaps they could exploit the gunman's request for bullet-proof vests and helmets, someone else said, and give him items that had been prepared with electricity or explosives.

How about summoning a prison chaplain who was adept at dealing with hardened criminals? Authorities could also hire a hypnotist—eye contact was not necessary to be effective, one advocate assured the police. Another person knew of an eccentric gentleman in London who had invented a device that transmitted sound waves that were said to trigger an epileptic fit. The police could, likewise, fire a silent dart laced with a muscle-paralyzing relaxant through one of the drilled holes—one person suggested tipping an arrow in the potent extract of the curare vine from the Amazon River basin. Someone else suggested using a flamethrower. A water cannon or powerful fire hose could also incapacitate the gunman and render his explosives inoperable.

Alternatively, the police could drop hundreds of soccer balls into the vault, thereby making it impossible for Janne to move. Ping-Pong balls were too small, cautioned one person from the northern city of Skellefteå. A massive amount of dried yellow peas could turn the confined space into a homemade pit of quicksand, and an immigrant from Hungary suggested spraying spicy paprika. Other people encouraged the police to send in an army of ants, a horde of black rats, or a swarm of hornets. How all these invaders would single out the gunman was, again, not always addressed.

When one caller suggested that the authorities clip the wings of a queen honey bee and drop her into the vault, thereby luring in the entire hive, a policeman asked him how they could prevent the bees from also stinging the hostages. The caller had not thought of that. Not missing a beat, he then proposed that they spray Janne and Clark with sugar water. The suggestions kept coming. The police should send down a skunk, or as another person proposed, his mother-in-law. She could clear any room, he said.

Contributions also came from abroad. A medical doctor in Great Britain suggested that the police depressurize the vault, which would cause the hostages to "float to the ceiling," as in outer space, thereby relieving the pressure of the nooses on their necks. The police could then send in a powerful gas and enter the vault, wearing astronaut suits, to rescue the hostages. The key would be in restoring the Earth's atmospheric pressure. If that failed, the power on the cervical spine or trachea would be intense, and, he warned, everyone could die.

Perhaps the key to victory, others said, lay in defeating Janne and Clark the moment that they left the vault. Lindroth and Thorander could order their men to mop the marble floor outside the door with soapy water, so that if Janne came out blasting his submachine gun, he would lose his balance, misfire, and presumably fall into the hands of awaiting police. A giant magnet could snatch his weapon out of his hands, or a laser beam seal up the opening of the barrel. Why not construct a wooden platform outside the bank entrance and station a team of well-trained policemen there? Release everyone at dark and then jump them when Janne and Clark exit. A musician in Uppsala suggested that the police bring back the getaway car and fit it with a specially constructed, remote-controlled seat that could catapult Janne through the roof.

A group of anonymous Gothenburg lawyers came up with a simpler plan: The police should reaffirm the promise to grant Janne and Clark free passage and then just arrest them when they left. But again, like many other suggestions, this advice failed to account for the fact that Janne still held a submachine gun, a bag of explosives, and hostages—and if this trap did not work, it could result in a shootout broadcast on live television.

There was also a plethora of other readers and callers who urged authorities to let the hostages depart with Janne and Clark, if they wanted. It was a free country, after all, and the hostages' wishes should be honored—that is, if it was not already too late. Could acquiescing to the gunman's demands, many people asked, actually be worse than the ordeal the hostages were enduring? Besides, how much was the entire police operation costing the taxpayers? Undoubtedly the tally far surpassed the ransom.

But money was not the issue, other people said. The most important priority must be to save the lives of innocent people, and the best way to do that was to allow the gunman to leave with the hostages. Several psychiatrists and psychologists also urged this course of action. The gunman was clearly desperate and dangerous. Wouldn't the authorities let them go, if the victims had been Olof Palme or his minister of justice, Lennart Geijer?

The police looked increasingly lost, concluded *Svenska Dagbladet*. They would have to consider just about anything, now that they had already squandered several opportunities to nip the crisis in the bud. Their strategy had thus far failed, *Expressen* agreed. Everyone, it added, could only hope that the standoff did not end in catastrophe.

36

Killing me softly with his song . . .

—As sung by Roberta Flack
and hummed by Clark Olofsson

THE VAULT REMAINED PITCH-DARK. DAY AND NIGHT BLURRED IN AN almost meaningless distinction. Captor and hostage alike took advantage of the break in the drilling process to appreciate what seemed like a heaven-sent reprieve. Until the police returned to their posts, Janne saw no reason to keep Kristin, Birgitta, Elisabeth, and Sven at their makeshift gallows. The nooses were removed from their necks, but remained, ominously, tied to the safety-deposit boxes.

Policemen in the surveillance room, meanwhile, listened with surprise to the microphones inserted in the ventilation shafts. Janne, Clark, and the four hostages were discussing their hopes, dreams, and ambitions like old friends. Conversation ranged from the serious to the mundane.

"It's damn smoky in here, yuck," Janne said.

Sven wondered aloud when he should quit smoking.

"Whenever," Janne said.

If it were so simple, Sven replied, everyone would quit.

"Everyone? I'm talking about you, aren't I?"

Janne asked the group how long they had sat in the vault. They tried to estimate the time by counting the days that had passed.

"A week has a hundred and sixty-nine hours," Clark began.

"Hell no, not a hundred and sixty-nine," interrupted Janne. There are twenty-four hours in a day, seven days in a week, he reminded, so the calculation 24 times 7 could not end in a 9. It was 168. He then switched back to talking about setting up another explosive charge.

One of the women—authorities often could not tell which one—commented on how their coworkers were so lucky because they had the day off.

"Yes, but you have had the day off since Thursday," Janne said.

Sven did not think their colleagues actually had a vacation. The bosses would likely have set them up in a temporary office. He was correct. The bank had moved the workers from the Norrmalmstorg branch to other offices around town. Only some of the usual meetings had been canceled.

After a short talk about check fraud and procedures for preventing it that intrigued Janne and Clark, the conversation turned to work in the bank itself. Janne wanted to know what it was like to spend their days in the midst of so much money.

"It is not our money," one of the women bank employees said. The microphone picked up so much static that it was again difficult to identify the speaker, though it was probably Kristin.

"It *is* your money," Clark said.

"No, no."

"All money is your money," Clark said.

"Let me ask you something," said one of the women, probably Elisabeth, taking their predicament as a starting point for a more philosophical turn. "Why are we alive?"

"You live because you have to," Clark said. "Nothing else."

"But *why* does one live?"

"To live," Janne said, spelling out the word for emphasis. "L-I-V-E!"

"But is it not in order to try to do everything as good [morally] as possible, to make it better, to try to improve everything?"

"Improve for whom?" asked Janne.

"For the world," one of the women said.

"We are doing that!" Janne said.

"Are you? By taking from others?"

"Of course we take everything we can from others," Clark said. That was just like in politics, business, and life, he added, provoking a reaction among the hostages.

"You shouldn't only think of yourself. That is the problem with the world, I guess. People only think of themselves."

"Yes, but those are the rules of the game," said Clark.

Sven asked Janne and Clark about where they wanted to go with all the money.

Janne mentioned South America or South Africa.

Clark disagreed. "What the hell would I do down there for the rest of my life?" He preferred Beirut, and started telling the group how much he loved that city, as he had gone there the previous year on one of his escapes from prison. Life there teemed with hope and promise, and every day seemed like a birthday. "I felt so bloody at home there."

It was the opposite experience when he was with his family. He could not communicate or relate with them because they had drifted so far apart. They spoke only of their jobs, bills, paychecks, lottery tickets, and television shows. All things, Clark said, he didn't "give a crap about."

One hostage asked what he was doing to make Sweden a better place.

"Sweden?" Janne asked.

"Nothing!" Clark said. "Not anymore." He was ready to leave the country. "If I have another chance to split, I'll never come back."

"Same here, ugh," said Janne.

"I will never, ever set foot here," Clark repeated. "Never!"

Then it would be nice if they received all the ransom money, one of the women suggested.

That would be a good way to get rid of them, Clark agreed.

Clark went on talking about his crimes and how no one really wanted to be a criminal and only opted for that difficult path for lack of "a better alternative." As for himself, he could not stand taking orders from anyone. He could, however, imagine running his own business. "I know I could do a crapload of things." To prove it, he started to talk about some of the coups he had pulled off in prison.

Janne said he ran his mouth too much. The police were listening.

"Come on, man. I must be allowed to speak!"

"They are listening everywhere."

"I don't give a shit," Clark said, and continued talking about crimes and contacts in the underworld. Janne cleared his throat and then protested again. Clark kept talking.

"I am completely certain of myself," Clark said. "I am in harmony with myself. There is no one who can keep me down, no way."

"Yes, there is," Janne said. "*I* can."

Clark told more stories, then turned to the microphones and addressed the eavesdroppers directly: Please bring us all some more cigarettes!

WITH THE TEMPORARY BREAK IN THE ACTION, REPORTERS VENTURED out in search of other angles to shed light on the extraordinary news story. It was "an exciting nonstop thriller," *GT* said, straight out of the cinema with tough bad guys, pretty women as hostages, police sharpshooters, and tense government leaders sitting in meeting rooms. Monday evening's *Aftonbladet* called the story "the most dramatic event in Swedish criminal history."

A *Dagens Nyheter* reporter caught up with Clark Olofsson's fiancée, Maria Wallin. She had remained in the background during the crisis, but could no longer stay silent about how authorities had treated her lover. Clark was innocent, she affirmed. He had known nothing of the plot to attack Kreditbanken and he had only worked since his arrival at the bank "to avoid a bloodbath."

In fact, not long after hearing the robber's demands for Clark, Maria had spoken on the phone with the minister of justice, Lennart Geijer. He had personally promised her they would not send Clark into the bank. Now, after watching in horror as it happened, she was angered to hear the same official accuse Clark of being the main instigator of the crime.

The reporter did not address why Janne had demanded Clark's release, but Maria gave her answer in an interview with *Aftonbladet.* Janne simply "idolized Clark," she said, and knew that he needed Clark's help to find a way out of his predicament. Above all, Maria said, she was "scared and worried." The government had placed Clark in a dreadful situation. The police and the press now blamed him for the hostage crisis and would, just as unfairly, hold him responsible for whatever happened.

In the best-case scenario, Clark would end up with a longer sentence; in the worst, she feared for his life. Maria wanted Clark returned to prison immediately. Authorities, she added, did not care at all about him or his safety.

Janne's younger brother, Åke, agreed about the long list of mistakes on the part of the police. Despite their refusal to listen to his warnings about Janne's state of mind and use him as an intermediary, Åke had arrived in the capital by plane the previous night. He still hoped that the police would let him reason with Janne.

Åke stressed that he himself was the only person who could reach his brother. Janne would never surrender, he said. The police should listen, if only for the sake of the innocent people held hostage. Åke went on to admit that he had hesitated to tell their mother, Olga Matilda, the news of Janne due to her heart condition. She had, of course, found out anyway, when she had been at the home of a couple she knew and heard it on the radio, just as they were about to have coffee. She had left at once.

Hour after hour, they had sat at his Helsingborg apartment in front of the television, with the radio also blaring. They felt "powerless" and "dejected," he said. Their mother was unable to sleep, except with the help of sleeping pills. She had wanted to come with him to Stockholm, but the police had discouraged it.

Janne's brother was soon joined at Norrmalmstorg by Elisabeth's parents, Erik and Estrid Oldgren. They, too, were more worried than ever. Asked about his opinion of the police methods, Erik said it was not the time to discuss whether the authorities had made errors. "The most important thing is that Elisabeth and the others make it out alive."

Sven's parents, Stig and Wera Säfström, by contrast, had no plans whatsoever to go to Norrmalmstorg. It was swarming with police, media, and beyond the barricades, a large crowd of spectators. "I do not believe that I could put up with seeing everything so closely," Wera said. It was bad enough to watch it on television.

37

One thing is clear: When Clark Olofsson sits locked up in a bank vault, instead of a prison, the whole country stops completely [to watch] television.

—*Dagens Nyheter*, August 27, 1973

A S THE MICROPHONES CONVEYED AMIDST THE STATIC CRACKLES, Janne, Clark, and the hostages went on talking in the dark vault. The hostages were particularly interested in life in prison. Clark explained to them that there really was no difference between inmates and everyone else. Janne agreed.

"Many of the people on the inside belong to the cream of Swedish society," he said, talking about their intelligence when one of the women interrupted him. The static in the reception again prevented the police from identifying the speaker exactly, though it was probably Elisabeth.

Didn't the fact that a person had been sentenced to prison prove that he or she had a different attitude toward other people?

"Nearly all the guys on the inside have at some point, in one way or another, been abandoned by society," said Janne.

"But don't you think that society has sometimes abandoned us?" She turned from the general to the specific: "Don't you think we are damned disappointed as we sit here?"

Clark launched into an exposition on the two types of prisoners. One group thought and acted pretty much as normal Swedes; the other group was a completely different and a more dangerous variety who had long ago abandoned hope of reintegrating with society. Fortunately, he thought, this was a small minority.

One of the hostages asked everyone what could be done to prevent these desperate criminals of the second category from causing harm.

"Prisons must exist" was Janne's answer.

"Hell yeah, they have to exist," Clark said. At the same time, prison staff must not abuse their power and torment the inmates.

"That is what they do," Janne agreed.

Why should a state have prisons, one of the hostages asked: Was it to lock up the criminals or an attempt to rehabilitate them into society?

It was about locking them up, Clark said. That prevented them from causing as much pain and damage to society as they would otherwise do.

"You don't think that one should attempt, in some way, to put the prisoner back on his feet?"

"Put him back on his feet?" Clark asked, as if surprised by the question. Criminals, he said, made so much money, without having to resort to what he dismissed as the plodding existence of the so-called honorable person.

Elisabeth did not appreciate how Clark denigrated the law-abiding citizen. Clark also seemed to be missing her point about reorienting the prisoner away from criminal activity.

"Little Elisabeth," Janne said. "You do not know at all what happens in prison." As for himself, he said that he did not, under any circumstances, want to return to that hell. He had a chance to stay out, he added, vaguely and provocatively, and turned to his partner: "You have one, too, Clark."

Clark started counting the years until his release in 1977, or perhaps in 1976.

They would sooner or later be free, Elisabeth said, but for them—the hostages—they would never have the chance.

He had not chosen his fate either, Clark said.

"No?"

"That's right!" Clark said. The news was wrong. He had never elected to come to the bank.

"You cannot trust everything that they say on the radio," agreed one of the female hostages.

Clark went on denying any advance knowledge of the plot at Norrmalmstorg.

Then, switching gears, Clark wondered how anyone could possibly put up with working a nine-to-five job. One of the hostages told him it requires patience, or rather endurance.

That was not his problem, Clark said. "You have endurance if you really have something to fight for," he added, and started talking about how he had organized prisoners to press for prison reform.

"If you have rights, you have responsibilities!"

"Yes, that's right!"

This was far from a unanimous view, Janne countered, and, with a laugh, turned to Clark.

"What do you mean? I have a lot of responsibilities," Clark said.

"And a lot of rights, too," Kristin added.

"My rights are bloody limited," Clark said. He could endure prison, but he certainly did not like it and the moment someone gave him an opportunity, he would not hesitate to take off.

Fleeing only made his sentence worse, objected one of the hostages.

Clark, ignoring the point, boasted that he had never relied upon social-welfare programs. Until that day came, he would continue living as he did. "I take what I have and do what the hell I want. I am responsible for myself."

Janne agreed. "Nobody but you can answer for what you do. There is no one else who commits your crimes."

TIME PASSED IN THE VAULT. THE BREAK IN THE DRILLING CONTINUED and the police kept listening in.

"*Vanity Fair!*" Clark said, all of a sudden, breaking a temporary silence. "This was the last book I read." He asked Elisabeth if she had read the William Makepeace Thackeray novel.

"*Vanity Fair*, yes."

"Boring book," Clark concluded.

Janne said he knew all about vanity fairs. He lifted weights every morning to strengthen his muscles. Elisabeth laughed. She went on to say how much she had enjoyed their conversations. Janne told her to keep her voice down. Satan was listening.

They turned on the radio just in time to hear the latest updates on Norrmalmstorg. The police, the broadcaster announced, had broken off negotiations with the bank robber.

How everyone seemed to "revel" in this story, Janne said.

"Poor Mamma and Pappa," said one of the hostages, thinking of how her parents would handle the news of the nooses.

The temperature dropped again as the evening wore on. Water from the coolant continued to drip into the vault. Kristin shivered. Clark offered her a blanket.

"No, I'll take the jacket," Kristin said, and put on the gunman's gray sweatshirt. Clark helped her.

"Is that my jacket?" Janne asked, pretending to be offended.

"Yes, yes, it is," Kristin said, "I have stolen your jacket, OK?"

"Damn, do you hear?" Janne said, speaking in the direction of the police bugs in the ventilation shafts, and continuing to act as if he had been a victim of theft.

"Yes, do you hear," Elisabeth played on, "the 'robber' has . . ."

"Janne. Say Janne," he corrected her, to laughter all around.

Elisabeth tried to take advantage of the growing camaraderie by steering the questions toward another discussion that had clear relevance for the hostages' predicament: Have any one of you ever thought you were right, only later to realize—and admit—that you were wrong?

"That's a helluva question," Janne said.

When she repeated it, Janne admitted that he had made mistakes and acknowledged them. "Many times."

"No, not so often actually," came Clark's response.

Later Clark told everyone that he had been accepted to study intellectual history at university, prompting skepticism from Janne and curiosity from the hostages.

Asked why he had stopped, Clark blamed it on prison authorities. It was "revenge," he said, for his failed attempt to run away from prison. The problem was, he added, that he had planned the escape too well. That was often the case in prison. "The people who are too smart, you know, usually have it the worst."

Elisabeth tried again to seize upon the increasing familiarity with Janne and Clark and made a suggestion: Why don't they move the cabinet out of the way so that they could all come out of the vault? There was still time to hit the town.

38

As this is being written early Monday morning, there is no one, besides the prime minister, Olof Palme, who dared to guarantee a happy ending to the bank drama.

— *Expressen*, August 27, 1973

NORRMALMSTORG REMAINED QUIET ON MONDAY AFTERNOON. THE most obvious change, *Skånska Dagbladet* thought, was that the blue Mustang was no longer parked outside the bank. Some journalists, returning to the square after the break in action, wondered if the robber had managed to flee in the car after all. They quickly learned that no one had left the vault.

"Are the hostages still alive?" asked *Sydsvenska Dagbladet* instead in its headlines that morning.

If so, how long could they survive this terrifying ordeal? There was so much uncertainty and despair at Norrmalmstorg, *Göteborgs-Posten* said, that the atmosphere felt like the morning after a defeat.

The police had now had time to rest and reflect. What would they do?

No one really had any idea, admitted *Östgöta Correspondenten*, because the robber's nooses had forced a fundamental reconsideration of strategy. Apparently, the authorities had no contingency plan, either, thought *Upsala Nya Tidning*.

The Stockholm police were understandably reluctant to announce their intentions, and speculation quickly filled in the gaps. Predictions about their next move ranged from the bold to the bizarre—from lacing the food with LSD to simulating a leak to flood the vault and then sending in rescue divers. Whatever the police did, it would have to be decisive. Janne and Clark, GT said, had shown their "sadistic inventiveness."

Kurt Lindroth and his advisers reassembled, as planned, on Monday afternoon. Of all the proposals to end the standoff, they found three broad alternative strategies most promising. The first was to station a sharpshooter at the hole to shoot Janne. The second was to rush into the vault, either by forcing open the door or entering through a new, larger hole that could be cut out of the ceiling. The third was to try again to drug Janne's food and drink, or perhaps, as mentioned, incapacitate him with an electric charge sent through some item that they could lower down into the vault.

No plan was perfect, but clearly some were less suitable than others.

The problem with the sharpshooter proposal was that Janne remained mostly out of sight. When he did move into the line of vision, he made sure to have one of the hostages in front of him. An attempt to rush into the vault would, likewise, require an undetermined amount of time—and would almost certainly provide too much opportunity for Janne and Clark to counterstrike. What's more, the entrance or hole in the ceiling might well be mined, as Janne had threatened.

As for the attempt to drug Janne, no one needed to remind Lindroth that the police had tried it without success and Janne would certainly be on his guard, perhaps forcing the hostages to eat or drink first. So despite the break in activity and the chance to weigh their options, the police had found no better solution to end the deadlock than to keep on drilling into the vault and pumping in gas.

The police would need several more holes to disperse the gas evenly throughout the room, and planned to begin drilling again that evening. The next four holes would be about five inches in diameter apiece and together form the shape of a clover.

But the drilling itself would serve another purpose. The constant, deafening roar would wear down the captors and weaken their resolve. Janne might surrender before they had to launch the risky gas attack. At the same time, even if he did not give up, Thorander reasoned, the drilling would, ironically, comfort them in a way silence would not. As long as the police drilled, Janne could be reasonably sure that they were not about to gas them. It was silence that heightened his fears and induced his panic.

BEFORE THE OPERATION RESUMED, THE POLICE NEGOTIATOR B-O Lövenlo called into the vault and adopted a more conciliatory approach. He complimented Clark for having a "cool head" and described how he had gone home last night, "dead tired" and "irritated." Now, however, he wanted to speak calmly, if Clark would do the same. B-O also had a peace offering of sorts: a dozen sandwiches, six cartons of milk, and three rolls of toilet paper. He also had the tampons, as requested.

"Yes, that was kind," Clark said.

"Listen, how is it going with her?" B-O asked.

"You can imagine for yourself." Two women were now menstruating. Clark reminded the negotiator about the request for cigarettes.

The plan was to toss down the toilet paper and tampons. After that, the police would lower the sandwiches and milk in a plastic bucket, which could then be filled halfway with water and used as a toilet.

Janne came to the line to tell the police not to throw down anything. There was too much water on the floor. What's more, he said, the lights should be turned on at once.

"Are they out now?"

They had been off for about thirteen hours, police estimated. B-O blamed it again on the drilling accidentally severing the wiring. Besides, didn't Janne have a flashlight in his bag?

"You are only messing with us!" Clark screamed in the background.

39

Instead of becoming broken down, I became for some strange reason STRONGER!

—Janne Olsson

AFTER HANGING UP THE PHONE, CLARK STUMBLED ABOUT IN THE darkness and accidentally stepped on one of the hostages.

"How clumsy you are, Clark!" someone said.

"Dammit, I don't know how you are lying."

"But don't you *feel* how you are stepping on me?"

"Yes, he is clumsy," Janne said, and started to tease him. One woman laughed.

"You don't have to start with that again," Clark said with obvious irritation.

Janne, Clark, and the hostages again waited on the police in the pitch-dark vault.

When the police finally lowered the bucket with the promised supplies Monday evening, Clark went to retrieve it and struggled to remove it from the wire. He was nervous standing under the opening. The police, he knew, could easily shoot him.

Janne, impatient with the delay, shouted at him.

"What the hell is it?" Clark asked.

"Shut your mouth!"

Janne then stopped himself, noting that such quarrels were exactly what the police wanted.

They started to divide the contents from the bucket.

"Can't we have some wet napkins or something to try to wash ourselves?" a woman asked.

"The flashlight, Clark!" Janne said.

All six men and women gathered around the table, with a paper bedsheet serving as a tablecloth and a battery-powered flashlight as a candle. A few people started to eat the sandwiches at once.

"A lot of goodies!"

"I don't give a crap what's in them."

"I don't give a crap if they poison me, either."

Someone with a mouthful of food mumbled about everything tasting delicious. One person had a ham sandwich, another one liver pâté. Clark did not like cucumbers. Kristin had not received her dinner yet. The police had sent down two sandwiches for each person. Janne advised them to take small bites to avoid a stomachache.

On the radio, broadcasters discussed different kinds of celery, which amused them. They got a kick, too, out of the news about Norrmalmstorg.

"Palme and Geijer, acid stuff," Janne scoffed. As for the police, "they are so phony that it is crazy!"

"Ah, I love you!" Kristin said, addressing the long-awaited food.

Janne laughed.

"You'll have to excuse me," Kristin said. "I'm going to drink a lot of milk."

As the news continued, Norrmalmstorg again dominated the broadcast.

"One thing is clear," Clark said. "If they had known what they know now, they would have shot you immediately." Clark then told everyone how the police had brought him to the bank. "They thought I would go down and fix everything here. I looked them straight in the eye and said, "Hell yeah, I'll go down there now!"

Kristin finished her sandwich and then tried to give her second one to Elisabeth.

"That's not wise," Elisabeth said. "I'd throw up."

Perhaps Birgitta wanted it.

No, they should save it for later, she suggested.

"Thank you, sweetie."

"It's like Christmas!" someone said.

For six days in August, Norrmalmstorg became the most watched street corner in the world.

Police rush to the scene in central Stockholm for what at first appeared to be a bank robbery.

A police sharp-shooter aims at the bank as the photographers beside him prepare to do the same.

Sharpshooters and observers take position in the park behind improvised barricades.

The hostage drama—broadcast on live television—attracted a large crowd of spectators. The atmosphere sometimes resembled a carnival.

Releasing Clark Olofsson into the bank was a risky, controversial move that more than a few policemen would soon regret.

Night falls on Norrmalmstorg, with no end of the hostage drama in sight.

Clark advised the media to keep their cameras ready. A blast soon rocked the lobby.

The police occupy the bank lobby and wait for orders.

Thanks to well-placed microphones, authorities listen in on the remarkable conversations in the vault between captor and captives.

Clark Olofsson, a charismatic outlaw who became a pop-culture icon. Stockholm syndrome, Clark said, resulted from his own manipulation of the circumstances.

Janne Olsson took pride in Stockholm syndrome. It was what he did—and did not do—that led to its discovery, he said. "I think that, in a way, I invented it."

Kristin Enmark, the most outspoken of the hostages, was the first person to be "diagnosed" with Stockholm syndrome. She still dislikes the concept today.

Birgitta Lundblad complimented Janne and Clark many times both during and after the ordeal. "We all felt strongly that we were in the same situation," she said.

Elisabeth Oldgren, the youngest of the victims, shifted between hope, fear, and despair. "I shook, I cried, I prayed; it was awful."

Sven Säfström did not recognize himself in the descriptions of Stockholm syndrome. "You don't see [the captors] as enemies," he said, "but they are not your friends, either."

A page from the notes Sven took during captivity.

The police lowered a Leica M4 camera through one of the drilled holes and took this chilling photograph. A controversy later emerged when a copy disappeared from the police files and turned up in Germany's *Bild am Sonntag*. The iconic image reportedly fetched one of the highest amounts that had been paid for a photograph.

The nooses from the vault.

Rare film footage captures the moment Janne exited the vault . . .

. . . and when Clark was arrested.

The end of the bank drama made front-page headlines around the world. Coverage of "Le Hold Up," as some French newspapers dubbed it, extended as far as Tunisia and Tanzania. It was "the bank robbery of the century," said the Dutch *Het Vrije Volk*.

Police chief Kurt Lindroth (left) and prime minister Olof Palme (right) celebrate at Norrmalmstorg.

All was calm at Norrmalmstorg, the broadcaster said, with no new developments. The standoff had now continued for more than one hundred hours.

"How on earth do they put up with this!" one of the women exclaimed with no small irony.

POLICE KEPT ARRIVING AT NORRMALMSTORG IN THE EVENING AND went to work in the bank lobby behind closed curtains. What they were doing, a reporter for *Skånska Dagbladet* said, was still anyone's guess. "A tense silence" prevailed, noted *Göteborgs-Posten*. The paper, like many other observers, also wondered if authorities were deliberately withholding the most "chilling news" from the public.

From time to time, Janne and Clark would complain of all the clatter that they heard coming through the ventilation: Hammering, sawing, banging, clanging, rattling, and other commotion. The police had to remove a small staircase to drill more holes into the vault.

Around nine p.m., the reverberations began to shake the walls again. Janne forced the hostages back up into the nooses. Ravel came on the radio. It was still completely dark in the vault. Janne and Clark whispered to each other.

The drilling drowned out the conversation for the police listening in the surveillance room.

As the night wore on, Janne allowed the hostages to take breaks. He let them stand in shifts, and even loosen the rope from around their necks, so that it could be pulled down to the shoulders or hidden under the collar of a sweater. This was, of course, provided that the hostages remained ready, at a moment's notice, to return the rope to its position. The police might look down through the holes and, if they did, Janne did not want them to think that he was bluffing.

Clark whispered to them, as he checked their nooses, that they were not in danger. He would cut them down if the gas came. Still, they grew tired of standing in the nooses. Elisabeth's thoughts turned to her family. "They had done so much for me," she later said, recalling what passed through her mind in those dark hours. "It would be unfair for them to lose me this way." The vault, at least, helped her realize her tremendous gratitude to her parents, as she had earlier felt that she was growing apart from them. Kristin concentrated on staying awake because she feared falling asleep with the noose around her neck.

The drill's coolant dripped from the holes in the ceiling, splashing into puddles. The water soon covered the soles of everyone's shoes.

Janne commented on how he was getting tired of staying there.

He and Clark were the only ones, Elisabeth said, who could end the ordeal.

Janne laughed.

Eleven of the twelve sandwiches the police sent down had been eaten. Janne groped around in the darkness with the aid of the flashlight until Clark found the last one floating in the vault's stagnating water. Janne wiped some butter off the bread with his thumb and used it to lubricate his sub-machine gun.

40

I had the impression that for him [Olof Palme] it was not a question of human life, but party politics. If this goes well, then the Social Democrats will receive more votes.

—Birgitta Lundblad

THE POLICE DRILLED ON RELENTLESSLY. JANNE AND CLARK USED the puddles of coolant water on the floor to wash their face, or quench their thirst. The exhausted hostages followed suit. There was enough water to last for weeks, Janne said. Blankets delivered earlier in the standoff helped counter the chill. Several people rested their feet on stools or on top of safety-deposit boxes yanked out of the cabinets.

For hours, the only light in the vault had come from either Janne's flashlight, or, indirectly, from the fixtures on the floor above that shone through the Plexiglas covering the drilled holes. During the early-morning hours, the police finally lowered a lamp through Hole Number 1, the largest of the openings.

Janne noticed that the cable holding the new lantern had a protrusion. He gave the cord a tug and heard something come loose. Moments later, the telephone rang. Don't play with the microphones, the police negotiator said. They are expensive.

With the lamp now illuminating the vault, Janne forced the hostages to stand again with their necks in the nooses. The police might try to take another look. Once again, as time passed, Janne relented and let the hostages rotate in shifts. Sven racked up the most hours of all, and even volunteered to stand for the others. "He was a real man," Janne said.

At one point, before 2:30 in the morning, the hostages heard rustling above one of the drilled holes. The sandbags and Plexiglas were being removed. Was this the beginning of the long-awaited attack?

"They are taking a photograph!" Janne said.

"No, they aren't," Elisabeth said.

The police had, in fact, obtained a small Leica M4 camera from SÄPO with a specially constructed remote-controlled trigger. It was then attached to a T-square and lowered down into the vault. Technicians had calculated the length that the device should disappear into the hole to obtain the best view. Inspector Jonny Jonsson lay on a mattress and navigated. At the signal, another man, police photographer Börje Oppmark, squeezed the rubber ball that served as the shutter button.

The result was a haunting image. Birgitta and Elisabeth sat on chairs beside the safety-deposit boxes. Sven crouched on the floor between them. Birgitta rested her head in her hands and clutched a pillow. Elisabeth stared straight into the camera with an expression of abject fear. Clark stood over them, looking more tired than threatening. Kristin could not be seen, and neither could Janne. But the photograph confirmed what the police feared. Just above the hostages, looped through the keyholes of the safety-deposit boxes, hung the nooses.

FIVE DAYS IN, MANY OF THE ESTIMATED 150 TO 200 JOURNALISTS FROM all over the world slept in shifts. Some headed for Palmhuset, or Hotell Stockholm. Others made do wherever they could. The photographer Bertil Haskel lay on a balcony, wrapped up with a blanket against the night chill, a cigarette dangling from his mouth. The wait for the final resolution went on. "The moment must come—eventually," said a reporter for GT.

During the early-morning hours, police microphones picked up something else surprising.

"Shall we burn up a little more dough now?" asked Janne.

Smoke soon came from the back of the dark vault. Clark was tossing money into a small fire that he had started with the help of the lighter that Thorander had loaned them on the first day. Clark and Janne were laughing. In the light of the flame, Clark looked like a real pyromaniac, Janne later said.

How much money had been destroyed?

Police microphones heard the words "half a million." Both *Expressen* and *Aftonbladet* soon put the figure at 1.5 million, as did many other papers around the country. The amount, however, was far less. The pile of ashes in the vault was too small for those sums, as was the evidence of smoke damage. Clark was in fact only putting one or a few bills at a time into the fire.

A more tantalizing question was why they were burning the ransom money. It was a protest demonstration, many people said, or perhaps a sign of desperation. *Aftonbladet*, for one, called it evidence that Janne and Clark had given up hope of ever leaving the bank. They were like Vikings burning their ships, ventured one psychiatrist.

But the real reason went unnoticed by police and press alike. Janne and Clark had burned the money as part of a contingency plan: Should they get arrested, the police would think any sums missing from the ransom money or the bank registers had been destroyed, when in fact they planned to help themselves to as much of it as possible.

———

BY 8 A.M. ON TUESDAY, AUGUST 28, 1973, THE POLICE HAD COMPLETED three holes in the vault ceiling. Janne blocked one of them by placing a chair on top of the filing cabinet and wedging the seat into the opening. He tried to close the other holes by using paintings taken down from the wall and filling in gaps with the newspapers that the police had sent in during the early days of the standoff.

Then, as the police finished making one of the holes in the clover formation and were pulling up the drill, Janne grabbed his submachine gun and shot up through the temporary opening. One policeman, who was trying to cover the hole with Plexiglas, Assar Karlström, ducked away, and the bullets struck the sandbags. Fortunately, the sand was wet from the coolant; otherwise he did not think the bag would have stopped the bullet.

Twenty minutes later, when the team returned to resume drilling, someone noticed that the Plexiglas had not been properly placed over the third hole. This was "our life insurance," police technician Olle Abramsson later said.

As one of the men went to correct the error, a bullet penetrated through the narrow gap and hit Abramsson in his hand. It struck his left index finger, exited out of his thumb, and reentered his cheek, lodging itself in his lower jaw. He had not even heard the shot. He was rushed to the hospital.

Photographers from all over the continent snapped pictures of the wounded man in his blood-splattered overalls.

When this shooting of a second policeman was announced on the radio, the microphones in the ventilation system picked up cheering from inside the vault.

"Finally we got one!" someone said.

When the drilling began anew, Clark thought that the police would either turn up the heat or adopt a more conciliatory stance to prevent harm from befalling the hostages. Janne, on the other hand, had no doubt that the police would make him pay.

From now on, Janne would force the hostages to spend more time either standing in the nooses at the safety-deposit boxes, or lying down directly underneath the drill, where chunks of concrete were expected to fall. He apologized to his "*Goldfinger* girls," as he called them, referring to the all-female squad of Pussy Galore's Flying Circus in the blockbuster James Bond film, as he sent them, once more, into harm's way.

"Stop! Cut it out! Stop drilling!" Kristin yelled at the police in the direction of the microphones. "You cannot drill any more . . . [The ceiling] will fall on our heads . . . Don't you understand? Do you hear what I'm saying? . . . It will fall on our heads! . . . We are lying underneath. Stop, please stop!"

The roaring, pounding drill went on without reprieve.

At one point, Clark wanted to move the girls out of harm's way, but Janne stopped him. "They will lie there. The decision is not ours."

"The hell it isn't," Clark said.

"No, it is them up there."

———

AT CHANCELLERY HOUSE, OLOF PALME WAS TALKING WITH THE national police chief, Carl Persson, about the Norrmalmstorg crisis. Over the weekend, the prime minister had given a speech outside Stockholm at Kolmården, the largest zoo in Scandinavia. "Violence can triumph in the short term," Palme said, "but in the long term, its prospect is hopeless."

Palme had continued this optimistic refrain throughout the first five days of the ordeal. In private, however, he was far less certain. He was feeling pressure from the Swedish public, which grew restless, fueled in part by the sensational coverage in the mass media. Tabloids kept churning out headlines, like *GT*'s that day: "Secret Microphones Reveal THE GIRLS IN TERROR FOR RAPE . . . DISGUSTING NIGHT IN THE BANK VAULT."

"Snipers with Infrared Light at New Holes," *Kvällsposten* headlined that afternoon. "NOW HE IS GOING TO DIE," the paper predicted of Janne. But it was, of course, not just Janne who was in danger. It was also Clark and the four hostages. The police had to be prepared in case Janne carried out his threats to strangle, crush, or shoot the victims if anyone tried to enter the vault. That was a risk, Carl Persson later said, that the authorities were prepared to take.

Palme and his advisers went to a lunch meeting to discuss their options.

41

The police have to be prepared for everything.

—Sven Thorander

SHORTLY AFTER ONE O'CLOCK TUESDAY AFTERNOON, THE BLUE MUS-tang getaway car pulled up again outside the bank. A helicopter flew over the square. Policemen controlled traffic beyond the barricades with increased vigor. Were the authorities about to yield to the robber's demands and let him leave with the hostages, or was it a trick to lure Janne and Clark out into an ambush? Rumors also circulated that the police would storm the vault at any moment. One hour later, reporters were still wondering what would happen next. An "eerie silence," *Expressen* wrote, had once more fallen on the square.

Olof Palme canceled his talk that afternoon. He declined interviews too. No wonder, *Aftonbladet* said. He probably had no answers for the questions everyone wanted to ask, or, if he did, he did not dare to reveal them to the public. The drama of Norrmalmstorg went on crowding out other news from headlines and broadcasts.

Despite B-O's repeated promises not to launch a gas attack, made no fewer than nine times in one telephone call that afternoon alone, Janne remained distrustful. One hole would suffice for communication or the delivery of supplies, so why would the police need to drill multiple holes if not to attack them? They were going to use gas, Janne told the hostages, just like the Nazis did to the Jews in the death camps.

This comment horrified Birgitta. Was Janne "completely insane"? she asked Clark.

This time, Clark had no comforting response.

Janne went on to tell Sven why he feared a gas attack: permanent brain damage, since the police would never be able to get them out in time to prevent it. He could not live with that, nor could he bear the thought of the hostages suffering from it either. He would then have to shoot all of them and then himself.

It was this comment that truly frightened Sven. "That was when I was scared as hell," he said.

Sven tried to reason with Janne, but got nowhere.

Authorities, meanwhile, continued to assume that they faced a rational, professional criminal who would not harm his hostages—or, at least, would not have the chance to do so before the police overpowered him.

AFTER A HEARTY LUNCH OF BEEF STEW AND RED BEETS, OLOF PALME and the cabinet approved the specific plan of the operation. It detailed every police action, minute by minute, sometimes second by second. Precision was of the utmost importance, Sven Thorander had said. Everyone would have to keep to the schedule. There was no room for deviation, or failure.

The plan was actually very close to the one on Sunday night that Janne and Clark had stopped. First, a team of specialists would deploy the CS tear gas, and then a group of policemen would enter the vault, defeat the gunman, and rescue the hostages. Palme had promised to stand behind any officer, who, in course of the rescue operation, "shot Jan-Erik Olsson or Clark Olofsson"—this, he apparently added on the phone to Kurt Lindroth, "regardless of what the courts say."

The police knew from a Leica photograph of the vault that Janne had barricaded the inner door with two heavy steel cabinets. Janne, Clark, and Sven had pushed the second one onto its side and wedged it between the first one and the nearby wall. The door could not open more than eight inches, Janne estimated.

A coin dealer in Östermalm who owned the same kind of cabinet had opened his shop in the middle of the night to allow the police to measure its dimensions. A bank employee on vacation in Copenhagen had then helped them estimate the amount of paper inside. As a result, the police calculated that the cabinet blocking their way into the vault weighed as much as 330 pounds.

Lindroth's men planned to force their way inside with the help of a jack and, if that failed, they would remove the door's hinges with a blowtorch. And if this in turn did not work, the police hoped to drill a large hole in the ceiling to enable officers to descend into the chamber. Such a plan would, of course, require a significant amount of time while also relinquishing any hope of catching Janne by surprise.

But was launching a gas attack and storming the vault really necessary? Some policemen inside the bank doubted it. The "exhaustion tactic" was working. Janne would soon surrender, they believed. There was no need to run this excessive risk.

Janne and Clark, in the meantime, counted the holes in the ceiling. There were six, and the authorities continued to drill a seventh. Kristin yelled at the police to stop. "If gas comes, we will be choked! . . . You have not done anything [to help]!"

"Are you not going to stop soon?" Clark said to the police. "I'm beginning to get tired of this."

Sven found some blank stationery and started taking notes. He would keep writing until he ran out of paper.

Janne prepared to set off a detonation. "It is not a threat; it is a promise!" he yelled. "OK, you are going to get what you want."

The drilling went on and the water dripped, splashing into the vault.

42

All or Nothing

—*Kvällsposten*, August 29, 1973

I T WAS GOING TO BE A RACE AGAINST TIME. THE POLICE WOULD HAVE, at most, fifteen minutes to apprehend the captors, free the hostages, and remove everyone before the point at which experts advised that the gas might prove dangerous. They had even less than that, of course, if the gunman, upon recognizing the attack, tried to harm the hostages or the police.

The actual time that the operation would start—H-Hour (*K-Klockan* in Swedish)—was not yet determined. The coded signal would be "Turn on the Lights." At that point, Thorander's team would deploy the gas by using an array of aerosol cans equipped with a special nozzle extension that enabled them to spray as a single unit. This was preferred over dropping tear-gas grenades, which might not explode if they landed on the vault carpet.

After the police pumped in the gas, Håkan Larsson and Jonny Jonsson, the leaders of the "break-in group," would enter the vault, bare-chested to prevent the gas from lodging in their shirts. Helmets could not be worn, because they would not fit over their gas masks. Bulletproof vests were to be avoided, too, for fear of being too heavy and unwieldy in the confined space.

Larsson and Jonsson had to be ready for a fight, even a shootout with Janne and possibly also Clark. Both policemen were excellent marksmen, though for this operation, they would have to wield a different weapon.

Police-issue pistols were too weak to be relied upon, and the submachine gun was too powerful, likely to ricochet. The sawed-off shotgun, on the other hand, was more suitable for short-range work, and had long been a favorite of criminals. It was Thorander who had proposed this solution.

It was Thorander, too, who had cut through the red tape to secure these particular weapons. This took some bureaucratic maneuvering, because the guns in question were illegal in Sweden and had actually been seized from the infamous bank robber Lars-Inge Svartenbrandt.

In addition to the sawed-off shotguns, Larsson and Jonsson carried service firearms in their shoulder straps. Knives were sheathed in the back of their pants to cut the nooses and prevent the hostages from being hanged. They tested the sharpness of the blades beforehand by cutting their own armpit hair.

OUTSIDE, PEOPLE STOOD ON BALCONIES, IN WINDOWS, AND AT THE BARricades on the surrounding streets. Everyone expected the final outcome—whatever it would be—at any moment. "At workplaces, in schools, on trains and tracks," *Göteborgs-Posten* wrote that day, "people sit and talk only of one thing: The Bank Drama."

In his column for Tuesday-evening's *Aftonbladet*, Christer Renström surveyed the situation after more than five days of tense standoff. The police, he wrote, had made "a fatal mistake" by sending Clark into the bank, and the gunman countered with his own significant strategic error, when he had retreated to the vault. The zero-sum prestige game waged by authorities, however, made matters worse. The best course of action, he argued, was to concentrate on the overarching objective of saving the lives of the hostages, even if it meant that Janne and Clark would get away with the ransom money.

This was also the view of Janne's brother Åke, who was spotted standing on a hotel balcony overlooking the square. He no longer felt that he could persuade Janne to surrender—he could have on Friday, he said, when he'd first offered his help. But not now; the crisis had gone on for too long. At any rate, the police had refused to let him try and he could now only see two chances for a peaceful outcome. Either the government yields, or Clark persuades his brother to surrender.

The latter option was certainly not going to happen, Janne's former lawyer, Göran Rise, told *GT*. Janne would never give up. The lawyer had a plan to avoid tragedy, though he hesitated to reveal it yet because he hoped to persuade the authorities to let him mediate. He would get no further with this request than Janne's brother had.

The worst outcome, many people said, was a police attack on the vault. A Helsingborg police officer who knew Janne told a reporter for *Expressen* that such a move would be very dangerous. Janne played by the precepts of the criminal underworld. Shooting an officer could carry prestige in that value system, and, if Janne felt threatened, the policeman warned, he would not hesitate to use his weapon.

Lost in the talk about nooses and submachine guns was something else that the police would be well advised to take into consideration: The robber's explosives were not just dynamite, but *sprängdeg*, a powerful military-grade substance used to destroy fortifications and large-scale structures. If it were detonated in only a fraction of the amount that Janne had brought with him, it would blast eardrums, rip up pulmonary tissue, and sear intestinal mucus. Internal bleeding would ensue. Perhaps all six people would be thrown with tremendous force against the walls. Very possibly everyone in the vault would die.

As the police finalized their preparations for gas, several psychiatrists and psychologists launched an energetic, eleventh-hour campaign to persuade the police to let the robber leave with the hostages. The man in the bank was desperate, with absolutely "nothing to lose," as the latest shooting of policeman Olle Abramsson confirmed. The authorities had no choice but to accept Janne's terms. Anything less than that would end in catastrophe, they argued.

A leading child psychologist, Gustav Jonsson, made this argument on television. Nine professors in the criminology department at Stockholm University likewise composed a joint statement in hopes of averting a tragedy. Other psychiatrists wrote in to the newspapers, including Karl Grunewald, who urged the police to rely more on the expertise of psychologists, nurses, social scientists, and, in particular, women. Not a single woman, he noted, was involved in the high-stakes negotiations, which had degenerated into a "game between men."

The police made no change to their plans. The bank drama, *Kvällsposten* feared, marched forward to its "bloody finale."

43

At any moment, [Janne] could be killed, or become a mass murderer.

—Åke Olsson

A T 8:55 P.M., SIX AMBULANCES PULLED UP OUTSIDE THE BANK. EACH one brought oxygen, breathing machines, vials of blood, and emergency medical kits. Stretchers were carried inside by policemen, who, given the danger of the situation, would assume responsibility for bringing out survivors.

Television cameras showered the darkened square in a surreal glow. The crowds behind the barricades remained largely quiet. Journalist Arne Thorén spoke of the "unreal atmosphere," while other reporters on the scene compared it to a gala opening of the opera or theatre.

The Stockholm police had already requested that the Swedish media "broadcast no alarming information" about its preparations. They did not want Janne to anticipate their moment of action. By the time of this communiqué, however, the radio had already reported the arrival of the ambulances. This news—along with the glaring lack of reported developments—did not calm anyone in the vault. The hostages sensed that something was about to happen.

The gas team, the drill team, the break-in team, and everyone else took their place. Experts prepared to pump the CS tear gas through three of the seven holes in the vault. Colleagues would shine lights down two other holes, while marksmen would wait at the last two holes in case they needed to shoot.

Larsson and Jonsson stood outside the vault. Farther away, behind walls of sandbags, crouched sharpshooters and a dozen other policemen in helmets and bulletproof vests, armed with submachine guns. The lobby looked like World War III, one observer said.

Lindroth had decided to strike at 9:05 p.m. The timing was significant. The operation would begin after the nightly news had just ended, and presumably catch Janne both distracted and lured into thinking that he had more time.

About 9:00 p.m., police microphones picked up some whispering. Clark mentioned something indecipherable and Janne responded, "That's crazy!" The police did not pay much attention to the exchange, but years later Clark said that he had wanted to attack by lobbing explosives at the police on the other side of the door.

At 9:03 p.m., as news about Norrmalmstorg blared on the transistor radio, the ventilation fan slowed to a stop. A giant spotlight lit up the vault door. The electric generator hummed. The drilling pounded again to divert attention.

At precisely 9:05 p.m., "Turn on the Lights!" The signal had been given.

A gray cloud poured into the vault. Janne, resting on a table, jumped up and ordered the hostages back into their nooses. But it was too late. Everyone went down. Choking, coughing, ducking low, they gasped for air as they pressed their faces into the standing water. The gas wheezed and hissed. Eyes burned. Everyone strained to breathe. Birgitta buried her face in a wet blanket. They writhed in pain and panic.

Kristin feared that they were all going to be shot, as Janne had threatened, if the police gassed them. She tried to squeeze herself between a cabinet and the wall.

Cries and screams emanated up the ventilation shaft. There was a lot of coughing.

The fan restarted, as planned, to disperse the tear gas throughout the vault.

"We give up!" someone yelled.

"Help! We give up! Help!"

All six men and women in the vault were screaming, coughing, and choking. Above and outside the vault, the police were yelling to one another all at once.

"Please open the door!" shouted a hostage. "Open the door!"

"Help us!"

Håkan Larsson ordered his police colleagues in the lobby to be quiet so that he could talk with the robber. Janne's submachine gun, he said, had to be placed on a hook on the rope and hoisted out through the large hole in the ceiling.

Janne started to hand over his gun. "I will not sacrifice you all," he told the hostages. "That was never my intention."

There was a lot of screaming and yelling.

"Do you know what I think?" Janne said. "They are going to beat me to death now when I come out."

Larsson shouted instructions, but Janne struggled to hear them, as they were muffled by his gas mask and drowned out by the noise of the policemen outside. The gas, all the while, attacked the eyes, lungs, and throats of everyone in the vault.

"Can't you open the door?" Elisabeth asked the police. "Hurry up!"

The lights came back on. Larsson stood on the threshold between the inner door and the outer door. The latter had now been opened from afar with the help of a string, in case it had been rigged with explosives.

Policemen in the lobby shouted to Larsson and one another, trying to figure out why Janne, Clark, and the hostages were not coming out. The gas was also starting to seep out of the vault into the lobby.

But Janne was trying to comply with the instructions. "I have taken a chance and I lost," he said to no one in particular.

Moments later, Clark grumbled something about what might have happened had he been a beast.

Send down the rope, Kristin yelled, so Janne could give them what they wanted.

"Send it down, dammit!" Janne said.

"Send down some cigarettes, first!" Clark said.

"You're only trying to torment us!" Janne said.

"Yes!" one of the women said.

Someone was crying, probably Elisabeth. Janne and Kristin tried to comfort her. There was more coughing, spitting, and clearing of throats.

Janne maneuvered the submachine gun, as instructed, to send it on the hook up through the hole. But the magazine got stuck.

Håkan Larsson's colleagues, standing on the other side of the door and not knowing the cause of the delay, seemed to be gripped by panic. Several officers yelled for the police to pump in more gas at once. Janne and Clark had to be defeated.

Sven Thorander gave the order.

It was not until 9:28 p.m. that Janne's submachine gun finally disappeared out of the drilled hole. The suffocating gas had now been in the vault for a full twenty minutes longer than anticipated.

And what about the explosives? they wondered.

Perhaps Janne would strap the dynamite to himself and try to blow up as many people as possible. The police in the lobby shouted warnings all at once. Jonsson told them again to quiet down. Larsson was conducting the negotiations.

Janne started to get angry. He had sent up his machine gun, just as he agreed. Did the police still not trust him?

Larsson handed his shotgun to a colleague and stood there, empty-handed, ready to receive the explosives. "You do realize," he said, "that I am going to go berserk if you blow off my arms?"

"You can trust him!" Kristin yelled.

"We need air in here!" Elisabeth screamed.

Janne handed over his explosives as he had promised.

Elisabeth was still crying. Clark tried to reassure her that they were no longer in danger.

"We are coming out," Kristin added. "Take it easy."

"It is completely full of gas here!" Elisabeth screamed.

Kristin and Sven both kept trying to comfort her.

The clock was ticking. After receiving the gun and explosives, the police still did not move with the urgency that the hostages had hoped. Instead, they had another demand: The hostages had to leave the vault first.

At this point, the hostages refused.

"We gladly let [Janne and Clark] go out first because they have been so very decent towards us," Birgitta said.

The police were taken aback. Officers in the lobby yelled for Larsson to insist that the hostages leave first. He ignored them.

They had now been in the vault for a half hour after the gas had been deployed. But they still could not leave. The steel cabinets blocked the inner door.

Trusting Larsson's assurances, Janne, Clark, and Sven worked to remove the heavy obstruction. They were exhausted, heaving and coughing with their eyes burning as they stood in water up to their ankles and struggled to get a footing. They pushed and pulled. Janne remained vigilant, fearful that a policeman might shoot him in the back through one of the holes in the ceiling.

Retreat to the far end of the vault, Janne told everyone, in case the police started firing at him.

Kristin gave him a hug and a kiss, and so did Elisabeth. Birgitta asked him to write to her.

44

The successful resolution was just as lucky as someone placing thirteen winning bets in a row . . .

—Anonymous policeman

ONE HUNDRED AND THIRTY-ONE HOURS AFTER THE ORDEAL BEGAN, Janne, Clark, and the four hostages were about to exit the vault. The transistor radio still played in the background. At 9:40 p.m., Radio Sweden interrupted a sports segment to broadcast the breaking news. The bank drama had come to an end.

"Hello, welcome out!" said Sven Thorander when he greeted the gunman.

The police handcuffed Janne "Stockholm-style," locking his right arm to Håkan Larsson and his left arm to Jonny Jonsson. Janne wondered what the police would do to him once they were away from eyewitnesses and had the opportunity. One policeman had already put a gun under Janne's chin and threatened to pull the trigger. Janne dared him to do it.

Janne then entered the lobby, exchanging words with the policemen at his side. Another officer escorted Elisabeth, who shielded her eyes from the bright lights. Kristin walked out by herself. Clark came next, handcuffed to two policemen, with a third detective inspector pointing a submachine gun at him and a fourth rushing in to help. Immediately behind him followed two additional officers with Birgitta. Last out of the vault was Sven.

Two policemen shoved Clark hard onto a stretcher and strapped him down tightly, using more force than necessary. Police film caught one of the men giving Clark a quick jab to the face and a knee to his thigh.

"Don't hit him!" Kristin yelled at the police.

Kristin sat on a nearby stretcher in the lobby. She was still wearing the gunman's oversized gray hooded sweatshirt. "We'll see each other again," she shouted to Clark, to everyone's further surprise.

The six men and women had spent more than thirty minutes in the gas-filled vault. They had been saved, ironically, by police errors. The aerosol cans were designed to spray horizontally, not vertically, and so a significant portion of the intended dosage had been wasted on the sides of the deep holes. At the last minute, too, Thorander had dismissed the experts who were meant to operate the spraying mechanism and put his own men in charge. Perhaps these non-chemists had bungled the operation, one of the dismissed scientists later suggested, thereby causing the powder in the canisters not to convert to gas and instead sink to the bottom of the vault, where it was absorbed in the water. At any rate, the concentration of gas was much weaker than expected, which was indeed fortunate. The original dosage had been calculated based on the expectation that everyone would be removed in fifteen minutes.

What had also saved the hostages, of course, was Janne's decision to spare them. Despite many threats to shoot, hang, or blow them up if the police gassed them, he had chosen to let them live. The so-called desperado had proven to be humane after all. And Janne, in turn, credited his captives for saving his life when they insisted that he come out first. Clark would say the same thing.

Out in Norrmalmstorg, blinding flashes of cameras lit up the square as five policemen, still wearing gas masks, led Janne out of the bank. Audiences around Sweden and the world now had their first live look at the man newspapers like London's *Daily Mirror* called "the Monster of Stockholm." He was tall and muscular, as the press had described him. Three buttons held together his drenched blue-striped shirt. Police dogs growled and barked while the crowd of mostly journalists jeered. Janne walked out proud, and erect, with his gaze fixed in the distance. He looked like a defiant general in Hitler's Waffen-SS, said *Vecko-Journalen*.

Detective inspectors Larsson and Jonsson led the handcuffed attacker to an ambulance, where he would be taken to the hospital for examination and then to jail. But they found that the barricades had been moved and the vehicle intended for Janne lay beyond a throng of photographers and reporters.

When they found a different, more accessible ambulance, the medical staff refused to take him. This vehicle was reserved for one of the hostages, the crew said, insisting that Janne would not receive the first ride out of Norrmalmstorg. Back the officers went, dragging Janne again in front of the booing, hissing crowd. Photographers and television cameras captured the commotion.

Janne blamed the police for a petty attempt to parade him around as a trophy and expose him to repeated catcalls and shouted insults. Larsson said he had actually hoped to shield him and apologized for the mix-up.

Clark and the hostages were carried out of the bank on stretchers. Kristin alone refused to lie down, as she had been instructed, and sat up, taking in the surreal scene of police dogs, fire trucks, medical staff, camera crews, and, in the distance, a crowd of spectators. She peered around as if looking for someone. Elisabeth hid her face under a blanket. Birgitta felt the fresh air of the late-summer night washing over her like a wave.

Each of the six people from the vault went by separate ambulance to one of five different hospitals around Stockholm to ensure maximum attention to each patient. Elisabeth, on her way to Karolinska, wondered what would happen to Janne and Clark, and thought that they deserved the same medical care that she would receive.

Janne's ambulance left for Seraphim Hospital on Kungsholmen. Five police officers rode with him. There was not a lot of conversation. Janne asked about the condition of the two officers he had shot, and learned that, unfortunately, neither one was doing well. He asked when he was going to get his beating. One of the men in the vehicle lost his temper and started insulting him, but Jonny Jonsson intervened. The police had won, Jonsson said, and there was no need to gloat.

As he exited, Janne thanked the ambulance crew for the ride.

Kristin, meanwhile, arrived at Sabbatsberg. Waiting for her was a bouquet of flowers from the prime minister and minister of justice. The card read: "In admiration for the perseverance and courage you showed." A reporter from *Expressen* that night found Kristin in reasonable health. Her cheeks and eyes were still red from the tear gas. She sipped coffee from a plastic cup. The sandwich on her paper plate remained untouched.

What she really wanted, Kristin said, was a cigarette and a toothbrush—and a good night's sleep in a real bed.

Sven went to St. Erik's Hospital on Kungsholmen. He lay sprawled out on the bed, exhausted, for about ten minutes before the staff helped him to call his parents. His grandmother, eighty-three-year-old Lilly Linderoth, already knew the good news. She had been watching television in Holmsund in northern Sweden and "cried tears of joy," when she saw Sven come out of the bank alive.

AGAINST ALL ODDS, THE NORRMALMSTORG HOSTAGE CRISIS HAD ENDED without a single loss of life. "It's all over," Sven Thorander announced at Norrmalmstorg, with a gas mask still around his neck. Police Chief Kurt Lindroth, megaphone in hand, regaled reporters about the police operation and thanked his staff for their contributions. Loud cheers greeted his words of triumph. He beamed with happiness.

Eager to show his own appreciation for the achievement, the prime minister hurried over to the spontaneous celebration that erupted in the Stockholm square. He strode right into the bank, with the country's national police chief, Carl Persson, at his side. Palme gave a speech, memorably, standing on a chair in the bank director's office. Policemen, raising their beers, toasted him.

The journalist Lennart Broström asked the prime minister how he felt at that moment.

"Exactly as all the other people in Swedish society: endlessly relieved."

Four innocent lives had been saved, Palme said, and, given the refusal to yield to the threats of violence, countless other lives in the future had also been spared. An open, lawful society had won at Norrmalmstorg.

In response to a question from the reporter Mikael Timm, Palme affirmed that he stood by his decision to adopt a firm stance against violence. "A society that arms two lunatics with pistols, places a car and three million crowns and two innocent people at their disposal—that society is sick in its core."

Olof Palme had spoken well, many people said. Other commentators, however, would soon criticize him for turning the Norrmalmstorg victory into an election speech.

45

Gladly let films, paperbacks, and television series depict crime dramas in black-and-white terms. Play along and pretend the world is divided into good and evil . . . But do not confuse that with the lawbreakers and victims of reality.

—Rune Moberg, *Se*, August 30, 1973

AT SERAPHIM HOSPITAL, CARDIOLOGIST DR. KJELL HELLSTRÖM PRE-pared the ER team to receive its contingent of Norrmalmstorg survivors. Janne and Clark were both on their way; the press, in fact, had beat them there. Some reporters had deduced the likely location by observing that the injured policeman, Olle Abramsson, had been taken there earlier that morning. Others probably acted on an insider tip.

Founded in 1752, Seraphim was considered the first modern hospital in Sweden. Upon arrival, Janne said that he had never seen so many physicians and nurses at one time in his life. They swarmed around him. Ordered not to remove his handcuffs, they had to cut off his shirt to check his vital signs. His clothes reeked of gas, sweat, and stale cigarette smoke from the vault.

The hospital staff doused him with a saline solution to prevent the sticky tear gas from burning his skin, and treated his eyes with bicarbonate. Håkan Larsson continued to follow Janne at every step, even into the shower. Janne earned respect from his keepers by making no complaints or objections—that is, until the flashes of cameras from photographers outside on the street lit up the room. He asked the staff to close the window.

Kerstin Westman, a nurse assistant on duty that night, returned Janne's watch after his shower. Keep it as a souvenir, Janne said. She declined. A policeman in the room joked that it was probably stolen. It certainly was not, Janne said.

After listening to Janne's heart and lungs, Dr. Hellström pronounced him fit enough to be transferred to the nearby jail, Kronobergshäktet. That night, Janne lay on a bunk in Cell 67—the first rest in a bed since Thursday morning. He struggled to sleep. Over and over in his head, he heard the cries of the hostages and imagined a drill boring down from the ceiling.

LIKE JANNE, CLARK HAD ARRIVED AT SERAPHIM FOR A SHORT EXAMINA-tion. He felt "shitty and sticky," as he put it, and his hair and beard were a mess. His stack of incoming telegrams kept piling up—there were already more than seventy, according to one nurse's count. Many of them were from young women who had enclosed photographs and telephone numbers.

After his health was checked, Clark was taken to the same jail as Janne. Clark, however, faced an additional challenge. Before leaving the vault, he had actually managed to smuggle out some cash. The police never knew how the money left the bank, but more than forty years later, Clark admitted what had happened: At the end of the siege, when the police were about to enter the vault, he had gone to the back, wrapped four 10,000 crown notes (approximately $60,000 today) with smaller bills, and inserted them in his rectum.

First, he had tried a bill or two, he said, but then surprised himself by fitting the whole lot. It was true, Janne said, adding that he had tried without success, even when using the leftover butter. For Clark, on the other hand, it was "whoop" and up it went.

Clark now had to figure out how to retrieve the money. Until he did, he knew only that he had to avoid eating. That meant playing up his real-enough feelings of despondency and shock. He eventually removed the notes in the shower. Rinsing off the large bills, he hid them in a sock and then laid them out to dry on his bed. If the authorities saw his loot, he knew, he would be charged with aggravated robbery. The 40,000 crowns would later leave his cell enclosed in a letter addressed to a friend and apparently mailed by his defense attorney, Olof Arvidsson, who thought the correspondence had already passed the censor. (Clark had found an envelope stamped with the words "examined by the prosecutor").

On Wednesday, August 29, 1973, all four hostages were relocated to private rooms at the newly renovated psychiatric department at St. Göran's Hospital on Kungsholmen. The clinic's staff worked under Dr. Lennart Ljungberg and Dr. Waltraut Bergman to restore the patients' sense of normalcy and address any traumas resulting from the ordeal. Treatment might require days, weeks, or months, though Ljungberg felt confident that it would ultimately prove successful.

Cards and flowers continued to arrive from family, friends, and sympathizers around the country. Bouquets of roses, lilies, and chrysanthemums came from the prime minister, and Kreditbanken sent each employee two dozen red roses. Birgitta also received a bouquet from her husband, who had picked the flowers from their garden himself.

The patients would be allowed to read the newspapers, watch television, listen to the radio, write letters, and speak on the phone. The clinic extended visiting hours to enable families to come as much as they liked. Birgitta passed the time by knitting and sewing. Kristin, in a nearby room, decorated wooden saltshakers. One thing off-limits, however, was talking with the media. No one, the psychiatrist said, was prepared for that yet.

Given the intense interest, the police posted guards at the clinic around the clock. The former hostages—Dr. Ljungberg liked that word—settled in to enjoy baths, pajamas, and clean sheets. Elisabeth threw away all her clothes from the vault, except for a suede jacket that she adored.

Insomnia, no surprise, plagued several of the veterans of the vault. Kristin received the barbiturate Diminal duplex. Still she lay awake and needed someone from the staff to sit beside her. She eventually dozed off about five in the morning with the help of Mogadon, a type of benzodiazepine or tranquilizer. She kept waking up throughout the early morning, wanting to hold someone's hand.

To avoid leaving difficult issues unresolved, the psychiatrists urged the patients to talk as much as possible about their experiences. The first question Kristin received, however, astonished her. It was not about how she felt, or how the staff could help her. A psychiatrist wanted to know if Kristin was in love with Clark.

After all she had experienced in the vault, it is no wonder that Kristin felt alienated by this initial inquiry. She did not think that the hospital's psychiatric team really wanted to help her, she later said, and, in fact, felt that she was the one being blamed. She never found out why one psychiatrist insisted on playing tape recordings of her screaming in terror in the vault.

At one point, Dr. Bergman told Kristin that it was "nearly unbelievable" that the men had not made a sexual advance. Kristin stuck to her story. They had not, she insisted.

"What I needed was trust, warmth, and assurances that [the hostage ordeal] was over and that I was safe," Kristin said. Not playing the tape of her screaming, or grilling her as if she were on trial.

Despite the repeated questions, the mind-set of the hostages remained largely unchanged. Kristin and Elisabeth, in particular, still saw Janne and Clark as protecting them from harm, and considered the police the real threat to their safety. When psychiatrists or the police later suggested otherwise, Elisabeth accused them of trying to brainwash her.

———

IT WAS AT THREE O'CLOCK THAT SAME WEDNESDAY AFTERNOON THAT two police inspectors, Leif Jermelid and Erik Skoglund, arrived at St. Göran's Hospital for the first questioning of the pretrial investigation. All four former hostages would describe separately, in their own words, what had happened at Norrmalmstorg. It was to be an informal affair conducted in the presence of a physician, who could intervene at any point.

Like the psychiatrists, the police seemed very much interested in possible "intimate relationships" in the vault, as Inspector Jermelid put it when he spoke with Sven.

"There was no intimate relationship," Sven said. "We all became very good friends."

What about rape?

Nothing like that had happened either, Sven said. "Janne was very pleasant and kind toward the women, and they had confidence in both him and Clark."

In her questioning, Elisabeth elaborated on the relationship. Clark was "a pretty amazing guy," she said, and he had comforted them in their distress. The real fear was that the police would fire on them in the lobby or later storm the vault, starting a deadly shootout. Clark had vastly improved the situation, she added, and she then praised Janne for his tenderness.

The media accounts of the supposed stranglehold were "a complete lie," Elisabeth said. There was no chokehold whatsoever. Janne had only grabbed her around the shoulders, she said, demonstrating for the inspector. "He did everything to calm us."

"So he did not threaten you or frighten you in any way?"

She denied it without qualification. He only used her and her colleagues to scare the authorities. She blamed the escalation of the crisis on the police. Janne, by contrast, was "an honorable thief."

When the physician motioned for the investigator to wrap up the day's questioning, the police inspector asked if there was anything else that happened in the vault that she wished to note.

"Yes," Elisabeth said. "You could have used much quieter microphones!"

Was that all she had to say?

"Yes, that is what I think."

The police interrogator asked her again if either Janne or Clark ever made a sexual move against them.

She denied it.

"Not against anyone?"

No, they had not, Elisabeth repeated.

Kristin was making similar statements—and denials—in her interrogation at the same time that afternoon. Inspector Erik Skoglund had barely opened the questioning when Kristin started criticizing the police action from the first minutes Thursday morning, when the officers came down the staircase and drew their guns.

But everything changed when Clark arrived, she said. "He calmed both the robber and us." At this point, the only thing she became afraid of, she said, was that the police would try something.

What about Janne?

No, she was worried about the police with guns she saw in the lobby, the staircase, or outside in the square and nearby park.

At this point, when Kristin spoke of Janne and Clark's actions in the vault, she used the plural "we" as in "We found Sven," or even, a few minutes later, "We shot at the police" and "We hit the officer."

The inspector asked her if Janne or Clark had acted in any way scandalously toward the women.

No, they had not.

As the inspector probed for more detail, Kristin replied that there was no rape or harassment whatsoever.

He then homed in on her testimony that Clark had held her hand, but

Kristin repeated that he had done nothing wrong. In fact, he had made "a real contribution."

Was there anything else she wanted to add?

"I think that there was a little too much politics in this," Kristin said.

"Anything else?"

"Yes, you should be completely clear that they did not do anything wrong toward us and I feel great and I am completely happy."

The inspector was struck, not least by her overwhelming confidence in Clark and Janne. Didn't she think that if the gunman shot at the police, he could also fire upon them?

"He said that he did not want to do us harm," Kristin said. "He was not out for our lives."

She closed by asking the police inspector to send her regards to Clark, along with a hug and a kiss.

46

I became the Stockholm syndrome.

—Kristin Enmark

WHEN DR. BEJEROT CAME OUT TO ADDRESS THE JOURNALISTS AT St. Göran's psychiatric clinic that day, reporters asked him about certain rumors already circulating in the media. Had Janne Olsson, one Danish reporter inquired, fallen in love with one of the hostages?

"No, it was the millions he was after," Bejerot said.

Another foreign correspondent asked if there had been a rape in the vault.

"None of the women have said so and there is no evidence," Bejerot said.

This was not, strictly speaking, a denial, several journalists noted, and ran with the story anyway. These allegations made headlines from London's _Daily Mirror_ to Vienna's _Die Presse_. Even the _New York Times_, citing "reliable policemen," reported that there was "no doubt [that] the women were subjected to sexual assault."

Other papers like Stockholm's _Expressen_ countered that nothing more had happened than hugs and handholding to comfort a fellow human being in distress. This is exactly what both Clark and Kristin later said, and nothing would emerge from the police investigations or the testimony in court to challenge this claim. Questions, however, persisted. "What really happened in the bank vault?" asked _Göteborgs-Posten_.

The most common early interpretation centered on the explanations put forth by the psychiatrists at St. Göran's. The hostages at Norrmalmstorg, Dr. Lennart Ljungberg said, suffered something resembling shell shock, a term that had come into use when describing the erratic behavior of veterans of the First World War.

Like the soldiers in the trenches on the western front, the hostages had been forced to remain immobile and passive, without control of their own destiny. Unlike the soldiers, however, the hostages had no time to prepare mentally, physically, or emotionally. They were immediately thrust into the vortex. At every moment, they had remained at the mercy of the gunman, or, for that matter, a stray bullet from a police sniper.

The hostages did not see it that way at all. Kristin, for instance, credited Clark for saving her life. She was enormously grateful for all his contributions—untying the ropes binding her, helping her to talk with her family on the telephone, reassuring and comforting her all the time that everything was going to be OK. In return, it did not seem fair that he was being punished. She wished that they had had a chance to speak, if only for a few minutes. She became angry, too, because she felt that the authorities treated her more like a villain than a victim of the crime.

For months after her rescue, Kristin had found herself thinking about Clark. She missed him and wondered how he was doing now that he was back in prison. By the summer of 1974, they started to exchange letters. First it was about general subjects, though over time, the contents became more intimate and explicit. They made plans to meet in person, of course, keeping it a secret. Norrmalmstorg was still front-page news in Sweden, even with stories far less explosive than this one would have been, had it reached the public.

The first meeting was supposed to be "discreet." It would take place on October 23, 1974. Clark had received a twenty-four-hour furlough to visit his lawyer, and they would use that occasion to meet for a lunch date at a restaurant at Stureplan in central Stockholm. Kristin arrived early to her table, almost giddy with excitement. "Hey, Kikki" she heard, his deep voice booming from across the dining room. Clark was about "as discreet as an elephant in a porcelain shop," she said.

It was a wonderful afternoon. They hugged and shared stories, though Kristin could not remember what they talked about, nor what they ate. But they certainly drank a lot of whiskey. The festivities continued at his lawyer's office. That evening, as Clark prepared to return to prison, he asked her to follow him to the train station and then onto the train itself. Her answer was a kiss. Kristin and Clark received more than a few looks of surprise when the fellow passengers spotted them together.

They checked into a small hotel near the train station in Norrköping. She felt like she was living in a thriller, she said, as she climbed the stairs to the room with the country's most notorious outlaw. "We threw off our clothes and set about doing everything that had been prohibited to us for so long." Clark had to scramble out afterward to rush back to prison. Kristin returned to Stockholm, as she put it, "hungover and with a dumb, happy smile stuck on my face."

Clark and Kristin would continue to exchange letters and talk on the phone. In November 1974, she visited him in prison twice. After the second time, Clark broke off contact, saying that he did not want them to see each other anymore in prison and they should postpone everything until he received his promised furloughs to study at Stockholm University. Kristin tried to understand.

Deep down, however, she knew that they were very different. Clark was also juggling several romantic relationships. By the end of the 1970s, when he gained permission to leave prison to attend class, they renewed their friendship. Kristin, meanwhile, had felt the urge to have children. She had had serious boyfriends, but no one seemed right. Not long after her thirtieth birthday, she asked Clark if he would father her child. He accepted on two conditions: that he would not be on any documents and that he would have no part in the upbringing.

After a few attempts, Kristin went to the hospital in considerable pain. Something was wrong. It was an ectopic pregnancy. Kristin was devastated.

47

I saw us as a team of specialists who, upon demand, would be able to charter a plane and fly over the globe and deal with similar stories.

—Dr. Nils Bejerot

THE POLICE, THE PRESS, AND THE PUBLIC WOULD LONG PUZZLE OVER the shocking, disorienting discoveries from the vault. Why had the hostages defended their captors and used the pronoun "we" when referring to their actions? Why, as Elisabeth asked Dr. Waltraut Bergman, did she not hate them? What about the swirling rumors of romance?

For Swedish psychiatrist Nils Bejerot, this event offered a unique opportunity to understand human behavior under extreme stress. He is traditionally credited with coining the term "Norrmalmstorg syndrome." The name later became "Stockholm factor" and then "Stockholm syndrome," as the story went global. Bejerot elaborated:

A paradox of common interest between hostage-taker and his victims arises. This can develop from understanding to sympathy and even lead to the victim developing strong emotional ties to the hostage-taker.

The captor, Bejerot further explained, had first established his authority by threatening to kill or harm the hostages, but as the siege progressed, he began to provide food, drink, and other basic needs. He even comforted the hostages, as they came to fear the attacks of the police, who were now regarded as outsiders, or enemies threatening to upset their fragile world.

Implicit in this captor-captive relationship, Bejerot said, was the potential for a highly volatile sexual component that could even develop into romantic love. Such an "intense emotional impress can easily become so strong that it lasts years after the resolution of the drama; in principle it can last a lifetime."

But the concept of "Stockholm syndrome" was actually not part of the original Norrmalmstorg narrative. Bejerot did not make a single mention of it in his published accounts of the hostage crisis that autumn, nor, for that matter, in his unpublished reports to the police. The term does not appear, either, in the extensive coverage in the Swedish or international newspapers. Even a *New Yorker* piece as late as November 1974 made no mention of the phenomenon.

So how exactly did the concept of Stockholm syndrome as terror bonding or trauma bonding come into being?

ON FEBRUARY 4, 1974, PATRICIA HEARST, A BERKELEY ART HISTORY major and heiress of the William Randolph Hearst fortune, was kidnapped from her apartment by members of a fledging underground outfit that called itself the Symbionese Liberation Army. Two months later, she was filmed, a sawed-off M1 carbine slung over her shoulder, robbing a bank with her captors. In tape-recorded messages broadcast worldwide, Patty, who adopted the name Tania, denounced her family, the establishment, and the FBI. The story had become a sensation. She would be on the cover of *Newsweek* no fewer than seven times.

Despite the close association today, Stockholm syndrome did not figure into the lavish media coverage of this affair, either, at the time. Nor did the concept surface during the trial, when Patricia faced charges of armed robbery, kidnapping, and many other crimes.

But Patty Hearst was a textbook example of Stockholm syndrome, concluded Special Agent Thomas A. Strentz, a terrorism expert and founding member of the FBI's Behavioral Science Unit. Strentz had watched the disturbing case unfold and later questioned Hearst following her arrest in September 1975. Outside of the FBI, however, there were still only a few people who made any link between the disorienting role reversals that Patricia Hearst underwent and the reactions of the hostages in the bank vault at Norrmalmstorg.

One person who did make the connection was Dr. Frederick J. Hacker. An eminent Viennese-born psychiatrist with a high-profile Beverly Hills clinic, Hacker had served as an expert witness at the Charles Manson trial and as consultant to West German government leaders after the massacre at the Munich Olympics. Ten days after the Hearst kidnapping, Hacker had been called in to advise the family. He warned them that Patty might come to "think fondly of her captors." Sure enough, the tapes began to surface with her praising her assailants and denouncing authorities, much as the hostages had done in Stockholm.

Hacker also helped Patty's fiancé, Steven Weed, try to understand this puzzling behavior. Weed described their consultations in his memoir, *My Search for Patty Hearst*, published to coincide with the Hearst trial in early 1976. Hacker summed up his own view in his account the same year:

> There is no doubt that strange feelings of camaraderie, closeness, empathy, friendship, even love often develop between hostages and captors, between victims and victimizers.

This phenomenon, he added, was called the "Stockholm Effect."

After briefly reviewing the case at Norrmalmstorg, Hacker stressed that "strong feelings of belonging" had developed in a group forged by "a common danger"; that is, the police and the authorities who tried to rescue them. For the hostages, their "initial calculated acquiescence" to their captor had changed into what he called a "willing submission and [an] enjoyment of dependency." The captor—now group leader—enjoyed the aura of "charismatic omnipotence."

By the time Hacker published his overview of the case, the FBI was developing its own hostage negotiations program at its academy in Quantico, Virginia. Strentz and his boss, Conrad V. Hassel, chief of the Special Operations and Research Unit, had been investigating many hostage crises and barricade situations across the country. "We were looking for a strategy," Strentz said, and that led them to the pioneering work of the New York Police Department.

There, Dr. Harvey Schlossberg, police psychologist, and Capt. Frank A. Bolz

Jr., chief hostage negotiator, had created the world's first and most acclaimed hostage-negotiation program. Until his retirement in 1982, Bolz and his team would rescue no fewer than 850 people in 285 separate hostage and hijacking incidents without a single loss of life. They encouraged, whenever possible, what Schlossberg had come to call Stockholm syndrome.

Schlossberg coined the term, he said, "to help cops understand what went on in the Stockholm incident." If they failed to grasp the phenomenon, he added, "they would miss an important aspect of the dynamic for handling complex emotions and interactions of a hostage situation." Bolz agreed on the importance of this concept to the person being held captive. "You will not experience a mental breakdown, or become a traitor, if you get along with your captors. It is what will keep you alive."

Thomas Strentz designed the FBI curriculum with "Stockholm syndrome" incorporated into the training protocols. Strentz went on to write one of the early and influential papers on the subject, "Law Enforcement Policy and Ego Defenses of the Hostage," published in April 1979.

Strentz outlined the general pattern of hostage reactions that began with denial ("This is not happening"); the delusion of reprieve ("It will soon be over"); busywork (counting objects, personal grooming); and then a stage of "taking stock" (evaluating one's life or planning the future if given "a second chance"). It was usually at the end of these phases that the bonds of affection emerged. By that point, the captive will have accepted the new reality and spent more time with the captor.

"The Stockholm Syndrome," Strentz wrote, "is an automatic, often unconscious, emotional response to the trauma of becoming a victim." It most often meant, he added, regressing to a childlike state of dependency. The perpetrator wielded nearly supreme power over the victim. Every single breath becomes a gift, Strentz said.

Understanding the complicated psychological processes of Stockholm syndrome would help police plan effective rescue missions. At the same time, Strentz cautioned, the police would experience a new range of challenges with this strategy, not least in the insults and curses from the hostages themselves. Authorities had to persist. "A hostile hostage," Strentz concluded, "is the price that law enforcement must pay for a living hostage."

The FBI training course, taught by Strentz, would also build upon the work of Frank M. Ochberg, a Johns Hopkins and Stanford–trained psychiatrist at the National Institute of Mental Health. Ochberg had been drawn to the Norrmalmstorg hostage crisis because it was, as he put it, then "the top news story in the world." He went on to study a number of hostage situations in Europe between 1975 and 1977 as part of his role on the National Task Force on Disorders and Terrorism. It was through this experience that he met FBI Special Agent Conrad V. Hassel. "Study the victim," Hassel advised him. "We know enough about the perpetrators."

Based on his interviews and observations, Ochberg began to see patterns of behavior as hostages confront the stress of captivity. Stockholm syndrome, he concluded, represents "the most clearly identified and acknowledged 'unique' psychological reaction associated with terrorist victimization."

Ochberg identified three basic components at work in what came to be the most widely accepted definition of Stockholm syndrome: First, the hostage developed some sort of attachment to the captor. Second, the attacker reciprocated the sentiment to the point of wanting the hostage to survive. Third, both the captor and hostages ended up distrusting the police and authorities. As for the exact nature of this "victim/terrorist alliance," it did not really matter. It could be love, gratitude, or friendly affection, he said. Like Strentz, Ochberg advised detectives to look for these bonds and encourage their development. Time, patience, empathy, and compromise then help make the victim, as Janne put it, "hard to kill."

From the New York Police Department and the FBI Training Division, the concept of Stockholm syndrome would spread to police departments across the United States. Strentz, Hassel, Bolz, and their colleagues would also teach crisis negotiations and hostage survival strategies in more than two dozen countries around the world. Demand for this specialized training continued to grow, even after the 1970s heyday of hijacking, skyjacking, and hostage-taking had passed.

DESPITE THESE CONTRIBUTIONS, SIGNS OF SKEPTICISM ABOUT STOCKholm syndrome emerged early. In 1981, in a piece for the *Chicago Tribune*, investigative reporter Daniel S. Greenberg criticized the "schlock science parading about as certified scholarship," and took issue in particular with the experts suddenly raised to "talk-show celebrity by invoking Stockholm Syndrome."

By this time, it was already clear that many hostages emerged from the ordeal of captivity without feeling anything remotely like the Stockholm syndrome. Later studies confirmed its rarity. An examination of more than 4,700 cases in the FBI's Hostage Barricade Database System showed that 73 percent of the victims showed no sign of Stockholm syndrome. Other studies have found it absent in as many as 92 percent of hostage incidents.

This is not surprising. Stockholm syndrome, Bejerot explained in 1981, occurred primarily under a certain set of circumstances. It was most likely when the perpetrator was a professional criminal who valued his hostages as leverage in the bargaining process. There was little chance that Stockholm syndrome would develop if the hostage-taker was irrational, delusional, mentally unstable, or under the influence of hard drugs. Nor was it probable if the aggressor and his cohorts were fanatics who acted on behalf of a religious, political, or ideological cause.

Nearly a half century after Norrmalmstorg, Stockholm syndrome still regularly appears in media discussions of high-profile hostage and kidnapping incidents, but there have been surprisingly few academic studies on the subject. Stockholm syndrome was neither then, nor now, listed in any standard classification system of psychiatry. It is not recognized in the *Diagnostic and Statistical Manual of Mental Disorders* or the *International Statistical Classification of Diseases and Related Health Problems*. It has not received its own Medical Subject Heading in the National Library of Medicine either. The closest related phenomenon is probably Acute Stress Reaction, which involves "an experience of intense fear or horror while exposed to a traumatic (especially life-threatening) event."

A review of the existing scholarship prompted one team of researchers, publishing in *Acta Psychiatrica Scandinavica*, to conclude that Stockholm syndrome is more a media phenomenon than a proper psychiatric diagnosis. Other professionals, such as the Austrian clinical psychologist Michaela Gufler and the Canadian family therapist Allan Wade, have highlighted the concept's lack of an empirical and scientific foundation.

After all, is it really necessary to coin a syndrome to account for what might be more simply explained as a basic human instinct to survive?

The hostages at Norrmalmstorg faced the terrifying, high-stress ordeal of captivity. As Kristin put it, "a crazy man with a submachine gun and a large knife" had seized her. There was no chance to run or hide, let alone overpower him. What was she supposed to do? "Our only chance was to become [his] friends," she said. The other hostages would make similar statements. The best strategy, it seemed, was to remain calm and obey the robber.

Then the police entered the picture. Stationing sharpshooters around the lobby terrified the hostages. Refusing to listen to their pleas infuriated them. The police tried to drug them and then locked them in a vault with a gunman that several authorities had called "crazy" and later withheld food, water, and other necessities, launching into torturous drilling and threatening to pump in gas, knowing well that the hostages stood with their necks in nooses. It is perhaps not surprising that the hostages feared the police.

Such a fear may not be irrational at all. Four years after Norrmalmstorg, a comprehensive study of seventy-seven hostage situations between August 1968 and June 1975 found that no less than 79 percent of hostage deaths occurred when the police or security forces launched an offensive to overpower the captor.

What's more, there is the issue of how much information an expert needs to evaluate a situation and assess motivation. Dr. Bejerot had a rare vantage point to observe the hostages during the crisis and listen to their conversations in the vault. He did not, however, have the opportunity to interview the hostages afterward. At St. Göran's, when he tried to speak with Elisabeth, she screamed, "Get out!" Kristin also refused to speak with him. As for Sven, Bejerot *never* tried to speak with him.

Was this because he was a man?

Feminist psychologist Hanna Olsson and political scientist Cecilia Åse have criticized just such a gender bias underlying the concept. Stockholm syndrome, Olsson wrote, emphasizes "weak-willed women in relationship with strong men." If these vulnerable female hostages started questioning the male authorities, rather than just being grateful for their rescue efforts, then the easy and convenient conclusion was that they must have suffered from a "syndrome." The women could then be silenced and ignored while the police escaped responsibility for any questionable action.

There is another point that should be noted. At the heart of Stockholm syndrome is the emotional bond between captor and captive. Ironically, at Norrmalmstorg, where it all began, the strongest attachment formed in the vault was between Kristin and Clark. But Clark was not the one who had rushed into the bank and started seizing hostages. He was not the one who tied Kristin or her colleagues up and threatened to shoot them. He wasn't even in the bank when the nightmare ordeal began. When he did arrive, he came unarmed with words of hope and comfort.

Clark was, in short, not really the captor. That is a big difference—or as Clark put it, "a big fucking difference."

48

[Olof Palme] can thank me, really.

—Janne Olsson

I N AN ARTICLE IN THE DECEMBER 1973 ISSUE OF *ESQUIRE* MAGAZINE, the writer Tom Wolfe reflected on the art of the perfect crime. In the 1950s, it was a murder committed with a frozen leg of lamb, which would then be thawed, cooked, and devoured, perhaps sprinkled with parsley and served with green mint sauce. In the 1970s, it was hostage-taking. Rebels, outcasts, and desperadoes could, as the Stockholm bank drama had shown, even give orders to a head of government, and, in the process, turn the world upside down.

Newspaper sales during the hostage crisis soared to historic heights. *Expressen* increased its daily print run from 600,000 copies to more than 900,000. *Aftonbladet* jumped from 450,000 to about 700,000, a figure that would not be surpassed until September 11, 2001. Even more triumphant was Swedish television. Ratings broke all records with viewership during the Tuesday-night finale hitting an estimated 5,098,600 people—an astonishing 73 percent of the entire country.

For six days, Norrmalmstorg had been the most watched street corner in the world. The bank became a tourist destination. Sightseers streamed into the square on bike or on foot, pushing baby carriages or walking dogs. Some people posed for photographs and pressed their noses to one of the windows, hoping for a glimpse behind the thick curtains. Businesses cashed in on the craze. Long lines formed at Palmhuset, prompting one waitress to say that she had never seen such crowds there before. A worker at the tobacco store compared the crush of customers to a stampede.

Long after the police, media, and sightseers had left, Norrmalmstorg would remain a national sensation. Headlines continued for months regarding what *GT* called the "drama that shook the world." Two journalists envisioned turning the story into a children's play, set in a fairyland with trolls and princesses. The Italian magazine *Corriere dei Ragazzi* planned to publish a comic-book adaptation.* A French company wanted to shoot a film. A British team drafted a screenplay. Hollywood began to show interest. John Schlesinger, the Oscar-winning director of *Midnight Cowboy*, nearly inked a deal for a major motion picture.

Norrmalmstorg had shown the cinematic potential of captor-captive bonding, as it came to be understood, and "Stockholm syndrome" would have a long life in film, television, and popular culture. Malcolm McDowell, the star of Stanley Kubrick's *A Clockwork Orange*, already recognized the attraction of the material as he sat that August in a restaurant near Norrmalmstorg and marveled at the spectacle. "Not even Hollywood screenwriters, in their wildest imagination," McDowell said, "could envision the drama that is now playing out in the bank in the middle of Stockholm."

———

THE HIGH-STAKES THRILLER HAD CROWDED SIGNIFICANT ISSUES OFF the front pages and out of the agendas of news programs. There was only so much space in the public forums, and the sensational Stockholm siege had hogged a large part of it.

In 1974, Gothenburg University professor Jörgen Westerståhl calculated just how much. Evening newspapers *Aftonbladet* and *Expressen* devoted a daily average of 71 percent and 62.7 percent, respectively, of their entire news coverage to Norrmalmstorg. Television was even more lopsided. The first day of the crisis consumed 75 percent, with the amount increasing by the end to

———

* *Corriere dei Ragazzi*'s comic appeared in the fall of 1973 with certain liberties. Janne becomes "Jack Ollson," Clark slaps Birgitta in the face, "*Terrore . . . Violenza!*" The story culminates with a fight in the vault.

almost 90 percent. The national election, by contrast, had received between 0 percent and 0.8 percent.

All the while, many journalists, swept up in the hysteria, indulged in rumor and speculation. "Everything to create sensation," concluded author Per Wahlöö. They also, as *Aftonbladet* put it, "analyzed when there was nothing to analyze . . . [and] reported despite the fact there was nothing to report." Other common critiques that emerged from a Radio Sweden survey of its audience included repetition, the revelation of police strategies to the benefit of the robber, and an overall lack of coordination between the two television stations. Did both of them really have to broadcast live at Norrmalmstorg at the same time?

The coverage would have been different, media executives said, had they known in advance that the bank drama would last six days. Repeatedly, the story seemed to be on the verge of reaching its climax, and no one wanted to shut off the cameras too soon. Some critics went as far as to call Norrmalmstorg a pseudo-event, in the sense of being created by the media, though that seems overstated, given that the prime minister sat locked in his office for days, and six lives in the vault were at stake.

Once the reporters caught their breath, several people began to question how this unprecedented focus on a single "made-for-television" event might affect the election.

The first 130 of the 131 hours of the bank drama had served up a picture of chaos and lawlessness. On its final day, the tabloid *GT* published a caricature of Olof Palme, sitting hunched over at a desk, his head in his hands, and staring with concern at a calendar turned to Election Day, September 16. The caption read: "The Last Day as Prime Minister?"

After the rescue of the hostages, however, Palme would be inundated with praise. Supporters called him a true statesman and inspiration to the world. He deserved the Nobel Peace Prize, another admirer said. A third letter compared his crowning speech about the rule of law conquering violence to Martin Luther King Jr.'s "I Have a Dream."

Amidst the euphoria, however, some people detected a distinct vulnerability. Critics began to dismiss Palme's actual significance in the outcome and accused him of trying to take credit for what was essentially a police triumph. Given how fast Palme had raced to Norrmalmstorg to give his victory speech, one person said the prime minister should be recruited for the national track team. "There cannot be a faster guy in this country."

Such impressions were somewhat misleading, if also understandable, given how Palme had remained for long periods of time out of the spotlight. But the prime minister was, of course, much more involved in the hostage crisis than it had seemed. Just looking at the two decisions Palme *admitted*— the transfer of Clark from prison to Stockholm and the refusal to allow Janne to leave with the hostages—shows that he and his cabinet had set the overall strategic parameters within which the police had to operate.

On September 15, 1973, the night before the country went to the polls, Sweden received the news that king Gustaf VI Adolf had died. Olof Palme went on to win one of the most closely contested elections in Scandinavian history. In record-setting voter turnout that approached 91 percent, his Social Democratic Party won 43.6 percent of the vote. With the support of the Communists, Palme's coalition increased its total to 48.87 percent over the opposition block's 48.80 percent. The margin of victory was only 0.07 percent of the vote.

Norrmalmstorg had come along at the right moment for Olof Palme, many of his critics later said. The peaceful resolution of the hostage drama seemed to have tipped the balance in his favor. Indeed of all the factors that led to Palme's reelection, it is difficult to imagine that one of them was not Norrmalmstorg. Many voters had, in this time of turmoil, proved reluctant to change the government.

————

THE TRIAL OF JANNE AND CLARK BEGAN ON A SNOWY AND BITTER-COLD January 9, 1974, at Stockholm's Fifteenth District Court. Janne entered the packed courtroom with handcuffs and a police escort, sporting tinted glasses, a trimmed mustache, and a tight sweater that showed off his muscular physique. He sat down at his table, pulled something from his pocket, and set it in front of him. It was a small yellow teddy bear.

Attention turned to his co-defendant, Clark, whose case was more complicated. It was the police, after all, who had brought him to the crime scene, and there was considerable evidence that, even though he had not been an angel, he had tried to find a peaceful resolution to the standoff. All four hostages would take the stand. Few people, a *Svenska Dagbladet* reporter said, dared to remove their fur coats in the warm, stuffy room for fear of missing any of the details.

At the end of the first week of the proceedings, Clark stunned the court with an announcement: He had fired his lawyer and wanted to defend himself. Critics accused him of sabotaging the trial or turning it into a farce. This was, after all, his second defense lawyer since his arrest. One reporter asked the judge, Wilhelm von Schéele, how many times Clark could dismiss his counsel. "It gets harder each time," the judge said.

But as the trial went on into its second and third weeks, many people would praise Clark's performance. He was articulate and aggressive. He showed a command of the complexities of the case that sometimes eluded the prosecution or the witnesses he cross-examined. Clark relished the opportunity to grill the policemen, including the chief of police.

"I have not done anything criminal," Clark told the court.

What about the 40,000 crowns he had smuggled out of the bank? No one had been able to pin that on him.

Janne knew, of course, and may have already started to resent the fact. "I still have not received my share," he said, years later. Clark, in contrast, said that Janne had chosen to hide "his share" in the vault (the police indeed found a wad of ninety-nine 1,000-crown notes in a small gap between the top of the safety-deposit box cabinet and the wall).* Perhaps it was a dispute over the money that caused the relationship between Janne and Clark to fray. Name-calling and insults eventually flew from both sides until the two men severed all contact. The trial would be the last time they would be in the same room together as allies.

The verdict came on March 19, 1974. Janne was convicted of kidnapping, extortion, attempted extortion, aggravated assault, and robbery, as well as possession of an illegal weapon, and sentenced to ten years at the maximum security prison at Kumla. This effectively added seven years to the sentence he had been serving when he had fled. There was no conviction for attempted murder, which was the only charge he denied.

Clark was convicted of being an accessory to robbery and aggravated robbery, along with complicity to extortion. Clark appealed the decision, and once again defended himself. This time, however, the court ruled in Clark's favor on all counts.

---

* Janne admitted that he had concealed the money there, but the correct amount was not 99,000. It was 100,000. Someone on the police force must have pocketed the difference, he said.

EPILOGUE

Why are we mean to each other? We live such a short life.

—Sven Thorander

FOR SOME TIME AFTER NORRMALMSTORG, THE STOCKHOLM POLICE enjoyed overwhelming acclaim. Praise poured in from the crown prince Carl Gustaf, the Danish prime minister Anker Jørgensen, and police chiefs from Rotterdam to Oslo. Munich police psychologist Georg Sieber complimented the Swedish team for its expertise in *Der Spiegel*, and a police delegation from Hamburg came north to learn from their example. August 28, one person suggested to the prime minister, should be renamed "Police Day."

At a banquet in September 1973, Kurt Lindroth thanked his staff for their hard work and handed out more than fifty plaques to physicians, nurses, chemists, firemen, bank employees, and other civilians who had contributed to the rescue of the hostages. The psychiatrist, Dr. Bejerot, received a special award for his years of service. "The Stockholm police have undergone a trial by fire," Kurt Lindroth wrote in an internal memo, and thwarted "an act of terror without equivalence in our country."

One person who never received the recognition that he deserved was Morgan Rylander. He had been one of the first policemen to arrive on the scene and spent more time than any other officer with the gunman during the crucial first hours when a hostage crisis is most volatile and the risks of panic are at their height. He had established a good rapport with the nervous gunman and managed to free more than a dozen people trapped inside the bank. Then, suddenly, after being sent home on Saturday morning, Morgan found himself confronting rumors that he was a hotheaded maverick who disobeyed orders. He returned to Norrmalmstorg only to be ordered to leave. Morgan was stunned. His career started to suffer. It was only later that he realized what had happened.

Morgan knew some inconvenient facts that threatened the official narrative about the police operation. For one, Janne had never put a chokehold on any of the women hostages—the justification that the police used for their controversial decision to send Clark into the bank. For another, Morgan always insisted that Janne had been much more considerate to the hostages than the authorities claimed. The police leadership, in turn, accused Morgan of suffering from "trauma," much as the hostages were said to have Stockholm syndrome. Morgan disagreed. The only trauma he experienced, he said, was at the hands of his superiors. Angry at the way he was treated, Morgan transferred to security duty at Arlanda Airport, where he remained for eleven years before leaving the police force altogether.

Another person who paid a personal price for the success at Norrmalmstorg was Ingemar Warpefeldt, the police inspector who had been shot in the hand during the first minutes of the crisis. Despite several surgeries, his middle finger remained about two centimeters shorter and lost about half of its mobility. Pain was almost constant, and it was often difficult to sleep. Still, he was glad that he had refrained from firing at the gunman, because he hated the thought of accidentally hitting a hostage. Warpefeldt would never work again and missed his job immensely. His family watched with sadness as he lost strength and his optimism drained.

The other policeman who had been shot at Norrmalmstorg, Olle Abramsson, lost the ability to grip with his left hand. His thumb remained almost an inch shorter and his index finger crooked. For a long time, he had difficulty eating because he could barely open his mouth. Like Warpefeldt, Abramsson held no grudge toward Janne and accepted the injury as an inherent risk in his job. He returned to work in early 1974, and, three years later, began lecturing at the police academy.

As accolades for the Stockholm police continued to accumulate, Kurt Lindroth discreetly appointed a committee to study the case of Norrmalmstorg and make recommendations. The group finished its work in May 1974.

One proposal was to establish a professional media spokesman. Another was to create the *piketpolis*, a specialized force designed for a quick response to a crisis, and similar to the Special Weapons and Tactics (SWAT) teams first instituted by the Los Angeles Police Department. Many other suggestions were made to improve organization, communication, and training, along with devising contingency plans for future crises. "We have a lot to learn from the experiences at Norrmalmstorg," Lindroth said.

IN SEPTEMBER 1973, KREDITBANKEN PURCHASED ADVERTISEMENTS IN Stockholm papers announcing that it had finished repairing the lobby and bank vault at Norrmalmstorg. Customers were welcome back. The bank awarded Birgitta, Sven, Elisabeth, and Kristin extended sick leave, three months' vacation, and a stipend of 10,000 crowns. It went ahead with its plans to merge with Postbanken to become PK-Banken (and later Nordea). The Norrmalmstorg branch closed in 1974. The location serves today as a showroom for the Swedish clothing design company Acne Studios.

Birgitta was the first to leave St. Göran's clinic. She was also the first to give an in-depth interview about her experiences to the press. In early September, she sat outside her villa with her two young daughters playing in her lap as she described the horrors of captivity. Years later, Birgitta credited her family for helping her cope with the immense difficulties of transitioning back to a reality that did not involve an ever-present threat to her life.

The hope was to make sure that her nightmare of being detained against her will did not make her a fearful person. In fact, Birgitta later thought, Norrmalmstorg had made her stronger than before. "I believe that I know how it feels to die, since I have been so close," she said. Birgitta returned to the bank in October 1973 and worked there until her retirement thirty years later. She lives today with her husband in Stockholm.

Sven also went back to work at Kreditbanken. Several months after Norrmalmstorg, he visited Janne in prison and brought him a chess set. Sven later saw Clark, too, by chance at a nightclub. Clark sat at one of the most prominent tables, entertaining a group of people and, when he saw Sven, invited him to join them. "It was a friendly talk," Sven said, and when Clark left, he gave him his table.

Forty-five years later, Sven harbored no ill will against Janne or Clark. At times, Sven said, he had to remember that *they* were the bad guys. It often had not seemed that way at the time. He still had questions, by contrast, about some of the police decisions, such as locking the hostages in the vault with the gunman. For some time, Sven considered writing a memoir. His working title summed up his 131 hours as a hostage: "I do not know if I was afraid, but I did not feel very brave."

After his retirement from the bank in 2011, Sven started to pursue his lifelong interests in home decoration and design. He crafted a sleek umbrella stand and a soap dish with a stainless-steel mounting plate. His designs have been acclaimed. At the time of writing, Sven's soap dish is a finalist for a prestigious Swedish Design Award.

Elisabeth and Kristin became friends after the Norrmalmstorg hostage crisis. In the fall of 1973, they took a vacation together to the island of Cyprus. The tabloids shadowed them from the beach to the nightclub. United Nations soldiers lined up to ask them to dance. It was a much-needed relaxation, but recovery from the stresses of captivity would not be an easy or quick process for either of them.

Elisabeth handed in her notice at Kreditbanken and moved back home with her family. "I shook, I cried, I prayed; it was awful," Elisabeth later said, describing her memories of the vault. At the trial, she was still fighting off feelings of terror and would long be plagued by nightmares. She went back to school and retrained as a nurse.

For some time, Elisabeth would speak out about her experiences. She gave interviews to several national and international papers. For the Swedish magazine *Se*, Elisabeth did a photo shoot with Kristin, where the two women posed in the lobby of the bank, examining the repaired ceiling after Janne's submachine-gun salvo. In another one, she and Kristin hold hands in the vault. Such experiences eventually became too much. Like Sven, she grew reluctant to speak with journalists. She let it be known that she did not wish to be contacted anymore about those terrible days at Norrmalmstorg that she just wanted to forget.

Kristin returned briefly to work at Kreditbanken in the autumn of 1973, but she, too, found the experience more difficult than she had expected. Her fear began almost as soon as she entered the building. She avoided the lobby as much as possible. Any number of sights or sounds could induce panic, such as someone lingering too long, or simply wearing a gray hood that she associated with Norrmalmstorg. She called it "a robber jacket."

Kristin would also suffer from nightmares. At home, she found herself wanting the lights on and interior doors open. She avoided cinemas and subways. Elevators brought back memories of the vault. Sirens from emergency vehicles made her flinch. After Norrmalmstorg, Kristin had become, she said, "afraid of being so afraid again."

For the first five years or so, Kristin thought of the hostage crisis virtually every day. Still today, memories of the ordeal come to her about once every week or two. She does not hold any grudge against Olof Palme after their telephone conversation. "I wanted to get out. I wanted to go away. I wanted to come home," Kristin said. There was not much the prime minister could have said to comfort her, and she respected him for taking her call. Kristin now agrees with Palme that letting the hostages leave the bank with Janne and Clark would not have been the ideal solution. But on one matter she had not changed her mind: the police's use of gas. She regards it as "attempted murder."

For years, talk of the Norrmalmstorg drama or the Stockholm syndrome would cause Kristin to freeze up, stare at the floor, and concentrate on her breathing. The term "Stockholm syndrome" was, forty-five years later, still not one that she liked. It made her feel that she was being viewed as sick— that is, as if she had indeed suffered from a "syndrome." She felt like she had done something wrong, or was being blamed for something. With time, however, she began to realize that that was not the case. She had carried out a strategy that had probably maximized her chances of surviving a terrifying ordeal.

All these experiences, at the same time, increased Kristin's desire to understand the root causes of crime. By the spring of 1974, she started pursuing a degree in social work. She gained valuable experiences working in a youth home and a night shelter, the latter frequented by many prostitutes and heroin addicts. Kristin specialized in psychotherapy and today runs a flourishing family therapy practice in Stockholm. She aims "to listen to those whom no one listens and respect those whom no one respects." In this way, Kristin gives her patients a dignity that, at Norrmalmstorg, far too often had been denied to her.

———

DESPITE HIS VICTORY IN THE COURTROOM, CLARK STILL, OF COURSE, had to serve out the remainder of his sentence that the bank drama had interrupted. He went back to his familiar prison activities of reading, writing, and plotting future action. In 1975, Clark escaped from Norrköping, robbed a bank in Copenhagen, and made his way to the French Riviera. He bought a sailboat and sailed for seven months around the Mediterranean before heading west to the Azores and then north to the British Isles.

In March 1976, with the police still in pursuit, Clark committed the largest single-person bank robbery in Swedish history at Svenska Handelsbanken in Gothenburg, making off with 930,000 crowns. The police caught up with him carousing in a hotel bar. That summer, only weeks after his latest sentencing, Clark escaped again. A group of his friends, wielding machine guns, had crashed a truck through three sets of prison gates, and spirited him and three other prisoners away to a waiting car. Once again, the predictable media circus ensued.

Clark would spend the next four decades in and out of prison. Convictions followed in 1980 for a knife attack and in 1984 for smuggling amphetamines, a charge that Clark adamantly denied. Upon release in 1991, Clark changed his name and moved to Belgium, with his new Belgian wife, Marijke, the daughter of a prominent businessman and member of the Demuynck tennis family. They had met at a train station in Germany on one of his flights from prison.

Vast sums of money flowed in—and out. Clark drove a string of flashy sports cars and lived, for a time, in a large villa that one visitor compared to a castle. Clark invested over the years in a wide variety of markets, including gold, diamonds, and high-yield Swiss bonds. The initial capital, he said, came from the money from the Gothenburg bank robbery, more than three-fourths of which had never been recovered.

In 1998, Clark was arrested in the Canary Islands on charges of smuggling amphetamines into Denmark and was sentenced to the strictest drug-trafficking punishment meted out at that time in Scandinavia. Clark, however, was released in 2005, only to be arrested in Sweden three years later on charges of smuggling amphetamines and cannabis from Holland.

Back in prison, Clark kept on reading Montaigne, Nietzsche, and Schopenhauer, as well as history and biography. He has written several books in Swedish, including three memoirs. One of them, *The Lottery of Justice*, depicts a judicial system in disarray, with the courtroom as a glorified casino in which the defendant draws a lot and hopes the draw comes his way.

In August 2018, at the age of seventy-one, Clark was released from prison. Reporters, photographers, and camera crews, once again, were waiting. Clark drove away to an undisclosed location in Sweden, where he lives today.

A FEW WEEKS LATER, I WAS ON MY WAY TO CLARK'S CURRENT ADDRESS.
We had spoken on the phone a few times, and he had invited me over to talk. We'd hang out by the pool, Clark said, and "I'll answer whatever the fuck you want."

After arriving in Stockholm, I booked a train and then flagged a taxi. Clark had told me to bring GPS or I'd never find him. The taxi driver drove us down one long country road after another. I could have flown here for less, he joked.

We pulled up to a white house behind large privacy fences. I could see that there was a swimming pool in the back. This seemed to fit the description. I walked up and knocked. No one answered. My phone did not have service out there. But the taxi driver loaned me his phone and I called Clark's mobile.

He would be right back, Clark said. "Go on inside, and make yourself some coffee."

Before I finished talking with the taxi driver, a large SUV came roaring around the corner. Out stepped Clark, tall and broad-shouldered. His hair and beard were now graying. He wore small-rimmed glasses, a black T-shirt, and black jeans. He looked young and energetic, and spoke in rapid-fire sentences that packed a punch.

That Clark was charismatic was no surprise. A few people, however, had warned me to be careful. He could be charming, but then all of a sudden become dangerous. I was advised to meet him only in public.

We went inside his house and sat down at a table in a room near the pool. We talked for hours. Norrmalmstorg, prison breaks, soccer, philosophy, writing. A guitar in the corner prompted talk of music. He had blasted Fleetwood Mac as he left prison one time. What album? *Rumours*, "the best record ever made." He also enjoys Merle Haggard, Johnny Cash, and Chet Atkins. As for the guitar, Clark had not played in many years. "I have been on 'vacation,'" he said.

Our talk was a free-ranging affair with no subject off-limits. Clark retold the story of Norrmalmstorg, replacing the names of some participants with monikers along the lines of "And then the idiot did this," or "the monkeys" (the police) did that. Clark laughed at the Stockholm police for actually turning him loose in the bank. It was like releasing a fox in a hen house, he said, and the situation for them "went from bad to worse."

From time to time, we'd take a break and go outside by the swimming

pool. It was a marvelous summer day. We talked of his attempted escape at
Kalmar, his telephone call with Janne at the prison office, his drive to Stockholm, his strategy in the bank, and so on. Clark introduced me to some of his
friends who arrived at the house. One of them had served time in prison for
his alleged involvement in another famous Swedish crime in which a group
of people stole a helicopter, landed it on the roof of a cash service depot, and
then smashed their way through its glass ceiling.

Clark and I went back inside the house.

Did he really hum Roberta Flack's "Killing Me Softly with His Song"
in the vault? I asked. Yes, he had, though he had almost forgotten. He then
started singing it for me. "It was not appropriate," he added, laughing.

With his intelligence and charm, it was perhaps easy to forget that he
was one of the country's most notorious outlaws of the last century. "A scruffy
Scandinavian mixture of Jesse James and Warren Beatty," one reporter said.
"The King of the Underworld," said another. Clark's face had adorned T-
shirts; his rebellious stance had raised him to a counterculture icon and sold
millions of newspapers over the years, penetrating even behind the Iron
Curtain. The Soviet Union's *Pravda*, for one, had written approvingly as he
attacked one arch-capitalist institution after another.

Bank robberies, prison escapes, and many, many other ventures—
Norrmalmstorg is clearly only one part of Clark's life, and actually a small
one at that. But it is a part about which he should be pleased. Even if Clark
had wanted to take advantage of the situation, very likely to get away with
the money, all four hostages affirmed that his arrival had been a source of
real comfort. He had eased the tension for everyone, including Janne, and
thereby reduced the risk of panic. Clark's contributions, moreover, were done
at considerable risk to himself, and the significance of his impact should not
be underestimated. Clark had been vital in preventing the bank drama from
turning into a tragedy.

What did he think about Norrmalmstorg after all these years, I asked.

Clark answered, as usual, without hesitation. "Fuck, it was very fun."

———

AT THE MAXIMUM-SECURITY PRISON AT KUMLA, JANNE PASSED HIS DAYS
between the workshop, the weight-lifting area, and his cell. It was in prison
that Janne developed a new interest in writing.

He began by answering letters from his pen pals, hour after hour, but he soon came to enjoy putting his thoughts on paper. His ambitions grew. He started to work on a memoir and later fiction. Writing, he said, helped him cope with life in prison.

One of his pen pals was a young teacher from northern Sweden named Gunilla. She started visiting him and then attended his trial. In 1975, Janne and Gunilla were married at the small prison chapel. The judge who had presided over his trial, Wilhelm von Schéele, performed the ceremony. Curiously, Kurt Lindroth, Sven Thorander, and Dr. Bejerot came to the wedding. Their attendance was controversial. More than sixty police officers signed a letter of protest and sent it to the minister of justice, Lennart Geijer. Geijer's response? He said he would have gone to the wedding, too, had he been invited. Together, Lindroth and Thorander gifted the newlyweds a painting. Dr. Bejerot gave a speech. These men had come to respect Janne and wanted to support his rehabilitation.

Janne was released on October 1, 1980, three years early, for good behavior. He was determined, as he had stated at the trial, to break away from crime for good. By this point, he had spent a total of almost twenty of his thirty-nine years in prison. That was enough.

Over the years, Janne would take up a wide variety of jobs. He bred pigs in southern Sweden; he made cabinets and doors in a town in the north; he taught judo for a while; later, when he and Gunilla returned to Helsingborg, Janne started fixing and selling used cars. At times, it was difficult to make ends meet.

The biggest challenge came with relinquishing the dream of pulling off the supreme heist that would lead to instant financial independence. He also missed the sheer excitement of the deed, not to mention the camaraderie of working with old friends who came with various schemes promising quick, easy cash. Sometimes these proposals were tempting, especially when money was tight, but Janne persevered.

"Sooner or later, you come to a crossroads," Janne said, "and my crossroads was at Norrmalmstorg."

Janne and Gunilla eventually went their separate ways, and divorced amicably. In 1989, Janne met Phian, a young woman from Thailand, and they were married. "She means everything to me," Janne said. In 1996, they moved to Thailand. Janne opened a grocery store in a village in the northeast, near the border with Laos. He purchased land, cultivated rice, raised cows and water buffalo, and became a Buddhist.

Many times over the years, Janne has been asked if he felt any remorse about the hostage crisis. Such feelings do no good, he said, but he admitted that he had made many mistakes in his life and foremost among these was Norrmalmstorg. He had no right, he said, to put those innocent people through so much suffering. "If I could rewind the tape to 1973, or 1960," Janne said, he would have channeled his restless energies into his interest in automobiles and "become a big car dealer." There was one other thing he would change: "I would not have spent a single day behind bars."

In 2011, Janne and Phian moved back to his hometown of Helsingborg. They purchased a property, a former flower shop, which they have renovated and Phian has redecorated. Janne today operates a used-car dealership.

———

IN SEPTEMBER 2018, I EXITED THE TRAIN STATION AT HELSINGBORG. THE weather was cool and overcast. Scanning the line of taxicabs and other vehicles outside the main entrance, my eye fell on a man sitting at the wheel of a gray car, smiling and waving. It was Janne Olsson.

He greeted me warmly. He scooped up my backpack with ease and tossed it into the back of his car. We went to eat at a Chinese restaurant around the corner. The staff treated him with much respect as we sailed through the dining room to a table of his choice. We talked about Norrmalmstorg, safe cracking, judo, cars, and the Thai language, which he speaks after having lived in Thailand for fifteen years. Time flew as we talked. He ate his chicken and rice, using a fork and spoon, a habit he had picked up in Thailand.

On our way back to his house, Janne pointed out various landmarks in his life, such as where he started his first car lot and where he had opened a big safe. I had been told that Janne would be stiff, formal, and intimidating. That was not at all my experience. There was a lot of laughter and genuine warmth.

He showed me photos of his children. He has nine. One is a lawyer, a second a policeman, and three have been members of a well-known motorcycle gang. His youngest son, Sakda, came in at one point to help Janne locate more pictures on his hard drive to show me. He was muscular and tattooed. When he left, Janne made sure I saw his shiny white Mercedes parked out front.

We spent most of the time in his office. A portrait of the king of Thailand hung on the wall behind his desk. We talked about how he had planned for Norrmalmstorg, down to the wig, makeup, and submachine gun, which he had purchased for 800 crowns. Janne retraced his movements inside the bank, marking them on a copy of the lobby's blueprint that I had brought.

"The party starts!" Janne said, repeating his lines at the opening of the bank drama for me. It was the first time I had heard him speak in English. His voice carried well and I could imagine it in the marbled lobby.

Janne told me where he had planned to go, had he and Clark gotten away, as he had always thought that they would. They would have driven to a certain spot where Janne had a sailboat waiting, and then made their way to France. I believed him. I had examined the map that he had brought with him to the bank. It was kept along with other objects that the police had retrieved from the crime scene in a warehouse outside of Stockholm. Sure enough, a route traced in red marker leads from Norrmalmstorg to a boathouse near the capital.

Hour after hour we talked. No subject had been out of bounds. As the day drew to a close, Janne ducked around the corner and came back with a present: Copies of two novels he had written and printed in Thailand. They told the fictionalized adventures of a resourceful criminal named "Janne Fräckis," a nickname, I remembered, that the police had given him for his ability to evade capture. He signed the books for me: "Janne, the Norrmalmstorg Robber."

Janne offered to drive me back to the train station. He took off at a fast clip, racing through the streets and around corners, as if pursued by the police. Occasionally he would slow down. "Cameras," he said, and pointed. There was a sense of play and an obvious enjoyment at beating the system. He then promptly gunned it again as we passed out of range.

ACKNOWLEDGMENTS

T O SPEND MORE THAN THREE YEARS OF FULL-TIME RESEARCH ON A six-day event has been a privilege and it is a pleasure to thank the people who made it possible. First, I would like to thank my agent, Suzanne Gluck, at William Morris Endeavor. She believed in the story from day one, when I first proposed it in 2012, and gave it such incredible support that once again proves that she is the best agent on the planet. My editor, John A. Glusman at W. W. Norton, showed immediate enthusiasm for the project and wonderfully improved the narrative with his insight. It is an honor, a privilege, and a sheer delight to work with John, and his influence, as always, has been extraordinarily beneficial.

There has never been a book on the Norrmalmstorg hostage crisis or the birth of Stockholm syndrome in the English language, or, for that matter, any other language besides Swedish. This is the first time, too, that both Janne Olsson and Clark Olofsson have been interviewed for the same book project, and I appreciate their support, especially as their own relationship has become strained, to say the least. Janne picked me up at the train station in Helsingborg, Sweden, showed me around his business and home, and gave me copies of novels he had written in Thailand. He answered all my questions without restriction or impatience, and never once tried to discourage me from pursuing any part of this story. Clark was extremely open from our first telephone call and invited me over to his place to speak more in person, promising to show me hospitality. He certainly did! He could not have been more generous in sharing his memories and reflections about the bank drama, and he let me examine his collection of photographs and newspaper clippings from decades in the headlines. Kristin Enmark and Sven Säfström went out of their way to help me understand the crisis at Norrmalmstorg, and answered all of my questions, no matter how difficult or painful it must have been to relive this experience as hostages. I am grateful for their generosity and their trust, as I know they usually refuse interview requests. Sven also gave me a copy of the notes he had written in the vault, and kindly read this manuscript to help me get the details of the six-day ordeal as correct as possible. I can't say how much all this wonderful support and encouragement mean to me, and the way everyone welcomed me into their lives is truly inspiring.

The Stockholm police files, to which I was given full access, offered a trove of valuable information. In addition to many hours of testimony from all the main people involved in the crisis, from hostages to policemen— many of the latter are no longer alive—this archival collection contained photographs, technical analysis of the crime scene, and indispensable transcripts from the bugged conversations in the vault. The police files were supplemented by the court records and the verbatim trial transcript. Morgan Rylander gave me his unpublished account of his experiences at Norrmalmstorg, which proved to be a vital source, and he spent many hours talking with me about his time in the bank lobby with the gunman and the hostages. Thanks, too, to Olli Kärki for relaying Morgan's earliest answers to my questions and sending along recorded elaborations, when Morgan was ill, and to Kristin Andersson for sending me additional commentaries from Morgan, along with photographs of him during his career. I appreciate all of Morgan's support. Another police officer who paid a high price for his contributions at Norrmalmstorg, Olle Abramsson, collected material for years about the hostage drama. His scrapbook was a valuable source with no lack of surprises. At one point, I opened a small envelope and found the bullet that surgeons had removed from him after the shooting.

Invaluable, too, was the rare 16 mm film footage from the Stockholm police and SÄPO. It captured not only the moment Janne, Clark, and the hostages left the vault, but also the police work in the lobby, the atmosphere on the bank's second floor, and many other vignettes of "everyday life" in the Norrmalmstorg hostage drama that would not ordinarily make their way into police reports, crime scene analyses, or radio, television, and newspaper coverage. The film footage also contained a reconstruction of the crime itself, along with images of the vault immediately after the siege. I knew from references in the police reports and the press that a short, edited film had existed at one point, but there was no sign of it in the archives of police and court files. It was, I later discovered, housed in a warehouse outside Stockholm—and it was with great excitement that I was able to watch the film and learn that there existed not just the edited version, but also raw footage from around the bank and the square. Special thanks to Jani Pellikka for allowing me access to this rich visual source, and for letting me examine the many objects the Stockholm police had retrieved from the crime scene at Norrmalmstorg. Among them were Janne's wig, his sunglasses, his radio, his canvas bag, and pieces of the drilled vault ceiling. Even Janne's toothbrush and the nooses were there, as was the lamp that the police lowered into the vault, with the microphone still attached. All this physical evidence has helped me understand the setting of the bank drama and complemented the dialogue, which, many times, was taken from the bugged conversations and recorded telephone calls. I am grateful for all of Jani's expertise, which he generously shared, and his help has been enormous.

I would like to thank the archivists and librarians at Stadsarkivet, Kungliga Biblioteket, Riksarkivet, and Polis Museet, for their help facilitating my work in Stockholm. Arkivarie Johanna Törnros welcomed me at Stadsarkivet with a professionalism that made it such a valuable and pleasant place to work. I was humbled, too, when Stadsarkivet, at one point, named me "researcher of the month." Such a warm reception meant a great deal to me, as I spent time away from my family on research trips to Sweden—two of my birthdays, it turned out. Kungliga Biblioteket, once again, proved to be another wonderful environment for conducting research. It housed not only many rare journals, such as the in-house communications for Radio Sweden's personnel, but also many other primary and archival sources that are difficult to obtain in the United States. I benefitted in particular from the Swedish television and radio archives, where the professional, friendly team made sure that I had a quiet room to watch hour after hour of the original broadcasts as well as go through the raw film footage, when the cameras were pointed at the bank, the square, or the getaway car, waiting for something to happen. As with the police film and the artifacts from the crime scene, this important visual source and commentary from reporters helped me understand the atmosphere that prevailed at Norrmalmstorg as well as the reasons why this story would, by its end, capture an estimated 73 percent of the country's audience.

I felt nostalgic returning to Stockholm where I spent some time in the 1990s and recall how I used to walk through Norrmalmstorg almost every day, without realizing the full extent of the drama that took place in this square. Kreditbanken is today the main branch of Swedish fashion house Acne Studios. Despite many changes, the general layout was immediately recognizable. One of the old vaults—not the customer safety deposit vault— is now a changing room. On one of the floors above, in a locker room at the Nobis Hotel Stockholm, you can still see where the police drilled into the vault. Thanks to Jonna Oxell and Adam Qvist at Acne Studios and Matt Ruiz at Nobis Hotel for their hospitality. I would particularly like to thank Helen Ardelius for sharing her knowledge about Norrmalmstorg and her notes from her interviews for her 1998 Swedish radio documentary *Norrmalmstorgsdramat*. It was wonderful to sit as we did, hour after hour, at the Norrmalmstorg restaurant, formerly known as Palmhuset, trading stories about the hostage crisis that had taken place just a few steps away.

In addition to the police files, court documents, and the extensive media coverage, as well as memoirs and my interviews, official investigations helped me sort through the successes and shortcomings of the affair. These include studies made by a parliamentary group (Riksdagens konstitutionsutskott, KU 1974:22), the Stockholm police (Arbetsgruppen, May 2, 1974, PHM: 1831, PM), the Justice Department (*Promemoria angående händelserna i samband med bankrånet vid Norrmalmstorg den 23 augusti 1973*), and "the people's judgment," as I pored over the large volume of mail that Prime Minister Olof Palme received (Statsrådsberedningen 1973, Statsministerns Korrespondens E I: 169, RA). The letters and telegrams—lavish in both praise and criticism—came from all over Sweden, as well as Denmark, Norway, Germany, Holland, Britain, and elsewhere. I would also like to thank the FBI Academy at Quantico for loan of library material, and Dr. Harvey Schlossberg, retired police psychologist of the New York Police Department, for answering my questions about how he came to coin the term "Stockholm syndrome."

My interviews and research in the archives benefitted from the work of many journalists, Swedish and foreign, radio, television, and newspaper, who poured into Norrmalmstorg to cover the story, hour after hour, day and night. Kungliga Biblioteket has an unsurpassed collection of newspapers from all over Sweden, as well as many from around Europe, along with the radio and television archives cited above. Several journalists wrote quick, short, though valuable, books or long essays in Swedish in the months after the crime: Börje Heed, Carl Olof Bernhardsson, and a special issue of Pockettidning R (Nummer 1, Årgång 4 [1974]), edited by Hans Nestius and Stig Edling, and published at the end of Janne and Clark's trial. These were followed by Professor Jörgen Westerståhl's study of the media coverage, a New Yorker article by Daniel Lang, and a 1977 sociological analysis by Gert Nilsson, half of which was devoted to Norrmalmstorg. Clark Olofsson did not participate in any of these projects, but he elaborated a great deal on his actions at the trial, along with writing a concise, insightful account in a 1977 issue of Nordisk Kriminalpolis (vol. 3, nr 1). This issue, edited by Ingemar Krusell, was another valuable source, as was the 1983 retrospective in the same journal, also edited by Krusell. It is a pleasure to acknowledge other journalists and researchers whose work I have also enjoyed and benefitted from, such as Helen Ardelius's above-cited Swedish radio documentary: Stig Edling's documentary on Clark Olofsson, Folkhems Desperadon (2001), Mikael Hylin's Norrmalmstorgsdramat inifrån (2003), Per Svensson's Dramat på Norrmalmstorg 23 till 28 augusti 1973 (2003), which he published with Håkan Lindhé, and an SVT1 episode of Veckans brott with Leif G. W. Persson and Camilla Kvartoft. Two other brief yet valuable accounts are Eric Rönnegård's Norrmalmstorgsdramat: den sanna historien (2013), particularly his own reflections based on his experiences as a policeman in the lobby, from his arrival on Saturday of the crisis, and Cecilia Åse's study Kris! Perspektiv på Norrmalmstorgsdramat (2014), with chapters featuring reflections on social contact, nationalism, and media theory. Thanks, too, to the producers of the upcoming Swedish television documentary on Clark Olofsson for enjoyable, informative conversations and for filming part of one of my interviews with Clark on the bank drama.

In addition to the treasured support of Suzanne Gluck and John Glusman, cited above, I would like to thank Helen Thomaides at W. W. Norton, Andrea Blatt at WME in New York, and Anna DeRoy at WME in Beverly Hills. Thanks to my longtime friend, Amitabh Chandra of Harvard University's John F. Kennedy School of Government for guidance in rendering 1973 Swedish krona to today's US dollar, and to Jeffrey Toobin at The New Yorker for information on the Patricia Hearst defense strategy at the trial. Thanks to my friends Peter Baniak and Linda Blackford of the *Lexington Herald-Leader* for advice on conducting interviews on complex, sensitive subjects. Thanks, too, to Gunnar Wesslén for sharing his memories about Norrmalmstorg and 1970s Stockholm over many enjoyable hours of conversations over coffee and wine—Gunnar had many exclusive interviews in the 1970s and 1980s and, had he not been away on vacation in August 1973, he would have had another scoop because Janne tried to call him before he made his move at Norrmalmstorg. Henrik Ericsson used his expertise at blowing up things to help me understand the explosives that powered Clark's escape attempt at Kalmar and Janne's threats in the bank vault. I would like to thank Joakim Berglund at Bilder i Syd in Malmö for his enthusiastic help, particularly for finding high-quality images. Pär Levander and Jacob Levander came bearing armfuls and sometimes suitcases full of Swedish books, and I always enjoyed their visits. Special thanks to my mother-in-law Annika Levander, who remembered Norrmalmstorg so vividly and believed in this story so strongly. I cherish her encouragement and would love to have shared this book with her. It is a pleasure, too, to thank Raymond F. Betts, David Olster, Jane Vance, Wanda Rodgers, and many other great teachers who have played such a formidable role in my life, and, of course, to my first teachers, my parents, Van and Cheryl King. My mom read the entire manuscript and made many helpful comments. It was heartwarming to hear that this might now be her favorite of my books.

"What is it with you and Sweden?" one of my Norwegian friends, Per-Ole Bratset, teased me, when he learned of this project. It is a good question. I would like to thank the J. William Fulbright Scholarship and the American-Scandinavian Foundation Fellowship for allowing me to spend almost two years in Sweden many years ago. These experiences certainly deepened my appreciation for the country, which I had already become fascinated with from my earlier brief visits. Of course, there is another, more important reason for my interest: My wife, Sara, who is Swedish. This is the first book I have written that originated from a suggestion, and it is fitting that it came from Sara. I liked the prospect immediately, but the more I thought about it, the more I realized that this was a really good idea. Sara was, as always, my first reader, and she made many helpful comments to improve the narrative, while also checking some of my translations from the original Swedish archives and interviews. Thanks again for all your help with this book and, even more, for all the joy you bring to my life! Our children, Julia and Max, have almost grown up with this story: Julia, now a high schooler and an enthusiastic vegan, enjoys yoga, art, and violin, while Max, now in middle school, still terrorizes soccer opponents with his goal-scoring wizardry. It is with much joy and, at the same time, not a little sadness, that I reach the end of this rewarding research journey, by saying, once again, thank you for being there, with all my love.

NOTES

ARCHIVES

KB Kungliga Biblioteket, Stockholm
PM Polismuseet, Stockholm
RA Riksarkivet, Stockholm
SA Stadsarkivet, Stockholm

CHAPTER 1

1 **"The day Stockholm":** *Aftonbladet*, August 24, 1973.
1 **"The party starts!":** Stockholms Tingsrätt Avd. 15:1 DB 248, Mål nr B 541/73, 13, SA.
2 **"Get up!":** Birgitta Lundblad, *Samtal*, August 29, 1973, Stockholms Tingsrätt Avdelning 15 Akter i brottmål B 541 del 2 Aktb. 40–42 1973 G1: 218, 257, SA.
2 **He seemed to be crazy:** Kristin Enmark, author interview and Helsinki's *Hufvud-stadsbladet*, August 24, 1973.
2 **At 10:02 a.m.:** *De Polisiära Insatserna i Samband med Norrmalmstorgshändelserna 23–28 augusti 1973, del 1/2*, PHM: 1831, PM.
2 **A small gathering of people:** Ingemar Åhman, *Protokoll över förhör*, Stockholms Tingsrätt Avdelning 15 Akter i brottmål B 541 del 1 Aktb. 1–39 1973 G1: 217, 184, SA.
3 **sounded like he was speaking German:** Torgny Wallström, *Protokoll över förhör*, August 24, 1973, Stockholms Tingsrätt Avdelning 15 Akter i brottmål B 541 del 1 Aktb. 1–39 1973 G1: 217, 180, SA.

3 **"What a fucking long time"**: Bo Nilsson, *Protokoll över vittnesförhör*, August 23, 1973, Förundersöknings Protokoll, Del 5, Stockholms Tingsrätt avdelning 15, B 541/73, G1 219, 146, SA.

3 **One of these police officers . . . The gunman, turning quickly:** Ingemar Warpefelt, *Protokoll över förhör*, August 24, 1973, Stockholms Tingsrätt Avdelning 15 Akter i brottmål B 541 del 1 Aktb. 1–39 1973 G1: 217, 192, SA, along with his interviews in *Svenska Dagbladet*, August 24, 1973, *Dagens Nyheter*, August 24, 1973, and on television, Rapport: Bankrånet i Sveriges Kreditbank, Norrmalmstorg, Stockholm, TV2, 1973–08–23 14.23–15.45, SMDB, KB. This scene also draws on the eyewitness accounts of the police officers on the stairs, as well as the police reconstruction in Teknisk Utredning, Del 3, Stockholms Tingsrätt Avdelning 15 Akter i brottmål B 541 del 2 Aktb. 40–42 1973 G1: 218, SA.

4 **"Yes, I am"**: Ingemar Warpefeldt, *Förhör*, January 29, 1974, GG Band 9, Stockholms Tingsrätt Avdelning 15 Akter i brottmål B 541 del 4 Aktb. 43–130 1973 G1: 219, 318, SA.

CHAPTER 2

5 **"When I realized"**: Bo Nilsson, *Protokoll över vittnesförhör*, August 23, 1973, Förundersöknings Protokoll, Del 5, Stockholms Tingsrätt Avdelning 15, B 541/73, G1 219, 146, SA.

5 **comparisons to John F. Kennedy:** Kjell Östberg, *När vinden vände. Olof Palme 1969–1986* (Stockholm: Leopard, 2012), 73, and Henrik Berggren, *Underbara dagar framför oss. En biografi över Olof Palme* (Stockholm: Norstedts, 2010), 315.

5 **Palme oozed too much affluence:** Claes Arvidsson, *Ett annat land. Sverige och det långa 70-talet* (Stockholm: Timbro Förlag, 1999), 42.

6 **one of the richest and most advanced economies:** Tony Judt, *Postwar: A History of Europe Since 1945* (New York: Penguin Books, 2005), 367.

6 **"land of tomorrow"**: Hans L. Zetterberg, *"Sweden: A Land of Tomorrow?"* in Ingemar Wizelius (ed.), *Sweden in the Sixties* (Stockholm: Almqvuist and Wiksell, 1967). For more on images of Sweden at this time, see Marie Cronqvist, Lina Sturfelt, and Martin Wiklund (eds.) *1973. En träff med tidsandan* (Lund: Nordic Academic Press, 2008).

7 **The bullet had entered:** Handkir. klin., Serafirmerlasarettet, October 15, 1973, Stockholms Tingsrätt Avdelning 15 Akter i brottmål B 541 del 1 Aktb. 1–39 1973 G1: 217, 196, SA.

7 **Blood dripped:** Ingemar Warpefeldt, interview, SVT, TV2 1979–09–29 21:00:00–21:43:55, Engman Kl 9, SMDB, KB.

7 **Beads of sweat:** Bo Nilsson, *Protokoll över vittnesförhör*, August 23, 1973, Förundersöknings Protokoll, Del 5, Stockholms Tingsrätt Avdelning 15, B 541/73, G1 219, 147, SA.

8 **"Bo," he told him:** Nilsson, *Protokoll*, and *Förundersökningsprotokoll Rånöverfall med Tagande av Gisslan i Sveriges Kreditbanks lokaler vid Norrmalmstorg i Stockholm 23.8–28.8* (1973), Stockholms Tingsrätt Avdelning 15 Akter i brottmål B 541 del 1 Aktb. 1–39 1973 G1: 217, 12, SA.

8 **"What's happening?"** . . . **He was adjusting the ropes:** Morgan Rylander, *Norrmalmstorgsdramat 23 till 28 augusti 1973*, Morgan Rylander Collection and Morgan Rylander, author interview.

9 **"Do you only speak"** . . . **"No, I am not":** Rylander, *Norrmalmstorgsdramat*, and Morgan Rylander, *Förhör*, February 8, Stockholms Tingsrätt Avd. 15:1, Band 17, B 541/73, G1: 220, 216, SA.

9 **"What's your name?":** Rylander, *Norrmalmstorgsdramat*, Rylander, *Förhör*, and Morgan Rylander, *Protokoll över förhör*, September 3, 1973, Stockholms Tingsrätt Avdelning 15 Akter i brottmål B 541 del 1 Aktb. 1–39 1973 G1: 217, 198, SA.

9 **the equivalent of the pre-tax income:** *Aftonbladet*, August 24, 1973.

9 **appeared to smile:** Janne Olsson's account, *Pockettidningen R* (1974), Årg 4, Nr. 1, 20.

9 **the country's most infamous criminal:** For more on the general view of Clark as the country's "most dangerous bank robber," see Ingemar Krusell "Norrmalmstorgsdramat i tioårigt perspektiv," *Nordisk Kriminalpolis*, Årg. 8, Nr 2 (1983), 77.

CHAPTER 3

10 **"Who I am does not matter":** SVT, Bankrånet i Sveriges Kreditbank, Norrmalmstorg, Stockholm, 1973–08–24, SMDB, KB.

10 **most influential opinion-makers:** Undated *GT* article, Clark Olofsson Collection.

10 **Six by his own count:** Clark Olofsson, author interview.

10 **"If you do not risk anything":** Clark Olofsson, *Vafan var det som hände?* (Livonia: Bokförlaget Upp med Händerna, 2015), 294.

11 **"Have you seen that":** Per Svensson i samarbete med Håkan Lindhé, *Dramat på Norrmalmstorg 23 till 28 augusti 1973* (Stockholm: Bonnier Fakta, 2003), 37.

11 **His father, Sten:** Clark Olofsson, *Personblad*, Stockholms Tingsrätt Avdelning 15 Akter i brottmål B 541 del 2 Aktb. 40–42 1973 G1: 218, 539, SA.

11 **"My enemies":** Clark Olofsson och Brita Lang, *Texter om Herr M:s Samhällsnyttiga Verksamhet* (Uddevalla: FörfattarFörlaget, 1977), 65.

11 **His favorite subject** . . . **"I like any kind of philosopher":** Clark Olofsson, author interview.

11 *The Concrete Paper: Betongbladet*, Julnummer 1 December 1970, Clark Olofsson Collection. The newspaper received more coverage that fall, such as *Aftonbladet*, August 24, *Dagens Nyheter*, August 25, 1973, and *Västmanlands Nyheter*, September 6, 1973.

11 **one journalist said:** Svensson (2003), 103.

11 **an international terrorist:** Rapport: Bankrånet i Sveriges Kreditbank, Norrmalmstorg, Stockholm, TV2, 1973–08–23 14.23–15.45, SMDB, KB, and policemen cited also in *Dala-Demokraten*, August 24, 1973.

12 **Janne's father:** Jan-Erik Olsson, *Levnadsberättelse*, September 3, 1973, Stockholms Tingsrätt Avdelning 15 Akter i brottmål B 541 del 2 Aktb. 40–42 1973 G1: 218, SA.

12 **She taught him to dance:** Janne Olsson, *Stockholmssyndromet. En självbiografi* (Telegram, 2009), 44.

12 **Janne liked music, sports:** Åke Olsson, interview, *Se*, September 6, 1973.

12 **Taking a job** . . . **In all honesty:** Olsson (2009), 51–53, 67–68, with reference to his "lawyer" in *Aftonbladet*, November 21, 1973.

13 **Janne had purchased:** *Förundersökningsprotokoll Rånöverfall med Tagande av Gisslan i Sveriges Kreditbanks lokaler vid Norrmalmstorg i Stockholm 23.8–28.8* (1973), Stockholms Tingsrätt Avdelning 15 Akter i brottmål B 541 del 1 Aktb. 1–39 1973 G1: 217, 8–9, SA.

13 **Avon bronzing powder:** The makeup in his bag, held today by PM in a warehouse outside of Stockholm.

13 **thirty-six shots:** *Bilaga C:1*, 1973–09–03, Teknisk Utredning, Brottsplatsundersökning, Del 3, Stockholms Tingsrätt Avdelning 15 Akter i brottmål B 541 del 2 Aktb. 40–42 1973 G1: 218, 93, SA.

13 **An older woman:** Olsson (2009), 12, and Janne Olsson in *Pockettidningen R* (1974), Årg 4, Nr. 1, 19.

CHAPTER 4

14 **"Ugh, how incredibly easy":** *Pockettidningen R* (1974), Årg 4, Nr. 1, 33.

14 **"Gun Girl":** *Daily Mirror*, August 24, 1973, and as symbolic of the affair, *Dagens Nyheter*, August 24, 1973.

14 **"Miss Sharpshooter":** *Expressen*, September 9, 1973.

14 **she thought he was cute:** Kristin Enmark, *Jag blev Stockholmssyndromet. Valvet, föraktet och mitt kärleksförhållande med Clark Olofsson* (Livonia: Ordupplaget, 2015), 19, and Kristin Enmark, author interview.

14 **less than half a minute:** Kristin Enmark, author interview.

15 **thin as an ink pen:** Bo Nilsson, *Protokoll över vittnesförhör*, August 23, 1973, Förundersöknings Protokoll, Del 5, Stockholms Tingsrätt Avdelning 15, B 541/73, G1 219, 158, SA.

15 **Kristin had enjoyed . . . vodka and Coca-Cola:** Kristin Enmark, author interview.

15 **She recalled the day . . . she thought of her family:** Enmark (2015), 20–21 and 25–26.

16 **Kristin had no idea, at the time:** Kristin Enmark, *Samtal*, August 29, 1973, Stockholms Tingsrätt Avdelning 15 Akter i brottmål B 541 del 2 Aktb. 40–42 1973 G1: 218, 303, SA. She later realized that she and her coworkers had been selected because they were women. Kristin Enmark, author interview. Their age as a factor comes from Janne Olsson, author interview.

16 **Janne sent Morgan to a black leather:** Morgan Rylander, *Norrmalmstorgsdramat 23 till 28 augusti 1973*, Morgan Rylander Collection.

16 **"Now you got your chance":** Morgan Rylander, *Protokoll över förhör*, September 3, 1973, Stockholms Tingsrätt Avdelning 15 Akter i brottmål B 541 del 1 Aktb. 1–39 1973 G1: 217, 199, SA.

16 **There had been an attempted rape:** Börje Heed, *Gentlemanna-Rånaren?* (Bromma: Williams Förlag, 1973), 12.

16 **"the real-life Martin Beck":** Per Svensson i samarbete med Håkan Lindhé, *Dramat på Norrmalmstorg 23 till 28 augusti 1973* (Stockholm: Bonnier Fakta, 2003), 26.

16 **He arrived at Norrmalmstorg:** *De Polisiära Insatserna i Samband med Norrmalmstorgshändelserna 23–28 augusti 1973*, del 1/2, PHM: 1831, PM.

17 **"What, does he know me?"**: Sven Thorander interview in *Lektyr,* June 26–July 2, 1978.

17 **"Stop right there!"** . . . **"especially desperate"**: *Promemoria angående händelserna vid Kreditbanken, Norrmalmstorg,* Stockholms Tingsrätt Avdelning 15 Akter i brottmål B 541 del 1 Aktb. 1–39 1973 G1: 217, 203–204, SA.

17 **"Spell it"**: *Förundersökningsprotokoll Rånöverfall med Tagande av Gisslan i Sveriges Kreditbanks lokaler vid Norrmalmstorg i Stockholm 23.8–28.8* (1973), Stockholms Tingsrätt Avdelning 15 Akter i brottmål B 541 del 1 Aktb. 1–39 1973 G1: 217, 13, SA.

17 **Thorander was beginning to think**: Sven Thorander, *Förhör,* February 6, 1974, Stockholms Tingsrätt Avd. 15:1, Band 16, B 541/73, G1: 220, 190, SA.

18 **At one point that morning**: Thorander's name is mentioned in several radio clips in the file that begins at 11 a.m., Sveriges Radio, Nyhetsstudion [Norrmalmstorgsdramat] 1973–08–23 11.00, SMDB, KB.

18 **"Thorander, that's you!"**: *Promemoria angående händelserna vid Kreditbanken, Norrmalmstorg,* Stockholms Tingsrätt Avdelning 15 Akter i brottmål B 541 del 1 Aktb. 1–39 1973 G1: 217, 205, SA.

18 **"You will not see"**: Sven Thorander, *Förhör,* February 6, 1974, Stockholms Tingsrätt Avd. 15:1, Band 16, B 541/73, G1: 220, 174 SA.

CHAPTER 5

19 **"One fine day"**: Börje Heed, *Gentlemanna-Rånaren?* (Bromma: Williams Förlag, 1973), 23, with the timing of the conversation in his *Anförande hållet vid presskonferensen i Jönköping i april 1974,* PHM: 1831, PM.

19 **"Clark could be quite charming"** and **"gangster buddy"**: Janne Olsson, *Stockholmssyndromet. En självbiografi* (Telegram, 2009), 23.

19 **The plan was**: Fångvårdsanstalten Kalmar, *Olofssons Rymningsförsök i Kalmarfängelset . . . teknisk undersökning med fotobilagor,* 1973–08–20, Stockholms Tingsrätt Avdelning 15 Akter i brottmål B 541 del 1 Aktb. 1–39 1973 G1: 217, SA; Olofsson (2015), 276–93, Olsson (2009), 24–27, Gunnar Wesslén, author interview, and *Aftonbladet,* August 23, 1983.

20 **on another occasion, she recalled**: Janne later denied it, but at least two hostages remembered hearing it, as did the police, *De Polisiära Insatserna i Samband med Norrmalmstorgshändelserna 23–28 augusti 1973, del 2/2,* PHM: 1831, PM. The movie was still showing in Stockholm, as advertised in *Aftonbladet,* August 23, 1973.

21 **"on a silver platter"**: Olsson (2009), 28.

21 **called his supervisor**: *De Polisiära Insatserna i Samband med Norrmalmstorgshändelserna 23–28 augusti 1973, del 1/2,* PHM: 1831, PM.

21 **The robber, however, preferred**: *Promemoria angående händelserna vid Kreditbanken, Norrmalmstorg,* Stockholms Tingsrätt Avdelning 15 Akter i brottmål B 541 del 1 Aktb. 1–39 1973 G1: 217, 204, SA.

21 **he whistled, told impromptu**: Morgan Rylander, *Protokoll över förhör,* September 3, 1973, Stockholms Tingsrätt Avdelning 15 Akter i brottmål B 541 del 1 Aktb. 1–39 1973 G1: 217, 200, SA.

21 **Elvis Presley's "Lonesome Cowboy":** Janne Olsson, author interview, and Morgan Rylander, author interview.

21 **"something completely unexpected":** Morgan Rylander, *Norrmalmstorgsdramat 23 till 28 augusti 1973*, Morgan Rylander Collection.

CHAPTER 6

22 **"We have experienced indeed":** SVT, Bakom rubrikerna. Vad gjorde massmedia på Norrmalmstorg? 1973–09–20, SMDB, KB.

22 **"Some robbers have barricaded"** and **"serious crisis":** Nyhetsstudion [Norrmalmstorgsdramat] 1973–08–23 11.00, SMDB, KB.

22 **one of Sweden's first media events:** Cecilia Åse, *Kris! Perspektiv på Norrmalmstorgsdramat* (Stockholm: Liber, 2014), 37–38.

23 **decided to send the idling TV bus:** Hans Hernborn in *Pockettidningen R* (1974), Årg 4, Nr. 1, 21.

23 **He would not leave:** Bo Holmström, *Lägg ut! Episoder ur ett journalistliv* (Stockholm: Natur & Kultur, 2011), 92.

23 **Traffic in the city center:** *Dagens Nyheter*, August 24, 1973.

23 **an occupied city:** *Svenska Dagbladet*, August 24, 1973.

23 **more like a battlefield:** *Expressen*, August 23, 1973.

24 **"There are people lying there"** . . . **"Let them out!":** Morgan Rylander, *Norrmalmstorgsdramat 23 till 28 augusti 1973*, Morgan Rylander Collection. See also Morgan Rylander, *Förhör*, February 8, Stockholms Tingsrätt Avd. 15:1, Band 17, B 541/73, G1: 220, 223–24, SA.

24 **the robber and his captives disappeared:** *De Polisiära Insatserna i Samband med Norrmalmstorgshändelserna 23–28 augusti 1973, del 1/2*, PHM: 1831, PM.

24 **Elisabeth poked her head up:** Elisabeth Oldgren, *Samtal*, September 6, 1973, Stockholms Tingsrätt Avdelning 15 Akter i brottmål B 541 del 2 Aktb. 40–42 1973 G1: 218, 362, SA.

25 **181931:** Elisabeth Oldgren, *Protokoll över förhör*, August 29, 1973, Stockholms Tingsrätt Avdelning 15 Akter i brottmål B 541 del 2 Aktb. 40–42 1973 G1: 218, 353, SA. This was correct, *Förundersöknings Protokoll, Del 5*, Stockholms Tingsrätt Avdelning 15 Akter i brottmål B 541 del 3 Aktb. 43–130 1973 G1: 219, 162, SA.

25 **"the world's worst desperado":** Elisabeth Oldgren, *Protokoll över förhör*, August 29, 1973, Stockholms Tingsrätt Avdelning 15 Akter i brottmål B 541 del 2 Aktb. 40–42 1973 G1: 218, 353, SA.

25 **yellow sweater, green skirt:** *Bilaga K2*, Teknisk Utredning, Brottsplatsundersökning, Del 3, Stockholms Tingsrätt Avdelning 15 Akter i brottmål B 541 del 2 Aktb. 40–42 1973 G1: 218, 117, SA.

25 **verifying a check:** Birgitta Lundblad, *Samtal*, August 29, 1973, Stockholms Tingsrätt Avdelning 15 Akter i brottmål B 541 del 2 Aktb. 40–42 1973 G1: 218, 257, SA.

25 **"the desperado":** Aktuellt: Bankrånet i Sveriges Kreditbank, Norrmalmstorg, Stockholm TV1, 1973–08–23 21.30–22.42, SMDB, KB.

26 **It was the first time:** Sven Thorander interview, *Lektyr*, June 26–July 2, 1978.

26 **asked for a cigarette . . . set the receiver down:** *Promemoria angående händelserna*

vid Kreditbanken, Norrmalmstorg, Stockholms Tingsrätt Avdelning 15 Akter i brottmål B 541 del 1 Aktb. 1–39 1973 G1: 217, 205–207, SA, and Sven Thorander, *Förhör*, February 6, 1974, Stockholms Tingsrätt Avd. 15:1, Band 16, B 541/73, G1: 220, 197–98, SA.

CHAPTER 7

27 **"I had absolutely nothing to run to"**: Clark Olofsson, *Vafan var det som hände?* (Livonia: Bokförlaget Upp med Händerna, 2015), back cover, 15–16.

27 **a bowl of pea soup**: Evald Olle Helmer Ivarsson, *Protokoll fört vid förhör*, September 6, 1973, Stockholms Tingsrätt Avdelning 15 Akter i brottmål B 541 del 1 Aktb. 1–39 1973 G1: 217, 217, SA.

27 **"Can't I at least"** . . . **"What is this about"**: Ivarsson, *Protokoll*. In some versions, Clark received the message in the exercise yard, but I have drawn on the accounts given by the guard, the interim prison director, and Clark himself at the trial. See, for instance, the testimony of Gunilla Arnerdal, February 6, 1974, Stockholms Tingsrätt Avd. 15:1, Band 16, B 541/73, G1: 220, 98, SA.

27 **"Oh yeah, who?"** . . . **Clark wondered**: Clark Olofsson, *Vafan var det som hände?* (Livonia: Bokförlaget Upp med Händerna, 2015), 295.

28 **"Do you want to come to my party"**: Olofsson (2015), 296, and Olsson (2009), 16.

28 **Clark grunted, mumbled** . . . **"What is this?"**: Gunilla Arnerdal, *Protokoll fört vid förhör*, September 6, 1973, Stockholms Tingsrätt Avdelning 15 Akter i brottmål B 541 del 1 Aktb. 1–39 1973 G1: 217, 213, SA.

28 **"the bedtime stories"** . . . **he had never thought**: Clark Olofsson, author interview.

28 **"precautionary measure"**: Justitiedepartementet, *PM angående händelserna I samband med bankrånet vid Norrmalmstorg den 23 augusti 1973*, 1974–01–22, PHM: 1831, PM. See also Ulf Bjereld, *Och jag är fri: Lennart Geijer och hans tid* (Stockholm: Atlas, 2015), 197–98.

29 **"You are not going to believe me"**: Olofsson (2015), 297. The guard Evald Olle Helmer Ivarsson also remembered Clark yelling across the yard to an inmate, *Protokoll fört vid förhör*, September 6, 1973, Stockholms Tingsrätt Avdelning 15 Akter i brottmål B 541 del 1 Aktb. 1–39 1973 G1: 217, 218, SA.

29 **"to balance on a knife's edge"**: Clark Olofsson, author interview.

30 **Officials at Norrköping Prison refused**: Justitiedepartementet, *PM angående händelserna i samband med bankrånet vid Norrmalmstorg den 23 augusti 1973*, 1974–01–22, PHM: 1831, PM.

30 **"We cannot send him"**: Gunilla Arnerdal, *Protokoll över telefonförhör*, October 16, 1973, Stockholms Tingsrätt Avdelning 15 Akter i brottmål B 541 del 1 Aktb. 1–39 1973 G1: 217, 215, SA.

30 **an irate telephone call**: *PM med vissa uppgifter angående regeringens åtgärder i samband med bankdramat vid Norrmalmstorg i Stockholm i augusti 1973*, KU 1974:22, 187, and more from the man who made the call, Ove Rainer, *Makterna* (Stockholm: P.A. Norstedt & Söners Förlag, 1984), 56–57.

30 **Around 1 p.m.**: Bror Axel Molin, *Skriftlig Berättelse*, October 18, 1973, Stock-

232 NOTES

holms Tingsrätt Avdelning 15 Akter i brottmål B 541 del 1 Aktb. 1–39 1973 G1: 217, 219, SA.

30 **Photographers and camera crews:** Rapport och Extra Rapport: Norrmalmstorgs-dramat 1973–08–23, TV Sändning, SMDB, KB.

30 **Did the police really think:** Olofsson (2015), 300–301, 306, 309.

30 **During the ride:** This draws on the account by Clark Olofsson as well as the police officers in the car, Bror Axel Molin, Jan Christer Högberg, Lars-Inge Johansson, and Tore Selevik. Molin's account is cited above, and the others are also at Stockholms Tingsrätt Avdelning 15 Akter i brottmål B 541 del 1 Aktb. 1–39 1973 G1: 217, SA, and Clark Olofsson, author interview.

CHAPTER 8

32 **"Personally, I believed":** Kurt Lindroth, interview in *Pockettidningen R* (1974), Årg 4, Nr. 1, 95.

32 **By noon, a reporter:** *Aftonbladet*, August 24, 1973. The crowd is already widely noted, for instance, *Dagens Nyheter*, August 24, 1973, *Upsala Nya Tidning*, August 24, 1973, *Östgöta Correspondenten*, August 24, 1973.

32 **they looked on the action:** *Svenska Dagbladet*, August 24, 1973.

32 **The chief of police, Kurt Lindroth, had arrived:** *De Polisiära Insatserna i Samband med Norrmalmstorgshändelserna 23–28 augusti 1973, del 1/2*, PHM: 1831, PM.

32 **"the kind policeman":** *Aftonbladet*, August 29, 1973.

32 **the police kept hearing:** One of them was the future Swedish criminologist and best-selling author, Leif G. W. Persson.

33 **Kaj, it was also said:** Information from one of Kaj's close friends, Nicolaas Cleyn-dert, *Protokoll fört vid förhör*, August 24, 1973, Stockholms Tingsrätt Avdelning 15 Akter i brottmål B 541 del 1 Aktb. 1–39 1973 G1: 217, 243, SA.

33 **"Guys, I think you should cut it out" . . . the most dangerous moment:** Morgan Rylander, *Norrmalmstorgsdramat 23 till 28 augusti 1973*, Morgan Rylander Collection, and Morgan Rylander, author interview. Radio Sweden on people passing police lines, Nyhetsstudion [Norrmalmstorgsdramat] 1973–08–23, SMDB, KB.

34 **the police decided to send in the ransom:** *Förundersökningsprotokoll Rånöverfall med Tagande av Gisslan i Sveriges Kreditbanks lokaler vid Norrmalmstorg i Stockholm 23.8–28.8* (1973), Stockholms Tingsrätt Avdelning 15 Akter i brottmål B 541 del 1 Aktb. 1–39 1973 G1: 217, 16, SA.

34 **Janne laughed:** Morgan Rylander, *Protokoll över förhör*, September 3, 1973, Stock-holms Tingsrätt Avdelning 15 Akter i brottmål B 541 del 1 Aktb. 1–39 1973 G1: 217, 199, SA.

34 **cut open the bag:** Morgan Rylander, *Förhör*, February 8, Stockholms Tingsrätt Avd. 15:1, Band 17, B 541/73, G1: 220, 227, SA.

34 **Janne soon allowed more people:** *De Polisiära Insatserna i Samband med Norr-malmstorgshändelserna 23–28 augusti 1973, del 1/2*, PHM: 1831, PM.

34 **"The robber had kind eyes":** *Expressen*, August 24, 1973.

35 **pointing to a small wastebasket:** Janne Olsson, author interview.

35 **the motivation was rather straightforward:** Birgitta Lundblad, *Samtal*, Septem-

ber 3, 1973, Förundersöknings Protokoll, Telefonavlyssning, Förhör, Övrige Avlyssningar mm, Stockholms Tingsrätt Avdelning 15 Akter i brottmål B 541 del 4
Aktb. 131–60 1973 G1: 220, 90, SA, and Kristin Enmark, author interview; Sven,
by contrast, saw it more as an unthinking mechanism, like the action of a "robot,"
but he came later and under different circumstances, author interview.

35 **a lobby with police officers hiding:** Kristin Enmark, *Samtal*, September 5, 1973,
Stockholms Tingsrätt Avdelning 15 Akter i brottmål B 541 del 2 Aktb. 40–42 1973
G1: 218, 309, SA, and Elisabeth Oldgren, *Protokoll över förhör*, August 29, 1973,
Stockholms Tingsrätt Avdelning 15 Akter i brottmål B 541 del 2 Aktb. 40–42 1973
G1: 218, 355, SA.

35 **"iron ring":** Extra Rapport: Bankrånet i Sveriges Kreditbank, Norrmalmstorg,
Stockholm TV2, 1973–08–23 13.25–14.20, SMDB, KB. The police used this description in the internal communication, *Våra Interna Aktualiteter i Stockholmspolisen*,
August 24, 1973, PHM: 1831, PM, as did other observers, such as Helsinki's *Hufvud-
stadsbladet*, August 24, 1973.

35 **"Here at Norrmalmstorg"** . . . **"We are prepared":** Extra Rapport: Bankrånet i
Sveriges Kreditbank, Norrmalmstorg, Stockholm, TV2, 1973–08–23 13.03–13.23,
SMDB, KB.

35 **"The tense, nervous expectation":** Extra Rapport: Bankrånet i Sveriges Kreditbank, Norrmalmstorg, Stockholm TV2, 1973–08–23 13.25–14.20, SMDB, KB.

35 **"do something"** . . . **"There are people sitting":** Morgan Rylander, *Norrmalmstorgsdramat 23 till 28 augusti 1973*, Morgan Rylander Collection, and Morgan
Rylander, author interview.

36 **Clark's caravan:** Justitiedepartementet, *PM angående händelserna i samband med-
bankrånet vid Norrmalmstorg den 23 augusti 1973*, 1974–01–22, PHM: 1831, PM.

37 **"Kaj Robert Hansson":** Account of this scene draws on the testimony of Ernst
Ahlbäck, Henry Bohjort, L-E Andersson, and Jonny Jonsson, Stockholms Tingsrätt
Avdelning 15 Akter i brottmål B 541 del 1 Aktb. 1–39 1973 G1: 217, SA, as well as
Clark Olofsson, *Vafan var det som hände?* (Livonia: Upp med Händerna, 2015), 302–
305, and his earlier account, "Klarspråk om Norrmalmstorg," *Nordisk Kriminalpolis*,
Årg. 3, Nr 1 (1977), 166–167.

37 **Worse, Clark suspected:** Clark Olofsson, author interview.

37 **"game over":** Olofsson (2015), 301.

37 **"That was unnecessary"** and **"You do not have to say":** Olofsson (2015), 305.

CHAPTER 9

38 **"In this decisive moment":** *Smålandsposten*, August 24, 1973.

38 **an already-scheduled press conference:** SVT, Rapport: Bankrånet i Sveriges
Kreditbank, Norrmalmstorg, Stockholm, 1973–08–23 23.56–00.10, SMDB, KB.

38 **Palme spoke too long:** *Svenska Dagbladet*, August 24, 1973.

39 **About a quarter after four o'clock:** *Rånöverfallet med Tagande av Gisslan i Sveriges
Kreditbank vid Norrmalmstorg i Stockholm den 23–28 augusti 1973*, Stockholms Tingsrätt Avdelning 15 Akter i brottmål B 541 del 1 Aktb. 1–39 1973 G1: 217, 167, SA.

39 **a fashionable blue-and-white sweater:** Bilaga J, *Förundersökningsprotokoll*,

Teknisk Utredning, Brottsplatsundersökning, Del 3, Stockholms Tingsrätt Avdelning 15 Akter i brottmål B 541 del 2 Aktb. 40–42 1973 G1: 218, 113, SA.

39 **"scruffy Scandinavian mixture":** John Vinocur, AP in *Herald Tribune*, August 10, 1976.

39 **"do a good deed":** Clark Olofsson, "Klarspråk om Norrmalmstorg," *Nordisk Kriminalpolis*, Årg. 3, Nr 1 (1977), 167–169, and Clark Olofsson, *Vafan var det som hände?* (Livonia: Upp med Händerna, 2015), 309. The scene also draws on the testimony of the other known people in the room: Kurt Lindroth, Sven Thorander, Nils Bejerot, and Jonny Jonsson, as well as police reports, including *De Polisiära Insatserna i Samband med Norrmalmstorgshändelserna 23–28 augusti 1973, del 1/2*, PHM: 1831, PM, and Clark Olofsson, author interview.

39 **"brain trust":** Olofsson (2015), 309.

39 **three weeks of freedom:** Clark Olofsson, author interview.

40 **heard on the radio that Clark had arrived:** Ingemar Krusell, "Norrmalmstorgsdramat i tioårigtperspektiv," *Nordisk Kriminalpolis*, Årg. 8, Nr 2 (1983), 79.

40 **"She is screaming.":** Stockholms Tingsrätt Avd. 15:1 DB 248, Mål nr B 541/73, 30, SA. See also *PM med vissa uppgifter angående regeringens åtgärder i samband med bankdramat vid Norrmalmstorg i Stockholm i augusti 1973*, KU 1974:22, 187, 189–90.

40 **to the chat staircase:** John Jonsson, *Promemoria*, Stockholms Tingsrätt Avdelning 15 Akter i brottmål B 541 del 1 Aktb. 1–39 1973 G1: 217, 228, SA; Kurt Lindroth, *Förhör*, February 6, 1974, Stockholms Tingsrätt Avd. 15:1, Band 16, B 541/73, G1: 220, 164–66, SA and Olofsson (2015), 311–12.

40 **"he is crazy enough to do anything":** Håkan Larsson, *Förhör*, February 1, 1974, Stockholms Tingsrätt Avd. 15:1, Band 16, B 541/73, G1: 220, 14, SA.

CHAPTER 10

41 **"If the police had been as cutthroat":** Clark Olofsson, *Vafan var det som hände* (Livonia: Bokförlaget Upp med Händerna, 2015), 314–15.

41 **Elisabeth dismissed it as false:** Elisabeth Oldgren, *Protokoll över förhör*, August 29, 1973, Stockholms Tingsrätt Avdelning 15 Akter i brottmål B 541 del 2 Aktb. 40–42 1973 G1: 218, 356, SA.

41 **it most certainly did not happen:** Morgan Rylander, author interview, Morgan Rylander, *Förhör*, February 8, Stockholms Tingsrätt Avd. 15:1, Band 17, B 541/73, G1: 220, 232, SA, and also in his notes, *Norrmalmstorgsdramat 23 till 28 augusti 1973*, Morgan Rylander Collection.

41 **Clark remembered the incident:** This scene has been doubted as too convenient for the police, but Clark also confirmed someone did come in with the news. Clark Olofsson, "Klarspråk om Norrmalmstorg," *Nordisk Kriminalpolis*, Årg. 3, Nr 1 (1977), 169, as well as in Olofsson (2015), 310, and Clark Olofsson, author interview. Other people in the room, including Nils Bejerot and Jonny Jonsson, recalled it as well; all three on February 6, 1974, *Förhör*, February 6, 1974, Stockholms Tingsrätt Avd. 15:1, Band 15 och 16, B 541/73, G1: 220, 129–31, 144–45, 164, SA.

42 **"We had more important things":** Börje Heed, *Gentlemanna-Rånaren?* (Bromma: Williams Förlag, 1973), 31, and *Aftonbladet*, January 9, 1974.

42 **Clark scanned the lobby:** Elisabeth Oldgren, *Samtal*, September 6, 1973, Stockholms Tingsrätt Avdelning 15 Akter i brottmål B 541 del 2 Aktb. 40–42 1973 G1: 218, 366, SA.

42 **"Are you a cop?"** . . . **"He is with us":** Morgan Rylander, *Förhör*, February 8, 1974, Stockholms Tingsrätt Avd. 15:1, Band 17, B 541/73, G1: 220, 227–28, SA.

43 **had inadvertently come to resemble Kaj:** Clark Olofsson, author interview.

43 **"Shaggy" and "What the hell":** Janne Olsson, *Stockholmssyndromet. En självbiografi* (Telegram, 2009), 18.

43 **huddled off to the side:** Morgan Rylander, *Protokoll över förhör*, September 3, 1973, Stockholms Tingsrätt Avdelning 15 Akter i brottmål B 541 del 1 Aktb. 1–39 1973 G1: 217, 201, SA.

43 **Janne nodded a few times:** Morgan Rylander, *Förhör*, February 8, Stockholms Tingsrätt Avd. 15:1, Band 17, B 541/73, G1: 220, 228, SA.

CHAPTER 11

44 **"For too long, we have had":** Harri Miekkalinna, *Dagens Nyheter*, December 30, 1973.

44 **Three large bags of cash:** Clark Olofsson, author interview with photograph of them at PHM: 1831, PM.

44 **Automatic carbines with riflescopes:** *De Polisiära Insatserna i Samband med Norrmalmstorgshändelserna 23–28 augusti 1973, del 1/2*, PHM: 1831, PM, and Kurt Lindroth, Transl.LH, PHM: 1831, PM.

44 **dumdum bullets:** Eric Rönnegård, *Norrmalmstorgsdramat: den sanna historien* (Stockholm: Jure Förlag, 2013), 40, with origin of the name in Irvin K. Owen, "What About Dumdums?" *FBI Law Enforcement Bulletin* 44, no. 4, April 1975.

45 **Morgan believed that he could reenter the bank:** Morgan Rylander, *Norrmalmstorgsdramat 23 till 28 augusti 1973*, Morgan Rylander Collection.

45 **the missing police officer:** Torgny Wallström, *Protokoll över förhör*, August 24, 1973, Stockholms Tingsrätt Avdelning 15 Akter i brottmål B 541 del 1 Aktb. 1–39 1973 G1: 217, 180, SA; Extra Rapport: Bankrånet i Sveriges Kreditbank, Norrmalmstorg, Stockholm, TV2, 1973–08–23 13.25–14.20 and TV2, 1973–08–23 14.23–15.45, SMDB, KB.

45 **"a ticking bomb":** Clark Olofsson, *Vafan var det som hände?* (Livonia: Upp med Händerna, 2015), 314. He used this description in particular for Morgan Rylander, whom he suspected carried a gun, as indeed he did, Morgan Rylander, author interview. Clark was in danger that afternoon, Ingemar Krusell, "Norrmalmstorgsdramat i tioårigt perspektiv," *Nordisk Kriminalpolis*, Årg. 8, Nr 2 (1983), 89.

45 **Clark estimated:** Clark Olofsson, author interview.

46 **A police officer with a view:** Erik Allan Johansson, *Protokoll över förhör*, September 5, 1973, Stockholms Tingsrätt Avdelning 15 Akter i brottmål B 541 del 1 Aktb. 1–39 1973 G1: 217, 237, SA.

46 **"They smelled good":** Janne Olsson, author interview.

46 **he bent it out of proportion:** *Förundersökningsprotokoll*, Teknisk Utredning, Brottsplatsundersökning, Del 3, Stockholms Tingsrätt Avdelning 15 Akter i brottmål B 541 del 2 Aktb. 40–42 1973 G1: 218, 22, SA.

46 **"It was impossible"**: Clark Olofsson, author interview.

46 **"Gas Money"**: Birgitta Lundblad, *Protokoll över förhör*, September 14, 1973, and again on September 27, 1973, Stockholms Tingsrätt Avdelning 15, B 541/73, Akter i Brottmål G1 218, 267 and 282, SA.

46 **Kristin and Elisabeth helped him count**: Kristin Enmark, *Samtal*, September 7, 1973, Stockholms Tingsrätt Avdelning 15 Akter i brottmål B 541 del 2 Aktb. 40–42 1973 G1: 218, 325, SA, and Elisabeth Oldgren, *Samtal*, September 6, 1973, Stockholms Tingsrätt Avdelning 15 Akter i brottmål B 541 del 2 Aktb. 40–42 1973 G1: 218, 368, SA.

46 **The vault was a long, rectangular**: *Förundersökningsprotokoll*, Avsnitt 2: "Kundvalvet," 1973-11-12, Teknisk Utredning, Brottsplatsundersökning, Del 3, Stockholms Tingsrätt Avdelning 15 Akter i brottmål B 541 del 2 Aktb. 40–42 1973 G1: 218, 30–31, SA.

47 **managed to lug into the room**: Birgitta Lundblad interview, *Dagens Nyheter*, September 7, 1973.

47 **Clark asked Birgitta**: Birgitta Lundblad, *Protokoll fört vid förhör*, September 27, 1973, Stockholms Tingsrätt Avdelning 15 Akter i brottmål B 541 del 2 Aktb. 40–42 1973 G1: 218, 279, SA.

47 **"Imagine meeting like this"**: Olofsson (2015), 321.

47 **Birgitta had mentioned where he could find**: Clark Olofsson, author interview.

47 **managed to reach the nanny**: *Aftonbladet*, August 25, 1973.

47 **"stuck at the bank"**: Kristin Enmark, *Jag blev Stockholmssyndromet. Valvet, föraktet och mitt kärleksförhållande med Clark Olofsson* (Livonia: Ordupplaget, 2015), 39.

48 **"You read about things like this"**: *Expressen*, August 24, 1973.

CHAPTER 12

49 **"He has captured me by force"**: Boris Pasternak, *Doctor Zhivago* (New York: Pantheon Books, Inc., 1958), 282–83.

49 **Clark had assumed**: Clark Olofsson, *Vafan var det som hände?* (Livonia: Upp med Händerna, 2015), 301.

49 **"our ticket out"**: Clark Olofsson, author interview.

49 **Clark watched the women**: Olofsson (2015), 322.

50 **brown blazer**: *Bilaga K4*, F Teknisk Utredning, Brottsplatsundersökning, Del 3, Stockholms Tingsrätt Avdelning 15 Akter i brottmål B 541 del 2 Aktb. 40–42 1973 G1: 218, 119, SA.

50 **What bad luck**: Janne Olsson account in *Pockettidningen R* (1974), Årg 4, Nr. 1, 30.

50 **Sven had gone into the supply room**: Sven Säfström, *Anteckningar*/Notes from the Vault, Sven Säfström Collection.

50 **someone falling down**: Sven Säfström, *Protokoll över förhör*, August 29, 1973, Stockholms Tingsrätt Avdelning 15 Akter i brottmål B 541 del 2 Aktb. 40–42 1973 G1: 218, 423, SA.

50 **windowpanes being smashed**: Sven Säfström, *Protokoll över förhör*, September 7, 1973, Stockholms Tingsrätt Avdelning 15 Akter i brottmål B 541 del 2 Aktb. 40–42 1973 G1: 218, 455, SA.

50 **He first thought** and **"Down on the floor!":** Sven Säfström, author interview.

50 **cruise ship** and **lack of direction:** *Aftonbladet*, August 25, 1973, with more on career choice in Daniel Lang, "A Reporter at Large," *The New Yorker*, November 25, 1974, 60.

50 **he asked himself:** Sven Säfström, author interview.

50 **"What the hell":** Sven Säfström, *Protokoll över förhör*, August 29, 1973, Stockholms Tingsrätt Avdelning 15 Akter i brottmål B 541 del 2 Aktb. 40–42 1973 G1: 218, 428, SA.

50 **"Look what I found":** Sven Säfström, *Protokoll över förhör*, September 3, 1973, Stockholms Tingsrätt Avdelning 15 Akter i brottmål B 541 del 2 Aktb. 40–42 1973 G1: 218, 436, SA, as well as on September 7 in the same file.

50 **"You must be very hungry"** and **the women, who seemed to be:** Sven Säfström, author interview.

50 **Clark discreetly encouraged:** Olofsson (2015), 328–29.

51 **sandwiches and beer:** Sven Säfström, *Anteckningar*/Notes from the Vault, Sven Säfström Collection.

51 **"Sven, we don't need any heroes":** Sven Säfström, author interview and Sven Säfström, *Protokoll över förhör*, September 7, 1973, Stockholms Tingsrätt Avdelning 15 Akter i brottmål B 541 del 2 Aktb. 40–42 1973 G1: 218, 462, SA.

51 **"Dear God":** *Gentlemanna-Rånaren?* (Bromma: Williams Förlag, 1973), 31.

51 **he had long suspected:** *Promemoria angående händelserna vid Kreditbanken, Norrmalmstorg*, Stockholms Tingsrätt Avdelning 15 Akter i brottmål B 541 del 1 Aktb. 1–39 1973 G1: 217, 206, SA.

51 **He turned the gun around:** Sven Säfström, author interview; Janne Olsson, author interview; Birgitta Lundblad, *Protokoll fört vid förhör*, September 27, 1973, Stockholms Tingsrätt Avdelning 15 Akter i brottmål B 541 del 2 Aktb. 40–42 1973 G1: 218, 281, SA.

51 **Years later, Janne would say:** Janne Olsson, author interview. For more, see Janne Olsson, *Stockholmssyndromet: en självbiografi* (Telegram, 2009), 21.

52 **"BANK ROBBER TOOK SIX"** and **"hundreds of policemen":** *Aftonbladet*, August 23, 1973.

52 **"A Man with a Submachine Gun"** and **"Demand":** *Expressen*, August 23, 1973.

52 **"The King Has Difficulty in Breathing":** *Aftonbladet*, August 23, 1973.

52 **"THE KING WORSE":** *Expressen*, August 23, 1973 and *Aftonbladet*, August 23, 1973.

CHAPTER 13

53 **"What is the burgling of a bank":** Bertolt Brecht, *The Threepenny Opera* (New York: Grove Press, Inc., 1964), 92.

53 **"two pistols and a fast car":** Kurt Lindroth, Transl.LH, PHM: 1831, PM.

53 **Sven was ruled out:** Kristin Enmark, author interview.

53 **Janne would later mock:** Janne Olsson, *Stockholmssyndromet. En självbiografi* (Telegram, 2009), 18.

54 **The cassettes of the bank's footage:** Many accounts, including some of the later police ones, put the burning of the film on Friday. This is a mistake. It was clearly Thursday, as hostages and participants said then and later. See, among many other

accounts, Birgitta Lundblad, *Samtal*, September 27, 1973, Stockholms Tingsrätt Avdelning 15 Akter i brottmål B 541 del 2 Aktb. 40–42 1973 G1: 218, 280, SA; Elisabeth Oldgren, *Samtal*, September 6, 1973, Stockholms Tingsrätt Avdelning 15 Akter i brottmål B 541 del 2 Aktb. 40–42 1973 G1: 218, 369, SA.

54 **Kristin helped:** Kristin Enmark, *Samtal*, September 5, 1973, and again, September 16, 1973, Stockholms Tingsrätt Avdelning 15 Akter i brottmål B 541 del 2 Aktb. 40–42 1973 G1: 218, 311–12, SA.

54 **Clark was still technically:** Clark was not really "released," lawyers concluded after the fact, because he was still in the bank and therefore legally in their custody, Ove Rainer, *Makterna* (Stockholm: P.A. Norstedt & Söners Förlag, 1984), 59, 61.

54 **another sharpshooter had entered:** *Dagens Nyheter*, August 24, 1973.

54 **"Negotiations with the robber continue":** *Svenska Dagbladet*, August 24, 1973.

54 **A handful of sharpshooters crept down:** This incident draws on *De Polisiära Insatserna i Samband med Norrmalmstorgshändelserna 23–28 augusti 1973, del 1/2*, PHM: 1831, PM; Lars Erik Karlsson, *Protokoll fört vid förhör*, August 24, 1973, Stockholms Tingsrätt Avdelning 15 Akter i brottmål B 541 del 1 Aktb. 1–39 1973 G1: 217, 233, SA, and also of Karl G. Åström on the same day in the same file, as well as author interviews with Janne Olsson and Clark Olofsson.

54 **"Take it easy, dammit!":** Börje Heed, *Gentlemanna-Rånaren?* (Bromma: Williams Förlag, 1973), 33.

55 **"a game of death":** Olsson (2009), 20.

55 **"No one dares"** . . . **"very irritated":** Rapport: Bankrånet i Sveriges Kreditbank, Norrmalmstorg, Stockholm TV2, 1973–08–23 19.09–20.17, SMDB, KB.

55 **"Get back!":** *Svenska Dagbladet*, August 24, 1973.

55 **The mass of spectators:** Crowds estimated by many papers at "thousands," with photos in *Dagens Nyheter*, August 24, 1973 and they continued to grow, *Göteborgs-Posten*, August 24, 1973.

55 **"excitement and exhaustion":** *Svenska Dagbladet*, August 24, 1973.

55 **Clark started reaching out:** Clark Olofsson, author interview.

55 **"It is cool and calm"** . . . **"terrorism of authorities":** *Aftonbladet*, August 24, 1973.

56 **In her article the next day:** *Aftonbladet*, August 24, 1973.

CHAPTER 14

57 **"We did not consider ourselves":** Kurt Lindroth, Transl.LH, PHM: 1831, PM.

57 **confusing and amusing:** Janne Olsson, author interview.

57 **"You've got to be kidding":** Bengt-Olof Lövenlo, *Protokoll fört . . . vid förhör*, September 4, 1973, Stockholms Tingsrätt Avdelning 15 Akter i brottmål B 541 del 3 Aktb. 43–130 1973 G1: 219, SA and *Expressen*, August 30, 1973.

58 **Less than one year before:** Dan Hansén and Ahn-Za Hagström, *I Krisen prövas ordningsmakten. Sex fallstudier av extraordinära händelser där det svenska rättsamhället har satts på prov* (Stockholm: Jure Förlag, 2004), 45–56, and Gustav Andersson and Per Gudmundsson, "Flygkapardramat," in Gunnar Davidsson (ed.), *Polisen griper in* (Stockholm: Lindfors, 1974), 151–95.

58 **The car they would offer:** *De Polisiära Insatserna i Samband med Norrmalmstorgshändelserna 23–28 augusti 1973, del 1/2*, PHM: 1831, PM, which notes the lack of keys though claims, incorrectly, that the car had a full tank of gas.

59 **At 7:40 p.m.:** Stockholms Tingsrätt Avd. 15:1 DB 248, Mål nr B 541/73, 18, SA.

59 **"The car, a sports car":** Rapport; Aktuellt: Bankrånet i Sveriges Kreditbank, Norrmalmstorg, Stockholm 1973–08–23 20.18–21.12, SMDB, KB.

59 **"It is possible that the dramatic":** *Ibid.*

59 **Clark kept working the telephone:** Clark Olofsson, author interview.

59 **"You understand"** . . . **"What do you have in mind":** *Dagens Nyheter*, August 24, 1973.

CHAPTER 15

61 **"Sweden was, despite everything":** Clark Olofsson, *Vafan var det som hände?* (Livonia: Upp med Händerna, 2015), 348.

61 **The hostages might then be exchanged:** *Smålandsposten*, August 24, 1973.

61 **"How much is the police promise":** *Skånska Dagbladet*, August 25, 1973.

61 **"See to it only that the plane":** *De Polisiära Insatserna i Samband med Norrmalmstorgshändelserna 23–28 augusti 1973, del 1/2*, PHM: 1831, PM.

62 **"We are going to take the bank":** *De Polisiära Insatserna i Samband med Norrmalmstorgshändelserna 23–28 augusti 1973, del 1/2*, PHM: 1831, PM.

62 **"And what the hell do we do"** . . . **"We have to kill him":** *Dagens Nyheter*, August 24, 1973.

63 **It was far from clear:** *Göteborgs-Posten*, August 24, 1973.

63 **one person said, a glass of whiskey:** Rapport; Aktuellt: Bankrånet i Sveriges Kreditbank, Norrmalmstorg, Stockholm 1973–08–23 20.18–21.12, SMDB, KB.

63 **hot dogs and French fries:** Sven Säfström, *Anteckningar*/Notes from the Vault, Sven Säfström Collection.

63 **no one had ordered them:** Clark Olofsson, "Klarspråk om Norrmalmstorg," *Nordisk Kriminalpolis*, Årg. 3, Nr 1 (1977), 173.

63 **an unidentified drug:** *De Polisiära Insatserna i Samband med Norrmalmstorgshändelserna 23–28 augusti 1973, del 1/2*, PHM: 1831, PM.

63 **"the boys"** . . . **"Say that it is Clark":** Börje Heed, *Gentlemanna-Rånaren?* (Bromma: Williams Förlag, 1973), 44, 39.

64 **"arrogant and intellectual fearlessness":** Olofsson (2015), 336.

64 **"One hell at a time":** Kjell Östberg, *När vinden vände. Olof Palme 1969–1986* (Stockholm: Leopard, 2012), 17–18.

64 **No one had tried to confirm that the caller:** Clark Olofsson, author interview. The person was Elisabeth, not Kristin as often reported first: Elisabeth Oldgren, *Samtal*, September 6, 1973, Stockholms Tingsrätt Avdelning 15, B 541/73, Akter i Brottmål G1 218, 377, SA.

65 **"I am going to shoot":** Per Svensson i samarbete med Håkan Lindhé, *Dramat på Norrmalmstorg 23 till 28 augusti 1973* (Stockholm: Bonnier Fakta, 2003), 87.

65 **The gunman started counting down:** Kurt Lindroth, Transl.LH, PHM: 1831, PM, and Janne Olsson, author interview.

CHAPTER 16

66 **"It was impossible to know what"**: Kristin Enmark, *Jag blev Stockholmssyndromet. Valvet, föraktet och mitt kärleksförhållande med Clark Olofsson* (Livonia: Ordupplaget, 2015), 31.

66 **Policemen, journalists, and photographers**: *Upsala Nya Tidning*, August 25, 1973.

67 **The biggest and most ominous development** and **"Swedish-American robber"**: Eko [Norrmalmstorgsdramat] 1973–08–24, SMDB, KB.

67 **Palmhuset restaurant**: Börje Heed, *Anförande hållet vid presskonferensen i Jönköping i april 1974*, PHM: 1831, PM.

67 **"The Monkey Cage"**: Per Svensson i samarbete med Håkan Lindhé, *Dramat på Norrmalmstorg 23 till 28 augusti 1973* (Stockholm: Bonnier Fakta, 2003), 63.

67 **"The Bank for You"**: This can be seen from time to time in the raw television footage, for instance, Rapport; Aktuellt: Bankrånet i Sveriges Kreditbank, Norrmalmstorg, Stockholm 1973–08–23 20.18–21.12, SMDB, KB.

67 **Kristin rested her head**: Kristin Enmark, *Samtal*, September 5, and September 7, 1973, Stockholms Tingsrätt Avdelning 15 Akter i brottmål B 541 del 2 Aktb. 40–42 1973 G1: 218, 316, 328, SA.

67 **He was popping little white pills**: Birgitta Lundblad, *Samtal*, August 29, 1973, Stockholms Tingsrätt Avdelning 15 Akter i brottmål B 541 del 2 Aktb. 40–42 1973 G1: 218, 261, SA. For more, see chapter 18.

68 **a night of terror**: *Aftonbladet*, August 24, 1973, and *Expressen*, August 24, 1973. Other papers also used this phrase, such as *Kvällsposten*, August 24, 1973.

68 **The sound of the bottles**: Håkan Larsson, *PM angående mina iakttagelser och åtgärder under bankockupationen vid Kreditbanken på Norrmalmstorg*, September 19, 1973, Förundersöknings Protokoll, Del 5, Stockholms Tingsrätt Avdelning 15 Akter i brottmål B 541 del 3 Aktb. 43–130, 1973 G1: 219, 137, SA.

68 **"murder him"**: Janne Olsson, *Stockholmssyndromet. En självbiografi* (Telegram, 2009), 32.

68 **"This is dead sick"**: Stockholms Tingsrätt Avd. 15:1 DB 248, Mål nr B 541/73, 40, SA.

CHAPTER 17

69 **"If you can shoot him, do it"**: *Aftonbladet*, August 29, 1973.

69 **contrasting the police sharpshooters**: *Svenska Dagbladet*, August 24, 1973.

69 **Olof Palme's offer**: *Dagens Nyheter*, August 24, 1973.

69 **"nerve-wracking night"**: *Expressen*, August 24.

69 **"brutal violent crime"**: *Dagens Nyheter*, August 24, 1973.

69 **It was Radio Sweden**: Eko [Norrmalmstorgsdramat] 1973–08–24, SMDB, KB.

70 **put his picture on the cover**: *Aftonbladet*, August 24, 1973, and *Expressen*, August 24, 1973. His photo appeared closer to his home in the south, *Skånska Dagbladet*, August 24, 1973, and around the world, for instance, in Amsterdam's *de Volkskrant*, August 25, 1973, or next to headlines like "The Face of Terror," London's *Daily Express*, August 24, 1973.

70 **"crimes, prisons, and crimes again"** . . . **"coldest and most talented"**: *Aftonbladet*, August 24, 1973.

71 **Both Dan and Nico:** *Promemoria angående händelserna vid Kreditbanken, Norrmalmstorg*, Stockholms Tingsrätt Avdelning 15 Akter i brottmål B 541 del 1 Aktb. 1–39 1973 G1: 217, 211, SA; Kurt Lindroth, Transl.LH, PHM: 1831, PM, Håkan Larsson in *Sambandet*, June 1993, and Sven Thorander piece in *Lektyr*, June 26–July 2, 1978, and for Dan Hansson, particularly Helen Ardelius's excellent radio documentary, *Norrmalmstorgsdramat*, Sveriges Radio, P1, 1998–08–15 11.03–12.00, SMDB, KB. Special thanks to Helen for sharing her notes from her interviews in the 1990s with Dan, Nico, and Kaj's mother.

71 **"Kaj, this is Dan":** Dan Hansson, *Protokoll fört vid förhör*, August 24, 1973, Stockholms Tingsrätt Avdelning 15 Akter i brottmål B 541 del 1 Aktb. 1–39 1973 G1: 217, 241, SA.

71 **about 6:10 a.m.:** *De Polisiära Insatserna i Samband med Norrmalmstorgshändelserna 23–28 augusti 1973, del 1/2*, PHM: 1831, PM.

71 **"I want to speak with you":** Dan Hansson, *Protokoll fört vid förhör*, August 24, 1973, Stockholms Tingsrätt Avdelning 15 Akter i brottmål B 541 del 1 Aktb. 1–39 1973 G1: 217, 241, SA.

71 **"Kaj, Kaj, this is your brother":** Janne Olsson, *Stockholmssyndromet: en självbiografi* (Telegram, 2009), 35.

72 **"Get out of here!"** and **"can't you see":** Nicolaas Cleyndert, *Protokoll, fört vid förhör*, August 24, 1973, Stockholms Tingsrätt Avdelning 15 Akter i brottmål B 541 del 1 Aktb. 1–39 1973 G1: 217, 242–43, SA.

72 **"Stop that shit":** Olsson (2009), 35.

72 **"You fucking idiots":** Olsson (2009), 35, and Dan Hansson interview in Helen Ardelius, *Norrmalmstorgsdramat*, Sveriges Radio, P1, 1998–08–15 11.03–12.00, SMDB, KB.

CHAPTER 18

73 **"It is not always reason":** Sven Thorander interview in *Pockettidningen R* (1974), Årg 4, Nr. 1, 90.

73 **"Talented cops":** *Pockettidningen R* (1974), Årg 4, Nr. 1, 24. Janne emphasized his point with three exclamation points and three question marks.

73 **under the influence of stimulants:** *Göteborgs-Posten*, August 25, 1973. Many others reported him under the influence, such as *Aftonbladet*, August 24, 1973 and *Svenska Dagbladet*, August 25, 1973.

73 **a drug addict:** *GT*, August 24, 1973.

73 **ephedrine:** Janne Olsson, author interview.

74 **probably his fiancée, Maria:** She later confirmed that she spoke with him on Friday morning, *Aftonbladet*, August 26, 1973.

74 **"Don't believe them"** . . . **"It's so ridiculous":** 24/8–73 kl. 8.06–8.50, *Påbörjat Samtal, Telefonavlyssning, Förhör, Övrige Avlyssningar mm*, Stockholms Tingsrätt Avdelning 15 Akter i brottmål B 541 del 4 Aktb. 131–60 1973 G1: 220, 45, SA.

74 **mattresses, pillows, and blankets:** Foto 18 and *Teknisk Utredning*, Brottsplatsun-

dersökning, Del 3, Stockholms Tingsrätt Avdelning 15 Akter i brottmål B 541 del 2 Aktb. 40–42 1973 G1: 218, 34, SA.

74 **The police chief, Kurt Lindroth:** *Promemoria angående händelserna vid Kreditbanken, Norrmalmstorg,* Stockholms Tingsrätt Avdelning 15 Akter i brottmål B 541 del 1 Aktb. 1–39 1973 G1: 217, 210, SA; *De Polisiära Insatserna i Samband med Norrmalmstorgshändelserna 23–28 augusti 1973, del 1/2,* PHM: 1831, PM.

75 **"a little dumb ignorant girl":** Kristin Enmark, *Jag blev Stockholmssyndromet. Valvet, föraktet och mitt kärleksförhållande med Clark Olofsson* (Livonia: Ordupplaget, 2015), 47. For more, see also Kristin's account, "Hur jag som gisslan såg på polisinsatsen - några synpunkter i efterhand med adress till polisledningen i Stockholm," *Nordisk Kriminalpolis,* Årg. 3, Nr 1 (1977). She was still upset at the police's approach and Clark's manipulation, years later: Kristin Enmark, author interview.

75 **conspiring to take over negotiations:** Olofsson (2015), 337–40.

75 **they could now do legally:** *Avlyssning av telefonapparat Nummer 213582,* August 23, 1973, Förundersöknings Protokoll, Del 5, Stockholms Tingsrätt Avdelning 15, B 541/73, G1 219, 160, SA.

76 **They played Tic-Tac-Toe:** Kristin Enmark, author interview, and paper with the games were later found by the Stockholm police, *Bilaga G1,* Teknisk Utredning Brottsplatsundersökning, Del 3, Stockholms Tingsrätt Avdelning 15 Akter i brottmål B 541 del 2 Aktb. 40–42 1973 G1: 218, 107, 109, SA.

76 **The bank drama was like a film:** *Dagens Nyheter,* August 25, 1973.

76 **"We are here as long as necessary":** *Expressen,* August 24, 1973.

76 **Janne had told the hostages:** Sven Säfström, author interview.

76 **Wienerschnitzel:** Sven Säfström, *Anteckningar/*Notes from the Vault, Sven Säfström's Collection.

76 **"That surely must be good enough":** Börje Heed, *Gentlemanna-Rånaren?* (Bromma: Williams Förlag, 1973), 56.

76 **"tug of war":** *Sydsvenska Dagbladet,* August 24, 1973.

76 **Olof Palme, Lennart Geijer, and the cabinet:** Clark Olofsson, author interview. Palme would need to take a tough stance, agreed the Italian Communist paper, *L'Unità,* August 26, 1973, and *L'Europeo* [September 1973] also portrayed him as playing politics.

76 **This was Sweden, after all:** Clark Olofsson, author interview.

76 **"He can blow the entire bank" . . . "Is this enough?":** Heed (1973), 56 and Bengt-Olof Lövenlo interviews in *Expressen,* August 30, 1973, and *Aftonbladet,* August 30, 1973.

CHAPTER 19

78 **"When you go down on your knee":** SVT, Bakom rubrikerna. Vad gjorde massmedia på Norrmalmstorg? 1973–09–20, SMDB, KB.

78 **It was the calmest period:** *Svenska Dagbladet,* August 25, 1973.

78 **Traffic lights blinked:** Raw television footage preserved of SVT for August 23 and August 24, SMDB, KB.

78 **"Sharpshooter Number 2"** ... **"I am not going to miss"**: *Aftonbladet*, August 25, 1973.

79 **"hyenas"**: *Aftonbladet*, August 24, 1973.

79 **The excessive media attention**: *Dagens Nyheter*, August 25, 1973.

79 **There had never been more**: *Kvällsposten*, August 25, 1973.

79 **"a city in shock"**: *Dagens Nyheter*, August 25, 1973.

80 **"Am I calling"** ... **"word of honor"**: 24.08–73 kl.15.17–17.03, *Telefonavlyssning, Förhör, Övrige Avlyssningar mm*, Stockholms Tingsrätt Avdelning 15 Akter i brottmål B 541 del 4 Aktb. 131–60 1973 G1: 220, 46–49, SA, and Eko [Norrmalmstorgsdramat] 1973–08–24. SMDB, KB.

81 **"a hero or villain"**: *Expressen*, August 24, 1973.

81 **"all the way to the bank"**: Per Svensson i samarbete med Håkan Lindhé, *Dramat på Norrmalmstorg 23 till 28 augusti 1973* (Stockholm: Bonnier Fakta, 2003), 103.

81 **"I am on the poor girls' side"** ... **"his damn money!"**: 24/8–73 kl.15.17–17.03, *Telefonavlyssning, Förhör, Övrige Avlyssningar mm*, Stockholms Tingsrätt Avdelning 15 Akter i brottmål B 541 del 4 Aktb. 131–60 1973 G1: 220, 49–50, SA.

CHAPTER 20

82 **"[In] 999 cases of 1,000"**: Elisabeth Oldgren, *Protokoll över förhör*, August 29, 1973, Stockholms Tingsrätt Avdelning 15 Akter i brottmål B 541 del 2 Aktb. 40–42 1973 G1: 218, 358, SA.

82 **"Dramatic interview"** and **"RELEASE THE ROBBER"**: *Kvällsposten*, August 24, 1973.

82 **did not hazard a prediction**: *GT*, August 24, 1973.

82 **Many people criticized Radio Sweden**: See, among many others, *Arbetartidningen*, September 5, 1973, SVT Bakom rubrikerna. Vad gjorde massmedia på Norrmalmstorg? 1973–09–20, SMDB, KB and Sveriges Radio, September 27, 1974, PHM: 1831: 13, PM.

82 **only one side of the story**: *Upsala Nya Tidning*, August 25, 1973.

83 **"I feel in good shape"** ... **"We are not four"**: 24/8–73 kl.16.36, *Telefonavlyssning, Förhör, Övrige Avlyssningar mm*, Stockholms Tingsrätt Avdelning 15 Akter i brottmål B 541 del 4 Aktb. 131–60 1973 G1: 220, 51–52, SA.

83 **Not knowing that:** Janne Olsson in *Pockettidningen R* (1974), Årg 4, Nr. 1, 29, 32.

83 **"The vault is mine"**: Daniel Lang, "A Reporter at Large," *The New Yorker*, November 25, 1974, 96.

84 **"The whole floor"**: Olsson in *Pockettidningen R* (1974), Årg 4, Nr. 1, 30.

84 **Elisabeth now walked out**: Elisabeth Oldgren, *Samtal*, September 6, 1973, Stockholms Tingsrätt Avdelning 15 Akter i brottmål B 541 del 2 Aktb. 40–42 1973 G1: 218, 373, SA, and Sven Säfström, *Protokoll över förhör*, September 26, 1973, Stockholms Tingsrätt Avdelning 15 Akter i brottmål B 541 del 2 Aktb. 40–42 1973 G1: 218, 502–503, SA.

84 **"I couldn't go far"**: Lang (1974), 63.

84 **"Why can't you go?"**: Elisabeth Oldgren, *Protokoll fört vid förhör*, October 3, 1973, Stockholms Tingsrätt Avdelning 15 Akter i brottmål B 541 del 2 Aktb. 40–42 1973 G1: 218, 418, SA.

CHAPTER 21

85 **"Palme was under incredible pressure"**: Carl Persson, *Utan Omsvep. Ett liv i maktens centrum*, i samarbete med Anders Sundelin (Stockholm: Norstedts, 1990), 242.

85 **"Kaj, this is Mamma speaking!"** . . . **"Give up, Kaj"**: Dagens Eko 1973–08–24 Bankdramat vid Norrmalmstorg, SMDB, KB, with the transcript reprinted in media and referenced abroad, for instance, Milan's Communist paper, *L'Unità*, August 26, 1973.

85 **his mother's telephone** and **neighbors began**: Helen Ardelius, *Norrmalmstorgsdramat*, Sveriges Radio, P1, 1998–08–15 11.03–12.00, SMDB, KB.

85 **"I beg you one last time"**: Dagens Eko 1973–08–24 Bankdramat vid Norrmalmstorg, SMDB, KB, and *Svenska Dagbladet*, August 25, 1973.

86 **laugh or cry**: Kristin Enmark, *Jag blev Stockholmssyndromet. Valvet, föraktet och mitt kärleksförhållande med Clark Olofsson* (Livonia: Ordupplaget, 2015), 62.

86 **It was probably later that afternoon**: No one seems to remember exactly when he removed his wig, including Janne himself. Janne Olsson, author interview. Sven thought that Janne still wore the wig when they heard Kaj's mother on the radio but took it off soon afterward. Sven Säfström, author interview. This was also the view of Kurt Lindroth, Transl.LH, PHM: 1831, PM.

86 **Sven, for one, was surprised**: Sven Säfström, *Protokoll över förhör*, September 7, 1973, Stockholms Tingsrätt Avdelning 15 Akter i brottmål B 541 del 2 Aktb. 40–42 1973 G1: 218, 464, SA.

86 **Kristin was the obvious choice**: Kristin Enmark, author interview.

86 **"Yes, my name is Kristin"** and **"He is coming now"**: Kristin Enmark, *Jag blev Stockholmssyndromet. Valvet, föraktet och mitt kärleksförhållande med Clark Olofsson* (Livonia: Ordupplaget, 2015), 191.

86 **"I am actually very disappointed"** . . . **"That is interesting"**: August 24, 1973, Kl. 17.03–17.45, Telefonavlyssning, Förhör, Övrige Avlyssningar mm, Stockholms Tingsrätt Avdelning 15 Akter i brottmål B 541 del 4 Aktb. 131–60 1973 G1: 220, 60–66, SA, with Palme's repetition in transcript at Enmark (2015), 206.

88 **"We shall see"** . . . **"Yes, I do"**: August 24, 1973, Kl. 17.03–17.45, Telefonavlyssning, Förhör, Övrige Avlyssningar mm, Stockholms Tingsrätt Avdelning 15 Akter i brottmål B 541 del 4 Aktb. 131–60 1973 G1: 220, 66–70.

88 **"This is also urgent"**: Enmark (2015), 219.

8 **"the election would go"** . . . **"Goodbye, and thanks for your help!"**: August 24, 1973, Kl. 17.03–17.45, Telefonavlyssning, Förhör, Övrige Avlyssningar mm, Stockholms Tingsrätt Avdelning 15 Akter i brottmål B 541 del 4 Aktb. 131–60 1973 G1: 220, 71–75, SA.

CHAPTER 22

90 **"The stranglehold the man placed"**: *Dagens Nyheter*, August 24, 1973.

90 **"playing chess"**: August 24, 1973, Kl. 17.03–17.45, *Telefonavlyssning, Förhör, Övrige Avlyssningar mm*, Stockholms Tingsrätt Avdelning 15 Akter i brottmål B 541 del 4 Aktb. 131–60 1973 G1: 220, 60, SA.

90 **"I liked Kristin for a lot [of reasons]"**: Janne Olsson in *Pockettidningen R* (1974), Årg 4, Nr. 1, 31.

90 **"village idiot"**: Clark Olofsson in Mikael Hylin documentary *Norrmalmstorgsdramat inifrån* (2003).

90 **"To whom am I speaking?"** . . . **she was upset at her daughter's:** Per Svensson i samarbete med Håkan Lindhé, *Dramat på Norrmalmstorg 23 till 28 augusti 1973* (Stockholm: Bonnier Fakta, 2003), 132–33, and Kristin Enmark, author interview. Gunnel Enmark's criticism of the media was also in *Aftonbladet*, September 2, 1973.

90 **"a big jerk"**: 24.08–73 kl.15.17–17.03, *Telefonavlyssning, Förhör, Övrige Avlyssningar mm*, Stockholms Tingsrätt Avdelning 15 Akter i brottmål B 541 del 4 Aktb. 131–60 1973 G1: 220, 47, SA.

91 **There must be a lot:** Kristin Enmark, *Jag blev Stockholmssyndromet. Valvet, föraktet och mitt kärleksförhållande med Clark Olofsson* (Livonia: Ordupplaget, 2015), 75.

91 **"Would it not feel good to die at your post?"**: Enmark (2015), 52, and Kristin Enmark, "Hur jag som gisslan såg på polisinsatsen - några synpunkter i efterhand med adress till polisledningen i Stockholm," *Nordisk Kriminalpolis*, Årg. 3, Nr 1 (1977), 163.

91 **fits almost seamlessly into the lacuna:** All of a sudden, Kristin says, "Now, Elisabeth says there are enough dead heroes, and I do not want to be a dead hero," which makes no sense given the conversation before or after. There is a break in the transcript immediately before, too, where the question fits without contradiction, August 24, 1973, Kl. 17.03–17.45, *Förundersöknings Protokoll*, Telefonavlyssning, Förhör, Övrige Avlyssningar mm, Stockholms Tingsrätt Avdelning 15 Akter i brottmål B 541 del 4 Aktb. 131–60 1973 G1: 220, 72, SA. When I asked Kristin about it, she thought it was indeed where it had happened, Kristin Enmark, author interview.

91 **Elisabeth had discouraged it:** *Telefonavlyssning, Förhör, Övrige Avlyssningar mm*, August 24, 1973, Stockholms Tingsrätt Avdelning 15 Akter i brottmål B 541 del 4 Aktb. 131–60 1973 G1: 220, 58, SA.

92 **"I can only hope that no one"**: *Expressen*, August 24, 1973.

92 **"between terror and hope"**: *Expressen*, August 25, 1973.

92 **expressed confidence in their son:** *Aftonbladet*, August 25, 1973.

92 **"The worst is the uncertainty"**: *Aftonbladet*, August 25, 1973.

92 **"the world's longest time"**: *Expressen*, August 25, 1973.

92 **"demonstration"**: *De Polisiära Insatserna i Samband med Norrmalmstorgshändelserna 23–28 augusti 1973, del 1/2*, PHM: 1831, PM.

92 **Clark, again, wondered** . . . **He would be cheered:** Clark Olofsson, *Vafan var det som hände?* (Livonia: Bokförlaget Upp med Händerna, 2015), 343.

CHAPTER 23

94 **"He still stood there with"**: Clark Olofsson, *Vafan var det som hände?* (Livonia: Bokförlaget Upp med Händerna, 2015), 351.

94 **It was probably going to be Birgitta:** *Kvällsposten*, August 25, 1973.

94 **"I cannot harm the girls"**: *Bandinspelning från den 13/9 1973 vid TV-utsändning,*

Intervju med Sven Säfström, Stockholms Tingsrätt Avdelning 15 Akter i brottmål B 541 del 2 Aktb. 40–42 1973 G1: 218, 511, SA.

94 **Janne promised Sven:** Sven Säfström, *Protokoll över förhör,* September 4, 1973, Stockholms Tingsrätt Avdelning 15 Akter i brottmål B 541 del 2 Aktb. 40–42 1973 G1: 218, 450, SA.

94 **"I do not know if I was afraid"** . . . **"OK, he is going to shoot me":** Sven Säfström, author interview.

95 **"It's only in the leg":** Janne Olsson, author interview.

95 **how much she regretted:** Kristin Enmark, *Jag blev Stockholmssyndromet. Valvet, föraktet och mitt kärleksförhållande med Clark Olofsson* (Livonia: Ordupplaget, 2015), 60, and Kristin Enmark, author interview.

95 **a boom rocked the lobby:** John Jonsson, *Promemoria*, Stockholms Tingsrätt Avdelning 15 Akter i brottmål B 541 del 1 Aktb. 1–39 1973 G1: 217, 230, SA.

95 **"Roll the cameras!":** SVT, Bankrånet i Sveriges Kreditbank, Norrmalmstorg, Stockholm, 1973–08–24, SMDB, KB.

95 **lack of damage:** *Göteborgs-Posten*, August 25, 1973.

95 **straight out of a nightmare:** *Svenska Dagbladet*, August 25, 1973.

95 **"My heart bled for him":** Janne Olsson, author interview.

95 **"so ashamed":** Clark Olofsson, author interview.

96 **Cash Register No. 1:** *Förundersöknings Protokoll*, Teknisk Utredning, Brottsplatsundersökning, Del 3, Stockholms Tingsrätt Avdelning 15 Akter i brottmål B 541 del 2 Aktb. 40–42 1973 G1: 218, 8, SA.

96 **ordering coffee and ice cream:** *De Polisiära Insatserna i Samband med Norrmalmstorgshändelserna 23–28 augusti 1973, del 1/2*, PHM: 1831, PM.

CHAPTER 24

97 **"The drama is beginning":** *Dagens Nyheter,* September 16, 1973.

97 **"full confidence":** SVT, Bankrånet i Sveriges Kreditbank, Norrmalmstorg, Stockholm, 1973–08–24, SMDB, KB.

97 **"absolutely no concessions":** *Expressen*, August 30, 1973.

98 **"How many lives":** *Skånska Dagbladet*, August 29, 1973.

98 **The hilarity of the film** . . . **"Such a [crime]":** *Expressen*, August 25, 1973.

98 **The old Sweden:** Per Svensson i samarbete med Håkan Lindhé, *Dramat på Norrmalmstorg 23 till 28 augusti 1973* (Stockholm: Bonnier Fakta, 2003), 57.

98 **"Who I am does not matter":** . . . **"What should I have done?":** SVT, Bankrånet I Sveriges Kreditbank, Norrmalmstorg, Stockholm, 1973–08–24, SMDB, KB, and police transcript at August 24, 1973, Kl. 16.36, *Förundersöknings Protokoll*, Telefonavlyssning, Förhör, Övrige Avlyssningar mm, Stockholms Tingsrätt Avdelning 15 Akter i brottmål B 541 del 4 Aktb. 131–60 1973 G1: 220, 54–55, SA.

98 **Kalmar prison guards:** The director informed Stockholm Police, noted Kalmar's *Barometern*, August 27, 1973.

99 **Kaj's mother:** *Expressen*, August 25, 1973, *Dagens Nyheter*, August 26, 1973, and *Svenska Dagbladet*, August 26, 1973.

99 **"desperate and tired of life":** *Aftonbladet*, August 27, 1973. This also draws on Åke Olsson's interviews in *Expressen*, August 27, 1973, *Kvällsposten*, August 26, 1973, and *Se*, September 6, 1973, along with Lennart Geijer's interview in *Pockettidningen R* (1974), Årg 4, Nr. 1, 108.

99 **"We don't know what":** *Göteborgs-Posten*, August 25, 1973.

99 **he had wanted to leave** and **"I could not do it alone":** Janne Olsson, author interview.

100 **Clark had opposed it:** Olofsson (2015), 348–50.

100 **did not think that they would dare:** Janne Olsson, author interview.

100 **a large blanket, or sheet:** Janne Olsson, author interview and Clark Olofsson, author interview. Kristin Enmark remembered the talk, too. Author interview. The blankets that the police brought in Friday morning were, however, not large enough, Janne said.

100 **they shut the inner door:** Sven Säfström, *Anteckningar*/Notes from the Vault, Sven Säfström Collection.

100 **"Pity we did not meet" . . . She wanted to go further:** Janne Olsson, *Stockholmssyndromet. En självbiografi* (Telegram, 2009), 73–74.

100 **Birgitta, on the other hand . . . she suggested that he take:** Birgitta Lundblad, *Protokoll över Förhör*, September 14, 1973 and September 27, 1973, Förundersöknings Protokoll, Telefonavlyssning, Förhör, Övrige Avlyssningar mm, Stockholms Tingsrätt Avdelning 15 Akter i brottmål B 541 del 4 Aktb. 131–60 1973 G1: 220, 99–100, 102–3, SA.

101 **Traces of semen:** *Bilaga M*, Statens Kriminaltekniska Laboratorium, 1973–11–12, Komplement till del 3, Undersökningsprotokoll angående rån mm hos Sveriges Kreditbank Norrmalmstorg 2, Stockholms Tingsrätt Avdelning 15 Akter i brottmål B 541 del 3 Aktb. 43–130 1973 G1: 219, SA.

CHAPTER 25

102 **"Under psychological pressure":** *Svenska Dagbladet*, January 24, 1974.

102 **climbed atop a nearby building:** *De Polisiära Insatserna i Samband med Norrmalmstorgshändelserna 23–28 augusti 1973, del 1/2*, PHM: 1831, PM, and Extra nyhetssändning [Norrmalmstorgsdramat], 1973–08–25, SMDB, KB.

103 **"wake" the robber:** Morgan Rylander, *Protokoll över förhör*, September 3, 1973, Stockholms Tingsrätt Avdelning 15 Akter i brottmål B 541 del 1 Aktb. 1–39 1973 G1: 217, 202, SA.

103 **"Was that you who shot?" . . . "Are you very tired?":** Morgan Rylander, *Norrmalmstorgsdramat 23 till 28 augusti 1973*, Morgan Rylander Collection and Morgan Rylander, author interview.

103 **"thrilling drama":** *Svenska Dagbladet*, August 26, 1973.

104 **Prime Minister Olof Palme urged his countrymen:** *Dagens Nyheter*, August 25, 1973.

104 **"Shoot the robber":** *Aftonbladet*, August 25, 1973.

104 **This viewpoint was particularly strong:** *Aftonbladet*, August 25, 1973.

104 **adopted such a passive stance:** *Västerbottens-Kuriren*, August 25, 1973.

104 **If a single gunman could incapacitate** and **"pornography of violence"**: *Aftonbladet*, August 25, 1973.

104 **"grotesque drama"**: *Barometern*, August 25, 1973.

104 **"Real Gentlemen"**: *Östgöta Correspondenten*, August 25, 1973.

105 **also stressed her fear of the police**: *Västerbottens-Kuriren*, August 25, 1973, using the TT news agency. See also *Skånska Dagbladet*, August 25, 1973 and *The Times* (London), August 25, 1973. Others expressed the sentiment more delicately as fear of police weapons, *Smålandsposten*, August 25, 1973. The situation was already noted abroad, from the *New York Times*, August 25, 1973, to *L'Unità*, August 26, 1973.

105 **"The Hostages Take"**: *Sydsvenska Dagbladet*, August 25, 1973.

105 **he lashed out at the media**: *Se*, August 30, 1973.

105 **"We are not dealing with idiots"**: *Dagens Nyheter*, August 26, 1973.

105 **"a saint and a superstar"**: *Aftonbladet*, August 25, 1973.

105 **"Tell Clark that he knows where"**: *De Polisiära Insatserna i Samband med Norrmalmstorgshändelserna 23–28 augusti 1973, del 1/2*, PHM: 1831, PM.

106 **The lobby looked almost deserted**: Håkan Larsson, *PM angående mina iakttagelser och åtgärder under bankockupationen vid Kreditbanken på Norrmalmstorg*, September 19, 1973, *Förundersöknings Protokoll*, Del 5, Stockholms Tingsrätt Avdelning 15, B 541/73, G1 219, 138, SA, and more on his belief that the robber might be watching him, *Dagens Nyheter*, August 26, 1973.

106 **if he left the door open**: Håkan Larsson interview in *Sambandet*, June 1993.

106 **Jack Malm** and **8-foot-long iron rod**: *De Polisiära Insatserna i Samband med Norrmalmstorgshändelserna 23–28 augusti 1973, del 1/2*, PHM: 1831, PM.

CHAPTER 26

108 **"It is, of course, a game of poker"**: *Östgöta Correspondenten*, August 27, 1973.

108 **Bejerot made another point**: Kurt Lindroth, Transl.LH, PHM: 1831, PM.

109 **"a bond of friendship"**: Daniel Lang, "A Reporter at Large," *The New Yorker*, November 25, 1974, 84. For more, see Kurt Lindroth, *Sammanställning av planeringen för befriandet av gisslan och gripande av gärningsmannen*, Stockholms Tingsrätt Avdelning 15 Akter i brottmål B 541 del 2 Aktb. 40–42 1973 G1: 218, 520, SA.

109 **By about 9:40**: *De Polisiära Insatserna i Samband med Norrmalmstorgshändelserna 23–28 augusti 1973, del 1/2*, PHM: 1831, PM.

109 **thought that they were going to storm**: *Svenska Dagbladet*, August 26, 1973.

109 **a rational, professional criminal**: Nils Bejerot, *Redogörelse för sina iakttagelser i Kreditbanken*, Stockholms Tingsrätt Avdelning 15 Akter i brottmål B 541 del 2 Aktb. 40–42 1973 G1: 218, 516, SA.

109 **At 9:51**: *De Polisiära Insatserna i Samband med Norrmalmstorgshändelserna 23–28 augusti 1973, del 1/2*, PHM: 1831, PM. This report identified Malm and Jonsson, noting an unnamed third man. This was Håkan Larsson.

110 **"What have we done?"**: Eric Rönnegård, *Norrmalmstorgsdramat: den sanna historien* (Stockholm: Jure, 2013), 60.

110 **Elisabeth was on the verge of panic**: Elisabeth Oldgren, *Protokoll över förhör,*

August 29, 1973, Stockholms Tingsrätt Avdelning 15 Akter i brottmål B 541 del 2 Aktb. 40–42 1973 G1: 218, 360, SA.

110 "a rat caught in a trap": Janne Olsson, *Stockholmssyndromet. En självbiografi* (Telegram, 2009), 70.

CHAPTER 27

111 "I never found out the answer": Sven Säfström, author interview.

111 "no-man's-land": Per Svensson i samarbete med Håkan Lindhé, *Dramat på Norrmalmstorg 23 till 28 augusti 1973* (Stockholm: Bonnier Fakta, 2003), 140.

112 "distribution of power": Kurt Lindroth, Transl.LH, PHM: 1831, PM.

112 Six plates, fourteen plastic cups: *Bilaga G1*, Teknisk Utredning, Brottsplatsundersökning, Del 3, Stockholms Tingsrätt Avdelning 15 Akter i brottmål B 541 del 2 Aktb. 40–42 1973 G1: 218, 107, SA.

112 Around 1 p.m., they obtained: *Förundersökningsprotokoll Rånöverfall med Tagande av Gisslan i Sveriges Kreditbanks lokaler vid Norrmalmstorg i Stockholm 23.8–28.8* (1973), Stockholms Tingsrätt Avdelning 15 Akter i brottmål B 541 del 1 Aktb. 1–39 1973 G1: 217, 21, SA.

112 one of the ventilation holes: Kurt Lindroth, *Sammanställning av planeringen för befriandet av gisslan och gripande av gärningsmannen*, Stockholms Tingsrätt Avdelning 15 Akter i brottmål B 541 del 2 Aktb. 40–42 1973 G1: 218, 523, SA.

112 It was a primitive system: Ingemar Krusell, "Norrmalmstorgsutredningen—några aspekter på förundersökningen med kända och okända fakta kring bankrdamat den 23–28 augusti 1973," *Nordisk Kriminalpolis*, Årg. 3, Nr. 1 (1977), 150, and Olof Frånstedt, *Spionjägaren. Säpo, IB, och Palme Del 2* (Stockholm: Ponto, 2014), 240.

112 Three officials sat in a cloakroom: Photo in collection, PHM: 1831, PM.

112 "Watergate apparatus": *Expressen*, August 27, 1973.

112 "It's me, B-O" . . . "How do you spell": Bengt-Olof Lövenlo interview and transcript was published in *Expressen*, August 30, 1973, with the order for provisions, Sven Säfström, *Anteckningar*/Notes from the Vault, Sven Säfström Collection.

113 B-O blamed the delay . . . "This gun is heavy": Kassetband C1, 73–08–25 Kl 14.20, Förundersöknings Protokoll, Del 5, Stockholms Tingsrätt Avdelning 15 Akter i brottmål B 541 del 3 Aktb. 43–130 1973 G1: 219, 31–34, SA.

114 "Hello . . . hello . . .": Kristin Enmark, *Protokoll över förhör*, September 16, 1973, Stockholms Tingsrätt Avdelning 15 Akter i brottmål B 541 del 2 Aktb. 40–42 1973 G1: 218, 340, SA.

CHAPTER 28

115 "The country was at a standstill": Daniel Lang, "A Reporter at Large," *The New Yorker*, November 25, 1974, 84.

115 Fortunately, there was not much crime: *Dagens Nyheter*, August 25, 1973. Vulnerability was acknowledged, Dag Halldin, *Anförande hållet vid Presskonferensen i Jönköping i april 1974*, PHM: 1831, PM.

115 **"to be there" and "open house":** Ingemar Krusell, "Norrmalmstorgsutredningen—
några aspekter på förundersökningen med kända och okända fakta kring bankdramat den 23–28 augusti 1973," *Nordisk Kriminalpolis*, Årg. 3, Nr. 1 (1977), 119.
115 **Wild West:** *GT*, August 25, 1973. For more critiques, see particularly Krusell, "Norrmalmstorgsutredningen," and Eric Rönnegård, *Norrmalmstorgsdramat: den sanna
historien* (Stockholm: Jure, 2013), 41, 59, and 66.
116 **Many of them actually seemed:** *Dala-Demokraten*, August 24, 1973.
116 **The atmosphere shifted:** *Dagens Nyheter*, August 24, 1973.
116 **"Is it really in society's interest":** *Östgöta Correspondenten*, August 25, 1973.
116 **that a safe and secure welfare:** *Svenska Dagbladet*, August 26, 1973.
116 **in the tens of thousands:** *Göteborgs-Posten*, August 26, 1973.
117 **"Nothing new at Norrmalmstorg":** Sveriges Radio, Extra nyhetssändning [Nor-
rmalmstorgsdramat] 1973–08–25, SMDB, KB and Sveriges Radio, September 27,
1974, PHM: 1831, PM.
117 **Attempting to drug:** Kurt Lindroth, *Sammanställning av planeringen för befriandet
av gisslan och gripande av gärningsmannen*, Stockholms Tingsrätt Avdelning 15 Akter
i brottmål B 541 del 2 Aktb. 40–42 1973 G1: 218, 521, SA.
117 **The police would need:** *De Polisiära Insatserna i Samband med Norrmalmstorgshändelserna 23–28 augusti 1973, del 1/2*, PHM: 1831, PM.

CHAPTER 29

119 **"That was our world":** Daniel Lang, "A Reporter at Large," *The New Yorker*,
November 25, 1974, 97.
119 **a reminder that despite everything . . . would her husband remember:** Birgitta
Lundblad, interview, *Dagens Nyheter*, September 7, 1973.
119 **Birgitta took notes:** Elisabeth Oldgren, *Protokoll fört vid förhör*, October 3, 1973,
Stockholms Tingsrätt Avdelning 15 Akter i brottmål B 541 del 2 Aktb. 40–42 1973
G1: 218, 416, SA.
120 **gave her a bullet:** Elisabeth Oldgren, *Protokoll över förhör*, September 16, 1973,
Stockholms Tingsrätt Avdelning 15 Akter i brottmål B 541 del 2 Aktb. 40–42 1973
G1: 218, 399, SA.
120 **"crazy":** *Norrköpings Tidningar*, August 29, 1973.
120 **"It was hard to believe" and "That was our world":** Lang (1974), 97.
121 **"the same boat" and "a common outside threat":** *Svenska Dagbladet*, August 26,
1973.
121 **"social community" . . . "great criminals":** *Aftonbladet*, August 26, 1973.
121 **"Killing Me Softly":** Kristin Enmark, author interview.
121 **"The girls absolutely want" . . . "excuse to give after the massacre":**
Förundersökningsprotokoll, Teknisk Utredning, Brottsplatsundersökning, Del 3,
Stockholms Tingsrätt Avdelning 15 Akter i brottmål B 541 del 2 Aktb. 40–42 1973
G1: 218, 54, SA.
122 **"Idiot!":** Janne Olsson, author interview.
122 **"No, you are not" . . . "I'm going to clip every fucker":** Kassettband B1 73–08–25

Kl17.40–19.05, Telefonavlyssning, Förhör, Övrige Avlyssningar mm, Stockholms Tingsrätt Avdelning 15 Akter i brottmål B 541 del 4 Aktb. 43–130 1973 G1: 219, 60–61, SA.

123 **"The Wrong Man was Brought"**: *Aftonbladet*, August 25, 1973. The error made headlines elsewhere, too, such as *Västerbottens-Kuriren*, August 25, 1973.

123 **"allowed themselves to be misled"**: *Aftonbladet*, August 25, 1973.

123 **"Every hour"**: *Expressen*, August 25, 1973.

123 **Men carried everything**: *Brandförsvarets insatser med anledning av råndramat vid Sveriges Kreditbank, Norrmalmstorg 2*, PHM: 1831, PM.

CHAPTER 30

124 **"Hard yet charming"**: *Expressen*, August 26, 1973.

124 **about thirty countries**: Sveriges Radio, September 27, 1974, PHM: 1831: 13, PM.

124 **the media's responsibility**: Bo Holmström, *Lägg ut! Episoder ur ett journalistliv* (Stockholm: Natur & Kultur, 2011), 97. See also the discussions in *Arbetartidningen*, September 5, 1973, and Swedish Television, Bakom rubrikerna. Vad gjorde massmedia på Norrmalmstorg?, broadcast 1973–09–20, SMDB, KB.

125 **He advised the police against**: *Svenska Dagbladet*, August 26, 1973, and *Dagens Nyheter*, August 26, 1973. For more on gas, see *Redogörelser för och synpunkter på gasbeläggningen i Kreditbankens lokaler Norrmalmstorg*, PHM: 1831, PM.

125 **figuring out the dimensions**: Kurt Lindroth, *Sammanställning av planeringen för befriandet av gisslan och gripande av gärningsmannen*, Stockholms Tingsrätt Avdelning 15 Akter i brottmål B 541 del 2 Aktb. 40–42 1973 G1: 218, 521, SA.

126 **310mm**: Bror Erik Österman, *Vittnesförhör*, September 25, 1973, Stockholms Tingsrätt Avdelning 15 Akter i brottmål B 541 del 2 Aktb. 40–42 1973 G1: 218, 245, SA; Martin Leidvik, *Redogörelse över utförda borrningar vid Kreditbanken Norrmalmstorg*, November 16, 1973, PHM: 1831, PM; Österman and Leidvik also in *Byggnadindustrin* Nr. 27 (1973).

126 **much like a regular Sunday**: Janne Olsson, *Stockholmssyndromet. En självbiografi* (Telegram, 2009), 98.

126 **"Worryingly quiet"**: *Svenska Dagbladet*, August 26, 1973.

126 **"We are not in a hurry"**: *Expressen*, August 26, 1973.

126 **"Why don't the police"**: *Sydsvenska Dagbladet*, August 26, 1973, and *Het Vrije Volk*, August 27, 1973.

126 **a long-distance phone call**: Kassettband D1, 73–08–26, Förundersöknings Protokoll, Del 5, Stockholms Tingsrätt Avdelning 15 Akter i brottmål B 541 del 3 Aktb. 43–130, 1973 G1: 219, 86–90, SA.

127 **"I'm perfectly capable"**: *Aftonbladet*, August 27, 1973.

127 **came close to revealing the identity**: *Svenska Dagbladet*, August 27, 1973.

127 **"He is hard, very hard"** and "DANGEROUS": *Expressen*, August 26, 1973.

127 **"The Beginning of the End"** . . . **"fight to the last drop"**: *Aftonbladet*, August 26, 1973.

CHAPTER 31

128 **"He says that it is easy as hell":** Kassettband E1, *Förundersöknings Protokoll*, Del 5, Stockholms Tingsrätt Avdelning 15 Akter i brottmål B 541 del 3 Aktb. 43–130, 1973 G1: 219, 108, SA.

128 **Thirst and hunger could be:** *GT*, August 26, 1973.

128 **already had such an opportunity:** *Svenska Dagbladet*, August 25, 1973. The sniper described his experiences, *PM beträffande skjutförbud i Kreditbanken, Norrmalmstorg*, PHM: 1831, PM.

129 **"politicize" the operation:** *Svenska Dagbladet*, August 27, 1973, with claims later picked up by many others, including *Expressen*, September 4, 1973.

129 **"The hostages find themselves":** *Dagens Nyheter*, August 27, 1973, and *Het Vrije Volk*, August 27, 1973.

129 **"Those who interviewed him":** Edward Hunter, *Brainwashing: The Story of Men who Defied It* (New York: Farrar, Straus, and Cudahy, 1956), 13.

129 **"The Calculated Destruction":** This was the 1951 edition. For more on novels and films using the new word, see Andreas Killen, *1973 Nervous Breakdown: Watergate, Warhol, and the Birth of Post-Sixties America* (New York: Bloomsbury, 2006), 90–91.

130 **"What will happen if the police storm":** *Dagens Nyheter*, August 27, 1973.

CHAPTER 32

131 **"We heard the screams":** Håkan Larsson, interview, *Pockettidningen R* (1974), Årg 4, Nr. 1, 86.

131 **"sharp knives":** Janne Olsson, *Stockholmssyndromet. En självbiografi* (Telegram, 2009), 99.

131 **"Help! . . . Stop, stop!":** Sven Ahlgren, *Iakttagelser vid tjg söndagen den 26.8 1973 kl 18.30–07.30*, September 6, 1973 B 3/SC, Förundersöknings Protokoll, Telefonavlyssning, Förhör, Övrige Avlyssningar mm, Stockholms Tingsrätt Avdelning 15 Akter i brottmål B 541 del 4 Aktb. 131–60 1973 G1: 220, SA.

131 **"He's raping her!":** Overheard by the skeptical Gunnar Arvid Strandberg, *Protokoll över förhör*, September 21, 1973, Förundersöknings Protokoll, Telefonavlyssning, Förhör, Övrige Avlyssningar mm, Stockholms Tingsrätt Avdelning 15 Akter i brottmål B 541 del 4 Aktb. 131–60 1973 G1: 220, 85, SA.

132 **"What the hell are you doing?" . . . "It made me feel":** Kristin Enmark, *Jag blev Stockholmssyndromet. Valvet, föraktet och mitt kärleksförhållande med Clark Olofsson* (Livonia: Ordupplaget, 2015), 77.

132 **"inferno of noise":** *Kvällsposten*, August 26, 1973. Kristin described the torture in "Hur jag som gisslan såg på polisinsatsen - några synpunkter i efterhand med adress till polisledningen i Stockholm," *Nordisk Kriminalpolis*, Årg. 3, Nr. 1 (1977).

132 **"the final act of the bank drama":** *Dagens Nyheter*, August 27, 1973.

132 **By 9:40 p.m., the police had drilled:** Carl Persson, *Utan Omsvep. Ett liv i maktens centrum*, i samarbete med Anders Sundelin (Stockholm: Norstedts, 1990), 246.

133 **"You fools!" . . . "Take it easy":** Kassettband E1, *Förundersöknings Protokoll*, Del 5, Stockholms Tingsrätt Avdelning 15 Akter i brottmål B 541 del 3 Aktb. 43–130 1973

G1: 219, 104–105, SA, and Lövenlo on using taunts as tactics, *Protokoll fört . . . vid förhör*, September 4, 1973, Stockholms Tingsrätt Avdelning 15 Akter i brottmål B 541 del 3 Aktb. 43–130 1973 G1: 219, 27, SA.

133 **"We are all going to die down here!" . . . "Listen," started B-O:** Kassettband E1, *Förundersöknings Protokoll*, Del 5, Stockholms Tingsrätt Avdelning 15 Akter i brottmål B 541 del 3 Aktb. 43–130, 1973 G1: 219, 105–9, SA.

CHAPTER 33

135 **"We didn't know what was true":** Birgitta Lundblad, *Samtal*, August 29, 1973, Stockholms Tingsrätt Avdelning 15, B 541/73, Akter i Brottmål G1 218, 261, SA.

135 **"Why can't the police"** and **she saw herself in an opera house:** Daniel Lang, "A Reporter at Large," *The New Yorker*, November 25, 1974, 102, 104.

136 **"Stop it!":** Telephone call, unspecified, though after the explosion, *Förundersöknings Protokoll*, Del 5, Stockholms Tingsrätt Avdelning 15 Akter i brottmål B 541 del 3 Aktb. 43–130 1973 G1: 219, 123, SA.

136 **"Turn on the lights!" . . . "Yes, there is no light":** Fortsättning på Kassettband E1, *Förundersöknings Protokoll*, Del 5, Stockholms Tingsrätt Avdelning 15 Akter i brottmål B 541 del 3 Aktb. 43–130 1973 G1: 219, 112, SA.

136 **"some tampons and water":** Fortsättning på Kassettband E2, *Förundersöknings Protokoll*, Del 5, Stockholms Tingsrätt Avdelning 15 Akter i brottmål B 541 del 3 Aktb. 43–130 1973 G1: 219, 115, SA.

137 **Kristin heard a few:** Kristin Enmark, *Jag blev Stockholmssyndromet. Valvet, föraktet och mitt kärleksförhållande med Clark Olofsson* (Livonia: Ordupplaget, 2015), 81.

137 **"We need some menstruation" . . . "Tampons!":** *Utskrift av stort Tandberg-band från Säk, Insp. 26–27/8–73, Natten, Snaran. S1, Sid 2, Ind. ca 1265 och framåt*, Telefonavlyssning, Förhör, Övrige Avlyssningar mm, Stockholms Tingsrätt Avdelning 15 Akter i brottmål B 541 del 4 Aktb. 131–60 1973 G1: 220, 120–21, SA.

137 **At 2:14 a.m.:** Carl Persson, *Utan Omsvep. Ett liv i maktens centrum*, i samarbete med Anders Sundelin (Stockholm: Norstedts, 1990), 247, and 253.

137 **The "gas group" . . . six stretchers:** Kurt Lindroth, *Sammanställning av planeringen för befriandet av gisslan och gripande av gärningsmannen*, Stockholms Tingsrätt Avdelning 15 Akter i brottmål B 541 del 2 Aktb. 40–42 1973 G1: 218, 524–25, SA.

137 **so desperate and shocking:** The unpredictable measure proved to be worse than the rumors imagined, for instance, *Hänt i veckan*, August 30, 1973.

137 **No one had seen:** Both Janne and Clark claimed to make the nooses, and no one in the vault saw it, which is not as unlikely as it first sounded, given the vault was pitch-dark until the police completed the holes. It is worth noting that the nooses were tied in two distinct ways. At any rate, forty-five years later, Kristin and Sven still thought it was Janne.

CHAPTER 34

138 **"The more inhuman a person is depicted":** Eric Rönnegård, *Norrmalmstorgsdramat: den sanna historien* (Stockholm: Jure, 2013), 67.

138 **"No, there is no gas at all"** . . . **"You hear what":** Fortsättning på Kassettband E2, *Förundersöknings Protokoll, Del 5,* Stockholms Tingsrätt Avdelning 15, B 541/73, G1 219, 123, SA.

138 **"possibly use gas"** . . . **"Have I":** Kassettband F i fortsättning, *Förundersöknings Protokoll, Del 5,* Stockholms Tingsrätt Avdelning 15, B 541/73, G1 219, 127–29, SA. They did hear talk of gas on the radio, as police microphones recorded and Kristin Enmark remembered, *Samtal,* August 29, 1973, Stockholms Tingsrätt Avdelning 15 Akter i brottmål B 541 del 2 Aktb. 40–42 1973 G1: 218, 296, SA.

140 **"What are we going to do now?":** Uncertainties were highlighted in Kurt Lindroth, *Sammanställning av planeringen för befriandet av gisslan och gripande av gärningsmannen,* Stockholms Tingsrätt Avdelning 15 Akter i brottmål B 541 del 2 Aktb. 40–42 1973 G1: 218, 524, SA. According to Carl Persson, his colleague, Åke Magnusson had to lie on the couch to keep from fainting at the news, *Utan Omsvep. Ett liv i maktens centrum,* i samarbete med Anders Sundelin (Stockholm: Norstedts, 1990), 248. The sense of crisis is also in the memoir of Ove Rainer, *Makterna* (Stockholm: P.A. Norstedt & Söners Förlag, 1984), 61.

140 **"Our negotiations with the robber"** . . . **"What plans":** Footage of this press conference can be seen at Bankrånet i Sveriges Kreditbank, Norrmalmstorg, Stockholm, SVT, 1973–08–24 [sic], SMDB, KB, with reporters' descriptions of him in *Expressen,* August 27, 1973 and *Aftonbladet,* August 27, 1973.

141 **"our power of judgment":** Kurt Lindroth, Transl.LH, PHM: 1831, PM.

CHAPTER 35

142 **"It was easier to predict":** Per Svensson i samarbete med Håkan Lindhé, *Dramat på Norrmalmstorg 23 till 28 augusti 1973* (Stockholm: Bonnier Fakta, 2003), 141.

142 **with tears in his eyes:** *Aftonbladet,* August 27, 1973.

142 **"a torture chamber":** *Dagens Nyheter,* August 28, 1973. Many other papers used it in Sweden, like *GT,* August 27, 1973, or abroad, such as *Journal de Genève,* August 28, 1973, and Melbourne's *The Age,* August 29, 1973.

142 **"Thank God that they":** *Kvällsposten,* August 27, 1973.

142 **"It was a thoroughly disgusting"** and **"tired, hungry":** *Expressen,* August 27, 1973.

143 **The police would then have no problem:** *De Polisiära Insatserna i Samband med Norrmalmstorgshändelserna 23–28 augusti 1973, del 2/2,* PHM: 1831, PM.

143 **"Shoot the bastards":** Carl Persson, *Utan Omsvep. Ett liv i maktens centrum,* i samarbete med Anders Sundelin (Stockholm: Norstedts, 1990), 243.

143 **A large number of other people:** *Våra Interna Aktualiteter i Stockholmspolisen,* August 27, 1973, PHM: 1831, PM.

143 **that hope was fading:** *Smålandsposten,* August 28, 1973.

144 **"We are not, in any way":** *Kvällsposten,* August 28, 1973.

144 **Eight people were soon:** *Våra Interna Aktualiteter i Stockholmspolisen,* August 30, 1973, PHM: 1831, PM.

144 **"a little James Bond":** *Kvällsposten,* August 28, 1973.

144 **a police officer asked:** Kriminalpolisöverintendent Dag Halldin, *Anförande hållet vid Presskonferensen i Jönköping i april 1974,* PHM: 1831, PM.

145 **"float to the ceiling":** Letter and a follow-up to Olof Palme in collection, Statsråds-beredningen 1973, Statsministerns Korrespondens E I: 169, RA.
146 **Their strategy had thus far failed:** *Expressen*, August 27, 1973.

CHAPTER 36

147 **"Killing me softly with his song":** Kristin Enmark, author interview.
147 **"It's damn smoky"** . . . **"Hell no":** *Telefonavlyssning, Förhör, Övrige Avlyssningar mm*, 73–08–27, Band I, Stockholms Tingsrätt Avdelning 15 Akter i brottmål B 541 del 4 Aktb. 131–60 1973 G1: 220, 123, SA, used with the second version of the same conversation in the same carton, *Prot. utskr. efter tekn. bearb. av band 1*, Bankvalvet, 73–08–27, Band 1, Sidan 1, 138, SA.
148 **authorities often could not tell:** Kristin, Elisabeth, and Birgitta are often depicted as only "F" for *flicka*, or "girl." For more on difficulties in the wire-tapping room, see for instance Sven Gösta Magnusson, *Protokoll fört . . . vid förhör*, September 6, 1973, Stockholms Tingsrätt Avdelning 15 Akter i brottmål B 541 del 4 Aktb. 131–60 1973 G1: 220, SA.
148 **"Yes, but you have"** . . . **"Yes, there is":** 73–08–27, Band I, Telefonavlyssning, Förhör, Övrige Avlyssningar mm, Stockholms Tingsrätt Avdelning 15 Akter i brott-mål B 541 del 4 Aktb. 131–60 1973 G1: 220, 124–27, and *Prot. utskriv. efter tekn, bearbeting av band 1*, Bankvalvet, 73–08–27, Band 1, Sidan 1, 139–41, SA.
148 **it was probably Kristin:** Kristin Enmark, author interview.
150 **"an exciting nonstop thriller":** *GT*, August 25, 1973.
150 **"the most dramatic event":** *Aftonbladet*, August 27, 1973.
150 **"to avoid a bloodbath":** *Dagens Nyheter*, August 26, 1973.
150 **"idolized Clark"** and **"scared and worried":** *Aftonbladet*, August 26, 1973.
151 **left at once:** *Expressen*, June 20, 1993.
151 **"powerless":** *Expressen*, August 27, 1973.
151 **"dejected"** and **"The most important thing is":** *Aftonbladet*, August 27, 1973.
151 **"I do not believe that I could put up":** *Expressen*, August 27, 1973.

CHAPTER 37

152 **"One thing is clear":** *Dagens Nyheter*, August 27, 1973.
152 **"Many of the people"** . . . **"Nobody but you":** 73–08–27 Band I, *Telefonavlyssning, Förhör, Övrige Avlyssningar mm*, Stockholms Tingsrätt Avdelning 15 Akter I brottmål B 541 del 4 Aktb. 131–60 1973 G1: 220, 128–31, and *Prot. utskriv. efter tekn. bearb. av band 1*, Bankvalvet 73–08–27 Band 1, Sidan 1, 142–45, SA.
154 **"Vanity Fair!"** . . . **"The people who are too smart":** 73–08–27 Band 1, *Telefonavl-yssning, Förhör, Övrige Avlyssningar mm*, Stockholms Tingsrätt Avdelning 15 Akter i brottmål B 541 del 4 Aktb. 131–60 1973 G1: 220, 131–34, and *Prot. utskr. efter tekn. bearb. av band 1*, Bankvalvet 73–08–27, Band 1, Sidan 1, 146–49, SA.
155 **hit the town:** The name of the speaker is written in the margins at 73–08–27 Band I, *Telefonavlyssning, Förhör, Övrige Avlyssningar mm*, Stockholms Tingsrätt Avdelning 15 Akter i brottmål B 541 del 4 Aktb. 131–60 1973 G1: 220, 135, SA. Elisabeth also

said it was her, *Samtal*, September 6, 1973, Stockholms Tingsrätt Avdelning 15 Akter i brottmål B 541 del 2 Aktb. 40–42 1973 G1: 218, 374, SA.

CHAPTER 38

156 **"As this is being written":** *Expressen*, August 27, 1973.

156 **The most obvious change:** *Skånska Dagbladet*, August 28, 1973.

156 **"Are the hostages still alive?":** *Sydsvenska Dagbladet*, August 28, 1973.

156 **the atmosphere felt like:** *Göteborgs-Posten*, August 28, 1973.

156 **No one really had any idea:** *Östgöta Correspondenten*, August 28, 1973.

156 **no contingency plan:** *Upsala Nya Tidning*, August 28, 1973.

157 **"sadistic inventiveness":** *GT*, August 27, 1973.

157 **three broad alternative strategies:** Kurt Lindroth, Transl.LH, PHM: 1831, PM and Carl Persson, *Utan Omsvep. Ett liv i maktens centrum*, i samarbete med Anders Sundelin (Stockholm: Norstedts, 1990), 250–51.

157 **no one needed to remind Lindroth:** *De Polisiära Insatserna i Samband med Norrmalmstorgshändelserna 23–28 augusti 1973, del 2/2*, PHM: 1831, PM.

157 **the police had found no better:** Kriminalpolisöverintendent Dag Halldin, *Anförande hållet vid Presskonferensen i Jönköping i april 1974*, PHM: 1831, PM.

157 **the shape of a clover:** Assar Karlström, *Berättelse*, 1973–09–11, Stockholms Tingsrätt Avdelning 15 Akter i brottmål B 541 del 2 Aktb. 40–42 1973 G1: 218, 251, SA. This can be seen today outside the gym at Nobis Hotel.

158 **"cool head"** . . . **"Listen, how is it going":** Kassettband G1, 73–08–27 Kl. 16.00–17.00, Stockholms Tingsrätt Avdelning 15 Akter i brottmål B 541 del 3 Aktb. 43–130 1973 G1: 219, 117, SA.

158 **"Are they out now?"** and **"You are only messing":** Kassettband G 1, 73–08–27 Kl. 16.00–17.00, 119–21, SA.

CHAPTER 39

159 **"Instead of becoming broken":** Janne Olsson in *Pockettidningen R* (1974), Årg 4, Nr. 1, 39, with slight variation in wording later in *Stockholmssyndromet. En självbiografi* (Telegram, 2009), 122, and a similar comment in the bank vault, Kassettband G1, 73–08–27, Kl. 16.00–17.00, Stockholms Tingsrätt Avdelning 15 Akter i brottmål B 541 del 3 Aktb. 43–130 1973 G1: 219, 118, SA.

159 **"How clumsy you are, Clark!"** . . . **"You don't have to start":** Bankvalvet 73–08–27, Klockan 18.20–19.30 Måndag, Band 1, Sidan 2, *Telefonavlyssning, Förhör, Övrige Avlyssningar mm*, Stockholms Tingsrätt Avdelning 15 Akter i brottmål B 541 del 4 Aktb. 131–60 1973 G1: 220, 154, SA, and second version, in same file, *Prot. utskr. efter Tek. bearb. av band 1*, 73–08–27 Kl. 18.20–19.30 Måndag, Band 1, Sidan 2, 164.

159 **Janne, impatient with the delay, shouted** . . . **"Can't we have":** *Prot. utskr. efter Tek. bearb. av band 1*, 73–08–27 Kl. 18.20–19.30 Måndag, Band 1, Sidan 2, Stockholms Tingsrätt Avdelning 15 Akter i brottmål B 541 del 4 Aktb. 131–60 1973 G1: 220, 165–66, SA.

160 **"A lot of goodies!"** and **"I don't give a crap":** *Prot. utskr. efter tekn. bearb. av band*

1, Bankvalvet 73–08–27 Klockan 18.20–19.30 Måndag Band 1, Sidan 1, *Telefonavl-yssning, Förhör, Övrige Avlyssningar mm*, Band 1, Sidan 2, Bankvalvet, Stockholms Tingsrätt Avdelning 15 Akter i brottmål B 541 del 4 Aktb. 131–60 1973 G1: 220, 158, SA.

160 **"Palme and Geijer"** . . . **"How on earth do they":** *Prot. utskr. efter tek. bearb. av band 1,* 73–08–27 Kl. 18.20–19.30 Måndag, Band 1, Sidan 1, *Telefonavlyssning, Förhör, Övrige Avlyssningar mm*, Stockholms Tingsrätt Avdelning 15 Akter i brottmål B 541 del 4 Aktb. 131–60 1973 G1: 220, 159–61, SA, and the second version, Bankvalvet 73–08–27 Klockan 18.20–19.30, Band 1, Sidan 2, in same file at 156.

161 **still anyone's guess:** *Skånska Dagbladet,* August 28, 1973.

161 **"A tense silence"** and **"chilling news":** *Göteborgs-Posten,* August 28, 1973.

161 **"They had done so much":** Daniel Lang, "A Reporter at Large," *The New Yorker,* November 25, 1974, 106.

162 **Janne wiped some butter off:** Sven Säfström, *Protokoll över förhör,* September 3, 1973, Stockholms Tingsrätt Avdelning 15 Akter i brottmål B 541 del 2 Aktb. 40–42 1973 G1: 218, 439, SA.

CHAPTER 40

163 **"I had the impression that for him":** Birgitta Lundblad interview in *Pockettidningen R* (1974), Årg 4, Nr. 1, 72.

163 **a protrusion:** It can be seen today on the lamp, which is housed today in a warehouse outside Stockholm.

164 **"He was a real man":** Janne Olsson in *Pockettidningen R* (1974), Årg 4, Nr. 1, 29.

164 **"They are taking a photograph!"** and **"No, they aren't":** *Prot. utskr. efter tekn. bearb. av band 3,* Bankvalvet 73–08–28 Klockan 02.37–04.10 Tisdag, *Telefonavlyssning, Förhör, Övrige Avlyssningar mm*, Stockholms Tingsrätt Avdelning 15 Akter i brottmål B 541 del 4 Aktb. 131–60 1973 G1: 220, 180, SA.

164 **a haunting image:** The photo first appeared in West Germany's *Bild am Sonntag,* September 2, 1973, followed by papers all over Sweden, Europe, and around the world.

164 **"The moment must come":** *GT,* August 28, 1973.

164 **"Shall we burn up a little more dough":** *Prot. utskr. efter tekn. bearb. av band 3,* Bankvalvet 73–08–28 Klockan 02.37–04.10 Tisdag, Telefonavlyssning, Förhör, Övrige Avlyssningar mm, Stockholms Tingsrätt Avdelning 15 Akter i brottmål B 541 del 4 Aktb. 131–60 1973 G1: 220, 181.

165 **"half a million":** *Utskrift av stort Tandberg-band från Säk, Insp. 26–27/8–73,* Natten, Snaran. S1, Sid 2, Ind. ca 1265 och framåt, Sid 1, Telefonavlyssning, Förhör, Övrige Avlyssningar mm, Stockholms Tingsrätt Avdelning 15 Akter i brottmål B 541 del 4 Aktb. 131–60 1973 G1: 220, 120, SA. Janne told B-O it would rise to 1.5 million, undated telephone call, Kasettband F1 fortsätter, *Förundersöknings Protokoll,* Del 5, Stockholms Tingsrätt Avdelning 15 Akter i brottmål B 541 del 3 Aktb. 43–130 1973 G1: 219, 132, SA.

165 **put the figure at 1.5 million:** *Expressen,* August 27, 1973, *Aftonbladet,* August 27, 1973, *Östgöta Correspondenten,* August 28, 1973, and *Le Figaro,* August 28, 1973,

among many others. One of the few skeptics of the amount, at this time, was Helsinki's *Hufvudstadsbladet,* August 28, 1973.

165 **like Vikings burning their ships:** *Sydsvenska Dagbladet,* August 28, 1973. For a slight variant, see also Amsterdam's *De Telegraaf,* August 30, 1973.

165 **Janne blocked one of them:** Kurt Lindroth, Transl.LH, PHM: 1831, PM and *De Polisiära Insatserna i Samband med Norrmalmstorgshändelserna 23–28 augusti 1973, del 1/2,* PHM: 1831, PM.

165 **the sand was wet:** Assar Karlström, *Berättelse,* 1973–09–11, Stockholms Tingsrätt Avdelning 15 Akter i brottmål B 541 del 2 Aktb. 40–42 1973 G1: 218, 252, SA, and *Förundersöknings Protokoll,* Teknisk Utredning, Brottsplatsundersökning, Del 3, Stockholms Tingsrätt Avdelning 15 Akter i brottmål B 541 del 2 Aktb. 40–42 1973 G1: 218, 59, SA.

165 **Twenty minutes later:** Olle Abramsson notes "Aug - 73" in Olle Abramsson Scrapbook, and *Våra Interna Aktualiteter i Stockholmspolisen,* August 28, 1973, PHM: 1831, PM.

165 **"our life insurance":** Olle Abramsson, *Förhör,* October 23, 1973, Stockholms Tingsrätt Avdelning 15 Akter i brottmål B 541 del 2 Aktb. 40–42 1973 G1: 218, 254, SA.

166 **cheering from inside:** Jonny Jonsson, *Förhör,* February 6, 1974, Stockholms Tingsrätt Avd. 15:1, Band 16, B 541/73, G1: 220, 134, SA.

166 **"Finally we got one!":** Accounts differ on the question of who exactly made this comment: Kristin Enmark, *Protokoll över förhör,* September 16, 1973, Stockholms Tingsrätt Avdelning 15 Akter i brottmål B 541 del 2 Aktb. 40–42 1973 G1: 218, 341, SA, and Birgitta's version, September 14, 1973, Stockholms Tingsrätt Avdelning 15 Akter i brottmål B 541 del 2 Aktb. 40–42 1973 G1: 218, 275, SA, and Elisabeth's, September 6, 1973, at 378.

166 **"Goldfinger girls":** *Prot. utskr. efter tekn. bearb. av band 3,* 73–08–28 Klockan 05.00–06.20 Tisdag Band 3, Sidan 2, Telefonavlyssning, Förhör, Övrige Avlyssningar mm, Stockholms Tingsrätt Avdelning 15 Akter i brottmål B 541 del 4 Aktb. 131–60 1973 G1: 220, 185, SA.

166 **"Stop! Cut it out! . . . "You cannot drill any more":** *Prot. utskrv. efter tek. bearb. av band 3,* 73–08–28 Klockan 05.00–06.20, Band 3, Sidan 2, Telefonavlyssning, Förhör, Övrige Avlyssningar mm, Stockholms Tingsrätt Avdelning 15 Akter i brottmål B 541 del 4 Aktb. 131–60 1973 G1: 220, 187, SA and Bankvalvet 73–08–27 Klockan 05.00–06.20 Tisdag, Band 3, Sidan 2, in same file, 183.

166 **"They will lie there" . . . "No, it is them":** *Prot. utskr. efter tekn. bearb. av band 4,* Bankvalvet 73–08–28 Kl. 06.20–09.05 Tisdag, Band 4, Sidan 1, Telefonavlyssning, Förhör, Övrige Avlyssningar mm, Stockholms Tingsrätt Avdelning 15 Akter i brottmål B 541 del 4 Aktb. 131–60 1973 G1: 220, 188, SA and second version Bankvalvet 73–08–28 Klockan 06.20–09.05 in same file at 193.

166 **"Violence can triumph":** *Expressen,* August 27, 1973.

167 **"Secret Microphones Reveal":** GT, August 28, 1973.

167 **"Snipers with Infrared Light":** *Kvällsposten,* August 28, 1973.

167 **That was a risk:** Carl Persson, *Utan Omsvep. Ett liv i maktens centrum,* i samarbete med Anders Sundelin (Stockholm: Norstedts, 1990), 251.

CHAPTER 41

168 **"The police have to be prepared"**: Sven Thorander interview, *Pockettidningen R* (1974), Årg 4, Nr. 1, 92.

168 **"eerie silence"**: *Expressen*, August 28, 1973.

168 **No wonder:** *Aftonbladet*, August 28, 1973.

169 **"completely insane"**: Birgitta Lundblad, *Förhör*, January 25, 1974, GG Band 8, Stockholms Tingsrätt Avdelning 15 Akter i brottmål B 541 del 4 Aktb. 43–130 1973 G1: 219, 298, SA, with slightly different wording in her *Samtal*, September 3, 1973, *Förundersöknings Protokoll*, Telefonavlyssning, Förhör, Övrige Avlyssningar mm, Stockholms Tingsrätt Avdelning 15 Akter i brottmål B 541 del 4 Aktb. 131–60 1973 G1: 220, 96, SA.

169 **"That was when I was scared"**: Sven Säfström, author interview.

169 **After a hearty lunch** and **"shot Jan-Erik Olsson"**: Carl Persson, *Utan Omsvep. Ett liv i maktens centrum*, i samarbete med Anders Sundelin (Stockholm: Norstedts, 1990), 251.

169 **"regardless of what the courts"**: Persson (1990), 251. See also Håkan Larsson interview, Helen Ardelius, *Norrmalmstorgsdramat*, Stockholm: SR, P1, 1998–08–15 11.03–12.00, SMDB, KB. See also the interviews with Håkan Larsson and Jonny Jonsson in *Sambandet*, June 1993. Lindroth defends the right of police officers to shoot under Swedish law, Transl.LH, PHM: 1831, PM.

170 **the police calculated:** Tekniska roteln, 1973–11–12 Avsnitt 2: "Kundvalvet," *Förundersöknings Protokoll*, Stockholms Tingsrätt Avdelning 15 Akter i brottmål B 541 del 2 Aktb. 40–42 1973 G1: 218, 32, SA.

170 **"exhaustion tactic"**: Kurt Lindroth, *Sammanställning av planeringen för befriandet av gisslan och gripande av gärningsmannen*, Stockholms Tingsrätt Avdelning 15 Akter i brottmål B 541 del 2 Aktb. 40–42 1973 G1: 218, 520, SA.

170 **"If gas comes"** . . . **"I'm beginning to get tired"**: *Prot. utskr. efter tekn. bearb. av band 4*, Bankvalvet 73–08–28 Kl. 06.20–09.05 Tisdag, Band 4, Sidan 1, Telefon-avlyssning, Förhör, Övrige Avlyssningar mm, Stockholms Tingsrätt Avdelning 15 Akter i brottmål B 541 del 4 Aktb. 131–60 1973 G1: 220, 188, SA.

170 **Sven found some blank stationery:** Sven Säfström, *Anteckningar*/Notes from the Vault, Sven Säfström Collection.

170 **"It is not a threat"**: *Prot. utskr. efter tekn. bearb. av band 4*, 73–08–28 Kl. 06.20–09.05 Tisdag, Band 4, Sidan 1, Telefonavlyssning, Förhör, Övrige Avlyssningar mm, Stockholms Tingsrätt Avdelning 15 Akter i brottmål B 541 del 4 Aktb. 131–60 1973 G1: 220, 189, SA.

CHAPTER 42

171 **"All or Nothing"**: *Kvällsposten*, August 29, 1973.

171 **"Turn on the Lights"**: *Minnesanteckningar hur arbetet gick för inbrytargruppen*, PHM: 1831, PM. See also Rolf Bångerud, *Redogörelse för och synpunkter på gas-beläggningen i Kreditbankens lokaler Norrmalmstorg*, PHM: 1831, PM.

171 **had to be ready for a fight:** Håkan Larsson, *PM angående mina iakttagelser och*

åtgärder under bankockupationen vid Kreditbanken på Norrmalmstorg, September 19, 1973, *Förundersöknings Protokoll,* Del 5, Stockholms Tingsrätt Avdelning 15 Akter i brottmål B 541 del 3 Aktb. 43–130 1973 G1: 219, 140, SA.

172 **The sawed-off shotgun, on the other hand:** Kurt Lindroth, *Sammanställning av planeringen för befriandet av gisslan och gripande av gärningsmannen,* Stockholms Tingsrätt Avdelning 15 Akter i brottmål B 541 del 2 Aktb. 40–42 1973 G1: 218, 523, SA. Håkan Larsson also saw this as best weapon, *Sambandet,* June 1993.

172 **"At workplaces, in schools":** *Göteborgs-Posten,* August 28, 1973.

172 **"a fatal mistake":** *Aftonbladet,* August 28, 1973.

172 **The latter option was certainly not:** *GT,* August 28, 1973.

173 **A Helsingborg police officer:** *Expressen,* August 28, 1973.

173 **several psychiatrists and psychologists:** Nils Bejerot, *Redogörelse för sina iaktagelser i Kreditbanken,* Stockholms Tingsrätt Avdelning 15 Akter i brottmål B 541 del 2 Aktb. 40–42 1973 G1: 218, 515, SA, and discussion of the matter later, *Arbetet,* August 20, 1974.

173 **"game between men":** *Expressen,* August 28, 1973.

173 **"bloody finale":** *Kvällsposten,* August 28, 1973.

CHAPTER 43

174 **"At any moment, [Janne] could be killed":** *Expressen,* August 27, 1973.

174 **Television cameras showered:** Extra Rapport: Norrmalmstorgsdramat, 1973–8–28, SMDB, KB.

174 **"unreal atmosphere":** *Sydsvenska Dagbladet,* August 30, 1973 with more in *L'Europeo,* September 1973.

174 **"broadcast no alarming information":** *Redogörelser för och synpunkter på gasbelägningen i Kreditbankens lokaler Norrmalmstorg,* PHM: 1831, PM.

174 **Experts prepared to pump:** *Redogörelser för och synpunkter på gasbelägningen* and Kurt Lindroth, *Sammanställning av planeringen för befriandet av gisslan och gripande av gärningsmannen,* Stockholms Tingsrätt Avdelning 15 Akter i brottmål B 541 del 2 Aktb. 40–42 1973 G1: 218, 525, SA.

175 **"That's crazy!":** *Prot. utskr. efter tekn. bearb av band 6,* Bankvalvet 73–08–28, Stockholms Tingsrätt Avdelning 15 Akter i brottmål B 541 del 4 Aktb. 131–60 1973 G1: 220, 209, SA.

175 **he had wanted to attack:** Clark Olofsson, author interview.

175 **"Turn on the Lights!"** Monica Ekman, Terttu Kallioinen, Nils-Olof Jonsson, *Tänd Lyset,* PHM: 1831, PM.

175 **Kristin feared that they:** Kristin Enmark, "Hur jag som gisslan såg på polisinsatsen - några synpunkter i efterhand med adress till polisledningen i Stockholm," *Nordisk Kriminalpolis,* Årg. 3, Nr 1 (1977), 164.

175 **"We give up!" . . . "Yes," one of the women:** Bankvalvet 73–08–28 Klockan 21.00–21.35, Band 6, Sidan 2, Telefonavlyssning, Förhör, Övrige Avlyssningar mm, Stockholms Tingsrätt Avdelning 15 Akter i brottmål B 541 del 4 Aktb. 131–60 1973 G1: 220, 210–211, SA, and *Prot. utskr. efter tekn. bearb. av band 6,* Bankvalvet 73–08–28 Tisdag, Band 6, Sidan 2, Förundersöknings Protokoll, Telefonavlyssning, Förhör,

Övrige Avlyssningar mm, Stockholms Tingsrätt Avdelning 15 Akter i brottmål B 541 del 4 Aktb. 131–60 1973 G1: 220, 214–15, SA.

177 **gripped by panic:** *Minnesanteckningar hur arbetet gick för inbrytargruppen*, PHM: 1831, PM.

177 **"You do realize":** Håkan Larsson, *PM angående mina iakttagelser och åtgärder under bankockupationen vid Kreditbanken på Norrmalmstorg*, September 19, 1973, Förundersöknings Protokoll, Del 5, Stockholms Tingsrätt Avdelning 15 Akter i brottmål B 541 del 3 Aktb. 43–130 1973 G1: 219, 141, SA.

177 **"You can trust" . . . "We gladly let them":** Bankvalvet 73–08–28 Klockan 21.00– 21.35, Band 6, Sidan 2, Telefonavlyssning, Förhör, Övrige Avlyssningar mm, Stockholm Tingsrätt Avdelning 15 Akter i brottmål B 541 del 4 Aktb. 131–60 1973 G1: 220, 212, SA and *Prot. utskr. efter tekn. bearb. av band 6*, Bankvalvet 73–08–28 Tisdag, Band 6, Sidan 2, Förundersöknings Protokoll, Telefonavlyssning, Förhör, Övrige Avlyssningar mm, Stockholms Tingsrätt Avdelning 15 Akter i brottmål B 541 del 4 Aktb. 131–60 1973 G1: 220, 216–17, SA.

178 **Kristin gave him a hug and a kiss:** Kristin Enmark, *Samtal*, August 29, 1973, Stockholms Tingsrätt Avdelning 15 Akter i brottmål B 541 del 2 Aktb. 40–42 1973 G1: 218, 298, SA.

178 **so did Elisabeth:** Elisabeth Oldgren, *Samtal*, September 6, 1973, Stockholms Tingsrätt Avdelning 15 Akter i brottmål B 541 del 2 Aktb. 40–42 1973 G1: 218, 377, SA.

178 **Birgitta asked him to write:** Olsson (2009), 138, and Janne Olsson *Pockettidningen R* (1974), Årg 4, Nr. 1, 42–43. See also Elisabeth Oldgren interview, *Se*, September 13, 1973.

CHAPTER 44

179 **"The successful resolution was just as lucky":** *Pockettidningen R* (1974), Årg 4, Nr. 1, 102 and Ingemar Krusell "Norrmalmstorgsutredningen—några aspekter på förundersökningen med kända och okända fakta kring bankdramat den 23–28 augusti 1973," *Nordisk Kriminalpolis*, Årg. 3, Nr. 1 (1977), 147.

179 **Radio Sweden interrupted:** Eko [Norrmalmstorgsdramat] 1973–08–28, Extra Eko Inslag 1: Gisslan och rånare förs ut (kl.21.40), SMDB, KB, and *Prot. utskr. efter tekn. bearb. av band 6*, Bankvalvet 73–08–28 Tisdag, Band 6, Sidan 2, Förundersöknings Protokoll, Telefonavlyssning, Förhör, Övrige Avlyssningar mm, Stockholms Tingsrätt Avdelning 15 Akter i brottmål B 541 del 4 Aktb. 131–60 1973 G1: 220, 217, SA.

179 **"Hello, welcome out!":** *Dagens Nyheter*, August 29, 1973.

179 **One policeman had already:** Janne Olsson, *Stockholmssyndromet. En självbiografi* (Telegram, 2009), 138 and Janne Olsson in *Pockettidningen R* (1974), Årg 4, Nr. 1, 44.

180 **"Don't hit him!":** Håkan Larsson, *PM angående mina iakttagelser och åtgärder under bankockupationen vid Kreditbanken på Norrmalmstorg*, September 19, 1973, Förundersöknings Protokoll, Del 5, Stockholms Tingsrätt Avdelning 15 Akter i brottmål B 541 del 3 Aktb. 43–130 1973, 142, SA, and Kristin Enmark, *Jag blev Stockholmssyndromet. Valvet, Föraktet och mitt kärleksförhållande med Clark Olofsson* (Livonia: Ordupplaget, 2015), 89–90. See also Amsterdam's *De Telegraaf*, August 30, 1973.

180 **"We'll see each other again":** Clark Olofsson, *Vafan var det som hände?* (Livonia:

Upp med Händerna, 2015), 401. This made it into many accounts outside of Sweden, too, for instance, *Washington Post*, August 30, 1973, and *Newsweek*, September 10, 1973.

180 **police errors:** BS Nilsson, *Protokoll fört vid diskussionssammankomst med spaningssektionens personal*, September 5, 1973, PHM: 1831, PM, and Christer Björklund in *Göteborgs-Posten*, August 29, 1973.

180 **"the Monster of Stockholm":** *Daily Mirror*, August 30, 1973.

180 **crowd of mostly journalists jeered:** This was despite their supposed impartiality, noted Hans Nestius in an interview in *Arbetaren*, September 21–27, 1973. See also *Pockettidningen R* (1974), Årg 4, Nr. 1, 118–19, and *L'Europeo*, September 1973.

181 **Janne blamed the police:** Janne Olsson wrote in his "prison diary," *Aftonbladet*, December 26, 1973; *Pockettidningen R* (1974), Årg 4, Nr. 1, 44, and Olsson (2009), 141. Years later, he had not changed his opinion, Janne Olsson, author interview.

181 **Larsson said he had:** Håkan Larsson, *PM angående mina iakttagelser och åtgärder under bankockupationen vid Kreditbanken på Norrmalmstorg*, September 19, 1973, Förundersöknings Protokoll, Del 5, Stockholms Tingsrätt Avdelning 15, B 541/73, G1 219, 142–43, SA.

181 **Birgitta felt the fresh air:** Birgitta Lundblad interview, *Dagens Nyheter*, September 7, 1973.

181 **asked when he was going to get his beating:** Information from Jonny Jonsson, *Expressen*, June 20, 1993.

181 **As he exited, Janne thanked:** *Provinstidningen Dalsland*, August 29, 1973, *Skånska Dagbladet*, August 29, 1973, and *Kvällsposten*, August 29, 1973.

181 **"In admiration for the perseverance":** *Expressen*, August 29, 1973.

182 **"cried tears of joy":** *Västerbottens-Kuriren*, August 29, 1973.

182 **"It's all over":** *Våra Interna Aktualiteter i Stockholmspolisen*, August 29, 1973, PHM: 1831, PM and *Svenska Dagbladet*, August 30, 1973.

182 **"Exactly as all" and "A society that arms":** Extra Eko: Rapport från Norrmalmstorg, 1973–08–28, SMDB, KB.

182 **election speech:** The author Per Wahlöö, for one, saw it as party propaganda, *Arbetartidningen*, September 5, 1973.

CHAPTER 45

183 **"Gladly let films":** *Se*, August 30, 1973.

183 **had to cut off his shirt:** Bilaga H, Teknisk Utredning, Brottsplatsundersökning, Del 3, Stockholms Tingsrätt Avdelning 15 Akter i brottmål B 541 del 2 Aktb. 40–42 1973 G1: 218, 112, SA.

183 **even into the shower:** Håkan Larsson interview in *Sambandet*, June 1993.

184 **"shitty and sticky":** Clark Olofsson, *Vafan var det som hände?* (Livonia: Upp med Händerna, 2015), 383.

184 **At the end of the siege:** Olofsson (2015), 376. The four 10,000 crown notes were seen in the vault, Elisabeth Oldgren told the police, October 3, 1973, Stockholms Tingsrätt Avdelning 15 Akter i brottmål B 541 del 2 Aktb. 40–42 1973 G1: 218, 415, SA, but indeed not found afterward in the vault or among the examined remains

of the burned notes, *Bilaga F,* Teknisk Utredning, Brottsplatsundersökning, Del 3, Stockholms Tingsrätt Avdelning 15 Akter i brottmål B 541 del 2 Aktb. 40–42 1973 G1: 218, 106, SA.

184 **First, he had tried:** Clark Olofsson, author interview.

184 **It was true, Janne said:** Janne Olsson, author interview.

184 **"examined by the prosecutor":** Olofsson (2015), 384.

185 **knitting and sewing:** *Dagens Nyheter,* September 7, 1973.

185 **suede jacket:** *Bilaga K3,* Teknisk Utredning, Brottsplatsundersökning, Del 3, Stockholms Tingsrätt Avdelning 15 Akter i brottmål B 541 del 2 Aktb. 40–42 1973 G1: 218, 118, SA.

185 **the barbiturate Diminal duplex . . . "What I needed was trust":** Kristin Enmark, *Jag blev Stockholmssyndromet. Valvet, föraktet och mitt kärleksförhållande med Clark Olofsson* (Livonia: Ordupplaget, 2015), 94 and 95–96.

186 **"intimate relationships" . . . "Janne was very pleasant":** Sven Säfström, *Protokoll över förhör,* August 29, 1973, Stockholms Tingsrätt Avdelning 15 Akter i brottmål B 541 del 2 Aktb. 40–42 1973 G1: 218, 434, SA.

186 **"a pretty amazing guy" . . . "Not against anyone?":** Elisabeth Oldgren, *Protokoll över förhör,* August 29, 1973, Stockholms Tingsrätt Avdelning 15 Akter i brottmål B 541 del 2 Aktb. 40–42 1973 G1: 218, 354, 356, 361, SA.

187 **"He calmed both the robber and us" . . . along with a hug:** Kristin Enmark, *Samtal,* August 29, 1973, Stockholms Tingsrätt Avdelning 15 Akter i brottmål B 541 del 2 Aktb. 40–42 1973 G1: 218, 291–303, SA.

CHAPTER 46

189 **"I became the Stockholm syndrome":** Kristin Enmark, *Jag blev Stockholmssyndromet. Valvet, föraktet och mitt kärleksförhållande med Clark Olofsson* (Livonia: Ordupplaget, 2015).

189 **"No, it was the millions he was after":** *Expressen,* August 30, 1973.

189 **"None of the women":** *Dagens Nyheter,* August 30, 1973.

189 **These allegations made headlines:** London's *Daily Mirror* and Vienna's *Die Presse,* for instance on August 30, 1973, and discussed widely elsewhere from Germany's *Bild,* August 29, 1973 to *Sydney Morning Herald,* August 30, 1973.

189 **"reliable policemen" and "no doubt [that]":** *New York Times,* August 30, 1973.

189 **hugs and handholding:** *Expressen,* December 28, 1973, emphasized that they were only rumors, as did the *Washington Post,* August 29, 1973, and *The Times* (London), August 30, 1973, which stressed Kristin's denials.

189 **"What really happened in the bank":** *Göteborgs-Posten,* August 30, 1973.

190 **credited Clark for saving her life:** Enmark (2015), 112; Kristin Enmark, *Samtal,* August 29, 1973, and September 5, 1973, Stockholms Tingsrätt Avdelning 15 Akter i brottmål B 541 del 2 Aktb. 40–42 1973 G1: 218, 294, SA.

190 **She became angry:** Kristin Enmark, author interview.

190 **She missed him . . . "as discreet as an elephant":** Enmark (2015), 133–35.

191 **Her answer was a kiss:** Clark Olofsson, *Vafan var det som hände?* (Livonia: Upp med Händerna, 2015), 444.

191 **"We threw off our clothes"** . . . **devastated:** Enmark (2015), 137–42, 172–75. They are still friends today, and they were set to have dinner together a few days after I spoke with them separately in the fall of 2018.

CHAPTER 47

192 **"I saw us as a team of specialists":** Nils Bejerot interview in *Pockettidningen R* (1974), Årg 4, Nr. 1, 77.

192 **"A paradox of common interest"** and **"intense emotional impress can easily":** Nils Bejerot, *"Svart Bokslut,"* FIB/Kulturfront 1981, Nr. 12, 13–17.

193 **The term does not appear:** This also goes for early short publications, Börje Heed, *Gentlemanna-Rånaren?* (Bromma: Williams Förlag, 1973), Carl Olof Bernhardsson, "Bankdramat på Norrmalmstorgs," in Gunnar Davidsson (ed.), *Polisen griper in* (Stockholm: Lindfors, 1974), and *Pockettidningen R* (1974), Årg 4, Nr. 1, which appeared in early 1974. The term did not appear in other early treatments, including the issue of *Nordisk Kriminalpolis* devoted to the bank drama [Årg. 3, Nr. 1 (1977)], and a sociological analysis of the same year, Gert Nilson, *Sociodramer. Rånardramat och Hylands Hörna* (Göteborg: Bokförlaget Korpen, 1977).

193 **Even a *New Yorker* piece:** Daniel Lang, "A Reporter at Large," *The New Yorker*, November 25, 1974.

193 **Nor did the concept surface during the trial:** Jeffrey Toobin, *American Heiress: The Wild Saga of the Kidnapping, Crimes and Trial of Patty Hearst* (New York: Anchor Books, 2017), 353. The focus was on brainwashing, 354–55, and Jeffrey Toobin email to the author.

193 **a textbook example:** Thomas Strentz, in an interview by Stanley A. Pimentel, June 23, 2009, Society of Former Special Agents of the FBI, National Law Enforcement Officers Memorial Fund at www.nleomf.org. Strentz also said he was relieved that the Hearst defense opted for brainwashing; apparently, F. Lee Bailey made an attempt to secure FBI files on "Stockholm syndrome," as the *New York Times* noted in November 1975 in one of the first uses of the term in print.

194 **"think fondly of her captors":** Frederick J. Hacker, *Crusaders, Criminals, Crazies: Terror and Terrorism in Our Time* (New York: W. W. Norton & Company, 1976), 114. Another person who predicted this response was Syracuse University psychologist Murray Miron, R. J. Gallagher to Mr. Gebhardt, Memorandum, April 17, 1974, HEARNAP, FBI.

194 **Weed described their consultations:** Steven Weed with Scott Swanton, *My Search for Patty Hearst* (New York: Warner Books, 1976), 141.

194 **"There is no doubt"** and **"Stockholm Effect":** Hacker (1976), 107.

194 **"strong feelings of belonging"** . . . **"charismatic omnipotence":** Hacker (1976), 111.

194 **"We were looking for a strategy":** Thomas Strentz, interview by Stanley A. Pimentel, June 23, 2009, Society of Former Special Agents of the FBI, National Law Enforcement Officers Memorial Fund at www.nleomf.org.

194 **the pioneering work:** Arthur A. Slatkin, "The Stockholm Syndrome and Situational Factors Related to Its Development," Doctor of Education dissertation (University

of Louisville, 1997), 26. See also Harvey Schlossberg, *Psychologist with a Gun* (New York: Coward, McCann, and Geoghegan, 1974); Frank A. Bolz and Edward Hershey, *Hostage Cop: The Story of the New York Police Hostage Negotiating Team and the Man Who Leads It* (New York: Rawson, Wade, 1979), 23–26, and Gary Noesner, *Stalling for Time: My Life as an FBI Hostage Negotiator* (New York: Random House, 2010), 32–33.

195 **what Schlossberg had come to call:** Harvey Schlossberg, email to author.

195 **"to help cops understand":** Harvey Schlossberg, email to author.

195 **"You will not experience":** Frank A. Bolz, Jr, *How to Be a Hostage and Live* (Secaucus, NJ: Lyle Stuart, 1987), 77.

195 **Strentz designed the FBI curriculum:** Strentz (2009), and teaching course in Ronald Kessler, *FBI: Inside the World's Most Powerful Law Enforcement Agency* (New York: Pocket, 1994), 279, and Don DeNevi and John H. Campbell, *Into the Minds of Madmen: How the FBI's Behavioral Science Unit Revolutionized Crime Investigation* (New York: Prometheus Books, 2004), 98, 117.

195 **"This is not happening"** . . . **"A hostile hostage":** Thomas Strentz, "Law Enforcement Policy and Ego Defenses of the Hostage," *FBI Law Enforcement Bulletin* 48, no. 4, April 1979.

196 **"the top news story":** Frank Ochberg interview, PTSD Questions & Answers with Joyce Boaz & Dr. Frank Ochberg, available at www.giftfromwithin.org.

196 **"Study the victim":** Frank M. Ochberg, "There is Reason in Action," in Charles R. Figley (ed.), *Mapping Trauma and Its Wake: Autobiographic Essays by Pioneer Trauma Scholars* (New York: Routledge, 2006), 140.

196 **"the most clearly identified":** Frank M. Ochberg, "A Case Study: Gerard Vaders," in Frank M. Ochberg and David A. Soskis (eds), *Victims of Terrorism*. Westview Special Studies in National and International Terrorism (Boulder: Westview Press, 1982), 31.

196 **"victim/terrorist alliance":** Ochberg and Soskis (1982), iii.

196 **"schlock science":** *Chicago Tribune*, March 13, 1981.

197 **An examination of more than 4,700 cases:** Nathalie de Fabrique, Stephen J. Romano, Gregory M. Vecchi, and Vincent B. Van Hasselt, "Understanding Stockholm Syndrome," *FBI Law Enforcement Bulletin* 76, no. 7, July 2007.

197 **Other studies have found:** G. Dwayne Fuselier, "Placing the Stockholm Syndrome in Perspective," *FBI Law Enforcement Bulletin* 68, no. 7, July 1999.

197 **surprisingly few academic studies:** M. Namnyak, N. Tufton, R. Szekely, M. Toal, S. Worboys, and E.L. Sampson, "'Stockholm Syndrome': Psychiatric Diagnosis or Urban Myth?" *Acta Psychiatrica Scandinavica* (2008), 117.

197 **"an experience of intense fear":** The International Statistical Classification of Diseases and Related Health Programs, ICD-10 (F43.0).

197 **Other professionals:** Michaela Gufler, *Mythos Stockholm Syndrom* (Innsbruck: Limbus, 2015), and Allan Wade, "Rethinking Stockholm Syndrome," lecture, available online at the youtube channel of Center for Response Based Practice [VanBC].

197 **"a crazy man":** Kristin Enmark, *Jag blev Stockholmssyndromet. Valvet, föraktet och mitt kärleksförhållande med Clark Olofsson* (Livonia: Ordupplaget, 2015), 20.

197 **"Our only chance":** *Expressen*, August 29, 1973.

198 **no less than 79 percent:** Brian Jenkins, Janera Johnson, David Ronfeldt, *Numbered Lives: Some Statistical Observations from 77 International Hostages Episodes*, July 1977, originally written for the US Department of State and Department of Defense and published by Rand Corporation, Sant Monica, 1977, 27.

198 **observe the hostages:** Nils Bejerot, *Redogörelse för sina iaktagelser i Kreditbanken*, Stockholms Tingsrätt Avdelning 15 Akter i brottmål B 541 del 2 Aktb. 40–42 1973 G1: 218, SA.

198 **"Get out!":** Kristin Enmark, author interview.

198 **Bejerot *never* tried to speak:** Sven Säfström, author interview.

198 **"weak-willed women in relationship":** Hanna Olsson, in Gunnar Wesslén and Kristin Enmark, *Jag blev Stockholmssyndromet. Valvet, föraktet och mitt kärleksförhållande med Clark Olofsson* (Livonia: Ordupplaget, 2015), 109; Cecilia Åse, *Kris!: Perspektiv på Norrmalmstorgsdramat* (Stockholm: Liber AB, 2014), 77.

199 **"a big fucking difference":** Clark Olofsson, author interview.

CHAPTER 48

200 **"[Olof Palme] can thank me":** Janne Olsson, author interview.

200 **reflected on the art:** *Esquire*, December 1973.

200 **increased its daily print run:** *Pockettidningen R* (1974), Årg 4, Nr. 1, 45.

200 **Ratings broke all records:** One arguable exception was the ice hockey match between Sweden and the Soviet Union in the championship finals in March 1970. This drew a slightly higher rating, but this event lasted only a few hours, as opposed to days. Norrmalmstorg commanded nine of the top ten slots for the week and sixteen of twenty. An earlier production of August Strindberg's novel *The People of Hemsö* also scored higher, but it was when there was only one television channel and significantly fewer people owned television sets.

200 **73 percent of the entire country:** Sveriges Radio, September 27, 1974, PHM: 1831: 13, PM.

201 **"drama that shook the world":** *GT*, August 29, 1973.

201 **"Not even Hollywood screenwriters":** Malcolm McDowell interview in *Expressen*, August 29, 1973.

201 **a daily average . . . betweeen 0 percent and 0.8 percent:** Jörgen Westerståhl, *Norrmalmstorgsdramat. En undersökning av Sveriges Radios nyhetsbevakning utförd på uppdrag av Radionämnden. Rapportserien 1974: 2* (Göteborgs universitet, 1974), 11–17. "Record low" interest in the election that fall was also noted by Karin Hallberg in *Antennen*, the journal for Radio Sweden's personnel, November 8, 1973, nr. 8.

202 **"Everything to create sensation":** *Arbetartidningen*, September 5, 1973.

202 **"analyzed when there was nothing":** *Aftonbladet*, September 13, 1973.

202 **The coverage would have been different:** "Bakom rubrikerna. Vad gjorde massmedia på Norrmlamstorg?" 1973-09-20, SMDB, KB and Sveriges Radio, September 27, 1974, PHM: 1831: 13, PM and KB.

202 **a pseudo-event:** See the discussion, for instance, in *Arbetartidning*, September 5, 1973 and *Arbetaren*, September 14–20, 1973.

202 **"The Last Day as Prime Minister?"**: *GT*, August 28, 1973.

202 **a true statesman**: Signed by "a housewife" in *Dala-Demokraten*, August 29, 1973.

202 **"I Have a Dream"**: Letter to Olof Palme, Statsrådsberedningen 1973, Statsministerns Korrespondens E I: 169, RA.

202 **"There cannot be a faster guy"**: *GT*, August 30, 1973.

203 **the two decisions**: Justitiedepartementet, *PM angående händelserna i samband med
bankrånet vid Norrmalmstorg den 23 augusti 1973*, 1974–01–22, PHM: 1831, PM.

203 **reluctant to change**: See, for instance, Kjell Östberg, *När vinden vände. Olof Palme
1969–1986* (Stockholm: Leopard, 2012), 63–64. The Social Democrats in Norway
and Denmark, by contrast, suffered major losses that fall, Henrik Berggren, *Underbara dagar framför oss. En biografi över Olof Palme* (Stockholm: Norstedts, 2010),
492–93.

203 **even though he had not been an angel**: *Expressen*, November 20, 1973.

203 **dared to remove**: Kerstin Hallert in *Svenska Dagbladet*, January 10, 1974.

204 **He had fired his lawyer**: Clark wanted to defend himself even before the trial
started, Clark Olofsson to Stockholms Tingsrätt Avd. 15, November 22, 1973, Stockholms Tingsrätt Avd 15:1, B 541/73, G1: 220, SA.

204 **"It gets harder each time"**: *Svenska Dagbladet*, January 16, 1974.

204 **"I have not done anything criminal"**: *Dagens Nyheter*, January 31, 1974.

204 **"I still have not received"**: Janne Olsson, *Stockholmssyndromet. En självbiografi*
(Telegram, 2009), 149 and 122.

204 **"his share"**: Clark Olofsson, *Vafan var det som hände?* (Livonia: Upp med Händerna,
2015), 342.

204 **The trial would be the last time**: Disputes were now starting to emerge in public,
this time over trial strategy, *Dagens Nyheter*, January 11, 1974.

204 **The verdict**: March 19, 1974, Stockholms Tingsrätt Avd. 15:1 DB 248, Mål nr B
541/73, SA.

204 **Janne admitted that he had**: Olsson (2009), 102. The police found the wad of bills,
Förundersökningsprotokoll, Rånöverfall med Tagande av Gisslan i Sveriges Kreditbanks lokaler vid Norrmalmstorg i Stockholm 23.8–28.8 (1973), Stockholms Tingsrätt Avdelning 15 Akter i brottmål B 541 del 1 Aktb. 1–39 1973 G1: 217, 24, SA.

EPILOGUE

205 **"Why are we mean"**: Sven Thorander, interview in *Pockettidningen R* (1974), Årg
4, Nr. 1, 92.

205 **Sieber complimented**: *Der Spiegel*, September 3, 1973.

205 **"Police Day"**: Letter from a private citizen to Olof Palme, Statsrådsberedningen
1973, Statsministerns Korrespondens E I: 169, RA.

205 **"The Stockholm police has undergone"**: *Våra Interna Aktualiteter i Stockholmspolisen*, August 30, 1973, PHM: 1831, PM.

206 **Morgan knew some inconvenient . . . The only trauma**: Morgan Rylander,
author interview, and Morgan Rylander, *Norrmalmstorgsdramat 23 till 28 augusti
1973*, Morgan Rylander Collection.

206 **Another person who paid a personal price**: Ingemar Warpefeldt interview, Gary

Engman, 21:00-21:43:55, Engman Kl 9, SVT, TV2 1979-09-29; Ingemar Warpefeldt interview by Gunnar Wesslén, *Aftonbladet*, October 13, 1977; *Helg-Extra*, January 1, 1975; *Hemmets Journal*, August 22–28, 1974, *Expressen*, November 9, 1975; Magnus Ihreskog, helagotland.se, June 24, 2018, and Helen Ardelius, *Norrmalmstorgsdramat*, Sveriges Radio, P1, 1998–08–15 11.03–12.00, SMDB, KB.

206 **The other policeman:** Olle Abramsson, *Förhör*, October 27, 1973, Stockholms Tingsrätt Avdelning 15 Akter i brottmål B 541/73, G1: 218; *Expressen*, November 20, 1973; *Aftonbladet*, January 9, 1974; and Olle Abramsson scrapbook.

206 **The group finished its work:** *De Polisiära Insatserna i Samband med Norrmalmstorgshändelserna 23–28 augusti 1973*, PHM: 1831, PM.

207 **"We have a lot to learn":** Kurt Lindroth interview, *Pockettidningen R* (1974), Årg 4, Nr. 1, 94.

207 **went ahead with its plans:** For more on the merger prior to the bank drama, see, for instance, *Svenska Dagbladet*, February 17, 1973.

207 **"I believe that I know":** *Svenska Dagbladet*, August 24, 2003.

207 **brought him a chess set:** Janne Olsson, author interview.

207 **"It was a friendly talk":** Sven Säfström, author interview.

208 **"I do not know":** Sven Säfström, author interview. See also *Bandinspelning från den 13/9 1973 vid TV-utsändning, Intervju med Sven Säfström*, Stockholms Tingsrätt Avdelning 15 Akter i brottmål B 541 del 2 Aktb. 40–42 1973 G1: 218, 514, SA, along with *Arbetet*, August 20, 1974.

208 **"I shook, I cried, I prayed":** *Dagens Nyheter*, January 24, 1974.

208 **"a robber jacket"** . . . **"attempted murder":** Kristin Enmark, author interview.

209 **"afraid of being so afraid"** and **"to listen to those":** Kristin Enmark, *Jag blev Stockholmssyndromet. Valvet, föraktet och mitt kärleksförhållande med Clark Olofsson* (Livonia: Ordupplaget, 2015), 187, 180. She connected her interest in social issues with her experiences at Norrmalmstorg here, as well as in an earlier interview with Gunnar Wesslén, *Aftonbladet*, June 5, 1977.

210 **Clark kept on reading:** Clark Olofsson, author interview.

210 *The Lottery of Justice:* Clark Olofsson, *Rättvisans Lotteri* (Stockholm: Prisma, 1986).

210 **undisclosed location:** *Kungsbacka-Posten*, August 2, 2018.

211 **"I'll answer whatever":** Clark Olofsson, author interview.

211 **"Go on inside"** . . . **"It was not appropriate":** Clark Olofsson, author interview.

212 **"A scruffy Scandinavian":** Associated Press in *Herald Tribune*, August 10, 1976.

212 **"The King of the Underworld":** *Expressen*, August 31, 1973.

212 **The Soviet Union's *Pravda*:** Clippings from Clark Olofsson Collection.

212 **"Fuck, it was very fun":** Clark Olofsson, author interview.

212 **a new interest in writing:** This was already detected in the "prison diary" Janne published in *Aftonbladet*, December 26, 1973, with an early example in *Pockettidningen R* (1974), Årg 4, Nr. 1. A photo of Janne's cell shows shelves filled with binders of letters and other texts, *Expressen*, August 22, 1974.

213 **more than sixty police officers:** *Expressen*, March 9, 1975 and *Expressen* March 10, 1975.

213 **The biggest challenge . . ."Sooner or later":** Olsson (2009), 206, 174.

213 **"She means everything":** *Expressen*, June 20, 1993, with more in Olsson (2009), 216–21.

214 **"If I could rewind the tape" . . . "Janne, the Norrmalmstorg Robber":** Janne Olsson, author interview.

ILLUSTRATION CREDITS

INDEX